ABERDEEN STUDENTS 1600–1860

Related titles available from the Queen Mother Library, University of Aberdeen

CROWN AND GOWN 1495–1995: An Illustrated History of the University of Aberdeen (1994)
Jennifer J Carter and Colin A McLaren

Quincentennial Studies Series

THE STUDENT COMMUNITY AT ABERDEEN 1860–1939 (1988)
R D Anderson

ABERDEEN UNIVERSITY 1945–1981: Regional Roles and National Needs (1989)
edited by John D Hargreaves with Angela Forbes

KING'S COLLEGE, ABERDEEN 1560–1641: From Protestant Reformation To Covenanting Revolution (1990)
David Stevenson

BAJANELLAS AND SEMILINAS: Aberdeen University and the Education of Women 1860–1920 (1991)
Lindy Moore

PROFESSORS, PATRONAGE AND POLITICS: The Aberdeen Universities in the Eighteenth Century (1992)
Roger L Emerson

THE ABERDEEN ENLIGHTENMENT: The Arts Curriculum in the Eighteenth Century (1993)
Paul B Wood

THE UNIVERSITY AND THE STATE: The Case of Aberdeen 1860–1963 (1993)
Iain G C Hutchinson

THE MODERNISATION OF MEDICAL TEACHING AT ABERDEEN IN THE NINETEENTH CENTURY (1994)
Carolyn Pennington

ACADEME AND EMPIRE: Some Overseas Connections of Aberdeen University 1850–1970 (1994)
John D Hargreaves

THE UNIVERSITIES OF ABERDEEN AND EUROPE: The First Three Centuries (1995)
edited by Paul Dukes

Cover design by Elmwood Scotland, Edinburgh

ABERDEEN STUDENTS 1600–1860

Colin A McLaren

With translations by Morton A E Gauld
and analytical tables by Rachel Hart

UNIVERSITY OF ABERDEEN

First published 2005

British Library Cataloguing in Publication Data

A catalogue record of this book is available from the British Library

ISBN 1 85752 300 8 (pbk)

Typeset, printed and bound in Hong Kong by Graphicraft Limited

To colleagues, past and present, who have cared for the special collections, manuscripts and archives of the University of Aberdeen.

Contents

List of Illustrations

Acknowledgements

To the British Library, the National Library of Scotland and the National Archives of Scotland, for permission to quote from manuscripts in their charge. To the Trustees of the National Library of Scotland for permission to reproduce the map of James Gordon, *Aberdoniae novae et Veteris descriptio* (1661).

Preface

Parts of this book first appeared as papers for seminars, conferences and journals. As a result, many academics, librarians and archivists have over the years generously given help, advice and criticism – too many to list individually. I have, however, expressed my gratitude in the footnotes to those who pointed me towards sources I might not otherwise have found. I wish to thank my very patient collaborators, Morton Gauld and Rachel Hart, and to make it clear that I take sole responsibility for any errors in the text. I also wish to thank staff of the Directorate of Information Systems and Services (DISS) of the University of Aberdeen; the Document Supply section of the Information Services division of the University of Kent; and, for assistance with illustrations, Mike Craig, Reprographics and Binding Manager (DISS), staff of the Marischal Museum (DISS), together with Dr M Pryor and Margaret McLaren. Finally, and especially, I must thank Jennifer Carter, my long-suffering editor, and Michelle Gait, the equally forbearing manager of the reading room of the Department of Special Libraries & Archives (DISS) at Aberdeen: without their help and support, the book could not have been completed. My debt, overall, to that department is expressed elsewhere.

Introduction

This is a study of the daily life of students at King's College, founded in 1495 in the Old Town of Aberdeen, and Marischal College, founded in 1593 in the New.[1] It begins in 1600, the date of the earliest surviving college register, and ends in 1860, when the colleges,[2] united by Act of Parliament, became the modern University of Aberdeen. It describes how the students were taught and how they learned; how they worshipped; how they relaxed; how they behaved in and outside the classroom; and, where the sources permit, where they came from (socially as well as geographically), and what they did when they left.[3] Originally planned as one of the Quincentennial Studies in the history of the University of Aberdeen, it keeps to the same modest size by reducing to a minimum the institutional and intellectual history of the colleges, and by focusing on students in the faculty of arts. Students following the four-year curriculum for the degree of Master of Arts (*artium magister*) were the core of the student body at both colleges throughout this period. Scientific subjects were incorporated in the arts curriculum, but there was no separate science degree until the late nineteenth century. Law, divinity and medicine (from the later eighteenth century) were also taught – usually as postgraduate degrees – though to smaller numbers than those in the arts cohort. In addition, there were many private students, especially at Marischal, who enrolled for particular courses rather than the full degree; little is known, however, about their college experience or their subsequent careers.

The first chapter covers the period from 1600 to 1639. It draws on sources that are unevenly distributed and often obscure. Among the most important are the college foundations – the New Foundation of King's and the Foundation Charter of Marischal,[4] which show, for the period around 1600 at least, what the students were taught and how they were expected to behave. The Foundations empowered the colleges to make laws for the regulation of their students. Only two sets of these laws have survived, both from Marischal: those of Principal Gilbert Gray in 1605 (the *Statuta*); and a shorter set, undated and of unknown provenance (the *Leges*).[5] Finally, there are registers of matriculation and graduation; complete for King's, irregular at Marischal.[6] They provide names and crunchable numbers but little more. These core sources are supplemented at King's by records of visitations (inspections) in 1619, 1623, 1628 and 1634;[7] at Marischal by registers of the town council of Aberdeen, which not only intervened in the affairs of what it considered to be the town's college, but jointly managed the bursaries (scholarships) founded there.[8] The students themselves are represented by their lecture notes, and by a 'Preceptive, Plauditory and Postulatory Panegyric',[9] delivered at King's with the help of a 'tear-inducing onion' by William Lauder (1628).[10]

Sources for the second chapter, covering the period from 1640 to 1717, are better for King's than for Marischal. King's has four codes of laws, and 'A set of rules for the table, Christian, salubrious, temperate and honourable', composed by Principal John Row.[11] In addition, there are minutes of college meetings (1640–50, 1663–89, 1700 onwards) and a continuous series of accounts (1652 onwards).[12] Marischal has neither laws nor minutes. Instead, there is a valuable series of policy papers drawn up by staff during negotiations with King's around 1675;[13] while the college accounts (1651–55, 1660 onwards) are rich in detail: 'ther being a visitation sitting in tyme of my entrie,' Principal William Leslie began his 'Dischairge and Compt' in 1661, 'the whole Visitors and particularly the Earl Marischall recommended to me, to repaire the College and schooles quhilk they lookit upon as ruinous.'[14] At King's, the matriculation register gives places (generally counties) of origin from the late 1640s onwards but, together with the register of graduation, is incomplete after 1680. At Marischal, matriculation alone is recorded regularly; again, only until 1680. The colleges' own archives are supplemented by records of general and specific visitations of the universities: in the 1640s by representatives of the General Assembly; after 1660 by commissioners of the state.[15] Concerned principally with what would nowadays be called quality assurance and compliance, the visitors also dealt with matters of discipline. Accordingly, their proceedings, along with those of local courts and the Privy Council, are an important source for the causes and consequences of the student disturbances that were a recurrent and distinctive feature of the period. Perhaps the most useful – certainly, the most readable – sources for this chapter are the letters written by students themselves and by their parents, tutors and masters, to be found scattered among family and estate papers.

Sources for the third chapter, covering the period from 1718 to 1825, are much as before at King's. The college laws were revised in 1765, 1794, 1799 and 1819;[16] alterations to the system of matriculation in 1812 improved the statistical record. At Marischal, in contrast, the range is greatly extended: new statutes were published in 1741 and reissued with revisions in 1799 and 1816;[17] college minutes survive from 1729 onwards;[18] matriculations record the name, occupation and parish of students' fathers from 1772 onwards; and numbers are more reliable after 1812. In addition, the extensive personal papers of Professor James Beattie illustrate his day-to-day dealings with Marischal students;[19] while those of William Knight (1798) record his years there as both student and professor.[20] Finally, there is the record of the reunions of the Marischal class of 1787–91, the earliest to survive in Aberdeen; buried in the Pickwickian prose are biographical details of class members unavailable elsewhere.[21] Among new printed sources are the colleges' contributions to the *Statistical*

Account of 1799 – part official histories, part prospectuses – to which the memoirs of former students provide an often astringent corrective.[22]

Sources for the final chapter, covering the period from 1826 to 1860, are dominated by the evidence and reports of the three commissions that were instrumental in bringing about the union of the colleges: the Scottish Universities Commission, 1826–30; the Aberdeen Universities Commission, 1836–37; and the Aberdeen Universities Commission, 1857. The 1826 commission published, in addition to its reports, verbatim transcripts of interviews with the staff of King's and Marischal, and returns of current, historical and statistical information.[23] The 1836 commission published returns only;[24] the 1857 commission, interviews and returns.[25] All three commissions were concerned primarily with governance, management and education at the two colleges: inevitably, however, they provide information about the condition and culture of the students. The oral evidence of the 1826 commission is especially important. While much of it refers to 1827, when the interviews were carried out, some is retrospective, drawn from the memories of long serving staff: 'I was,' said 84-year-old Professor Robert Hamilton at Marischal, 'a member of the College [in 1786], and I am the only one surviving.'[26] Letters and diaries of former students are by this time often incorporated in published memoirs or biographies. Most of these concern students who rose from plough to pulpit – sometimes to a peerage – by virtue of the bursary system and are heavy on gratitude and nostalgia. Alexander Bain (1836), formerly of Marischal, certainly shows gratitude in his autobiography, but his main aim was 'to indicate the stages of [his] mental growth, under the circumstances of the time.'[27] There is a return to nostalgia in the college novels of George MacDonald (1840) and Neil Maclean (1853), both graduates of King's. Macdonald is said to have put much of his own experiences at King's in the 1840s into *Alec Forbes of Howglen* (1865) and *Robert Falconer* (1868).[28] Maclean, having published in 1872 a factual account of student life at King's in the 1850s,[29] turned it into a semi-documentary novel, *Life at a Northern University*.[30] All three novels depict life in and outside the college: MacDonald focuses on the individual; Maclean, on the group; inevitably, however, neither can resist scenes in which overworked but underfed students expire degreeless in their garrets. There were some efforts to compile records of classes of the 1850s: the most elaborate was for the two classes of 1859, the last to enter before King's and Marischal ceased to be separate institutions.[31]

Chapter 1

An Honourable Education, 1600–1639

In 1603, Thomas Burnet of Leys entered King's College as a student in arts.[1] He was the son of a Kincardineshire laird, who preferred to see his heir educated at the venerable, conservative college in the Old Town, rather than entrust him to the fledgling establishment founded by the Earl Marischal in the New. It was to Marischal College, however, that Alexander Jaffray was sent in the same year. His father, having progressed from a bakery to a seat on the town council,[2] was keen to show his confidence in what was commonly called the 'college of new Aberdene'.[3] Thomas and Alexander were admitted by their colleges because they professed the reformed faith, were proficient in Latin, and had fathers who could afford their fees, bed and board there. Other boys, who qualified on the first two grounds but whose families could not support them, depended upon college bursaries.[4] At King's, these were provided under the New Foundation; at Marischal, they were created by private benefactors like the Aberdeen physician and mathematician, Duncan Liddel.

Looking around the quadrangle, Thomas would have seen King's much as it was when it was built in the early sixteenth century. On the north side was the chapel, with its crown tower and spire, classrooms and a library. On the east stood the common school, where the entire college could assemble; above it was the hall, where staff and students ate. The remaining sides were formed by two residential blocks with spired towers called 'capitols' at their southwest and southeast corners. What had once been 'a fabrick firme and faire',[5] however, was now shabby and dilapidated, and there was no money to restore it: when the crown of the tower was blown down in 1633, it was rebuilt only after a public appeal for funds. Marischal was no better. It was housed near the centre of the New Town, off Broadgate, in the former Franciscan convent. The residences had been turned into classrooms, a common school, a dining hall and living quarters. They were, the staff later complained, 'mean and incapable to lodge our Students, or allow conveniency for our publick Solemnities';[6] a problem aggravated in 1639, when part of the college was destroyed by fire.

Thomas entered King's when morale there was low. Following the Reformation the college had been purged then reconstructed: teaching was re-focused upon arts and theology, and delivered by a slimmed-down staff. This change of strategy was embodied in the 'New Foundation', modelled on the new constitutions created for the universities of Glasgow and St Andrews by the Reformer, Andrew Melville. Intended to re-energise King's as a centre of learning and a powerhouse of the Reformed Church, the New Foundation succeeded only in dividing it. Not until the robust chancellorship of Patrick Forbes, bishop of Aberdeen (1619–35), did the college recover; its gifted scholars teaching an arts course centred upon the works of Aristotle, reinterpreted in the light of new ideas and methods from the Continent. Marischal, in contrast, was buoyant. Founded in 1593 as an assertion of Protestant supremacy in the still resistant North East, its charter was modelled on the New Foundation and vigorously implemented by men like Gilbert Gray, principal from 1598 to 1614. Marischal's university status was unclear, however, and its relationship to King's uncertain. Nevertheless, by the time Alexander entered, its first graduates were already distinguishing themselves; and under Principal Patrick Dun (1621–49) it matched King's luminary for luminary.[7]

Both colleges provided what their Foundations called 'an honourable education'. Over a period of four years Thomas and Alexander were instructed not only in philosophy and religion but also in piety and morality. In accordance with what the New Foundation called the 'right fashioning of youth', they read Cicero's *On Duties* in their third year, partly to improve their Latin, partly 'for the better shaping of [their] morals.' They were required, in return, to be diligent in their studies, dutiful in their religion and seemly in their conduct, living in harmony with their fellow-students under a strict code of discipline. They were also expected to be grateful; showing their gratitude not simply by paying their fees on time but by supporting their colleges in later life. Bursars, as recipients of college or private charity, were judged by even higher standards.

Students had obligations, then, but few rights. Thomas enjoyed the long-established immunities of King's: he was subject to the jurisdiction of the chancellor and not 'obliged to answer before any other judge or judicatory whatsoever.'[8] Alexander was liable, within the walls of Marischal, to 'all . . . iurisdiction that to ane frie college within this realme be law and practick is knawin to apertene'; beyond them, he was subject 'to the iurisdiction of the provest, baillies and counsaill of the . . . burgh of abirdene.'[9] Additionally, under the Foundations they were entitled to participate in the election of their rectors by voting in one of the four student 'nations': Mar and Buchan (comprising the diocese of Aberdeen), Moray (the North) and Angus (the South).[10] Beyond this, however, they had no say in college government and no appeal against it: at matriculation they bound themselves freely and without qualification to obey the principal, his colleagues and the laws of the college.

Toil away, night and day

Under the Foundations students in arts accumulated their knowledge and skills 'step by step'. There are occasional references to the traditional, intermediate qualifications: at King's, it was said, 'in the third [year] there is the degree of bachelor; in the fourth, the licenciate'.[11] At Marischal, according to the *Leges*, 'students of the third class . . . may be adorned with the first grade of honour which they call the baccalaureate.' Generally, however, the course was seen as a four-year continuum, culminating in the degree of Master: William Lauder (1628), in his 'Panegyricus', grandly compared it to an Olympiad.

Preparations for the academic year began in September, when the colleges advertised their vacant bursaries. The session itself began on 1 October, although the preliminaries must have taken longer than the single day prescribed for them. Prospective entrants were to be tested on their Latin and the proficient admitted; competitors for bursaries were to be tested on their Latin, their conduct and their means, and the most deserving selected; and matriculated students were to begin to present themselves, one by one, for the examination that would determine whether or not they would proceed to the next class. At King's, by the 1620s, there had been some slippage, and students assembled gradually over several weeks.[12] The visitation of 1634 tightened things up: students were to convene on 29 September, easing the process of admission, and a fortnight was set aside for examinations. At Marischal, the *Statuta* already allocated a full month to these.

Teaching began as soon as examinations were over. Neither of the Foundations prescribed a timetable, but the programme imposed at King's in 1634 probably reflects the original structure of the ten-month session. The first three classes were to have lectures from 15 October to 15 July. The fourth class was to finish lectures on 3 May and to 'continew in repeitting' (revising) until 15 June. It then proceeded to 'examinatioun, tryallis and graduatioun',[13] the last taking place in July. At Marischal, under the *Statuta*, all four classes were taught through July. There were no vacations. Both Foundations were concerned 'that no loss be incurred to either morals or letters by the interruption of studies'. By the end of the period, however, King's had a regular break at Christmas (below, p. 35). Once the colleges had dispersed, students had August and September to themselves.

Teaching at King's at first followed the traditional practice of 'regenting', in which a single master took students through all four years of their course.[14] The New Foundation had, in fact, rejected this practice, prescribing instead the 'professorial' system, in which students were taught each year by a different master, who became something of a specialist in that year's portion of the curriculum. This was not introduced into the college effectively, however, until 1628. Students in the first class were also coached in Latin and rhetoric by the grammarian (or humanist), whom some would have encountered already in his school in the college grounds. At Marischal, they were taught from the start by the professorial system: the principal and three masters were each responsible for a year of the course until 1620, when a fourth master was appointed to free the principal's time. In the same year the master of the town grammar school was hired to teach Latin to the first class, presumably in emulation of King's, but he withdrew soon afterwards.[15]

Students at both colleges spent up to 50 hours a week in the classroom. From Monday to Friday they worked from 6 am to 9 am, excluding college prayers, and from 10 am until noon. On two afternoons they resumed from 1 or 2 pm until around 6 pm; on the remaining three, when they had games, they recommenced at 4 pm. When the evenings grew light they reconvened from 8 until 9 pm.[16] On Saturday the nature and pattern of their work changed, but the hours were much the same. When William Lauder spoke of students sweating over their studies, he was – for once – not exaggerating.[17]

Fundamental to their studies was the knowledge of Greek as well as Latin, since the Foundations, true to their Melvillean principles, ordained that all texts should be studied in their original language. At King's, therefore, the first class consolidated its skill in reading and writing Latin until March; it also began Greek, concentrating upon this from March onwards. The students were taught from 'the easiest and best authors' in both languages, presumably a concession to their mixed abilities. A note on the progress of the class of 1604 in its first year shows that Thomas Burnet's brother, Robert, had committed to memory the ninth book of the *Iliad*, two chapters of Nonnus, three orations of Isocrates, the 'praxis of Antesignanus', a letter of St Basil and the catechism in Greek.[18] The second class continued with Latin and Greek but focused on the study of eloquence and rhetoric; learning how to assemble information, construct an argument, and present it in writing or speech. It followed 'as easy a method as [the regent may choose]'; not a concession this time, but a nod towards the works of Peter Ramus, the Continental educator, whose ideas Andrew Melville had imported into Scotland.[19] The class was expected to emerge from these studies 'more fitted to grasp the rules of philosophy', which dominated the remaining two years of the curriculum. The third class studied logic, ethics and politics from the works of Aristotle, and mathematics. The fourth read Aristotle on physiology (natural science) and biology; going on to geography, astronomy, history and cosmography (including navigation); then it began to learn Hebrew. At Marischal, students studied the same subjects in the same order. Under the *Statuta* and the *Leges*, however, they were pushed harder, earlier, and studied core subjects such as logic – 'the key of the whole College and the courss therof verie long'[20] – over two years. In the first class they not only did Latin and Greek but also learned the basics of eloquence and rhetoric; in the second, they began logic and continued it in the third, when they started natural science, completing this in the fourth. In the 1620s the first and second classes were also taught elementary mathematics as part of a scheme to give the subject greater prominence.[21]

The standard mode of instruction in the classroom was the lecture, delivered daily, usually in the first teaching period. Masters often dictated their lectures, the fluent stream of Greek text and Latin commentary frequently taxing the penmanship of the students, to judge from what may be the earliest surviving Marischal notebook, of 1602–03.[22] Some students made fair copies of these 'dictates', selling them on to their successors: the 'Compendium of Logic' written up by a student in the second class at Marischal in 1622 was re-used by Robert Dunn (1623) there two

1 Sir Thomas Burnett of Leys, 1636, a 'sober, grave man'. Aberdeen University Picture Collection.

years later. Dictates taken down in the first and second classes generally comprised line-by-line readings of literary texts, like the 'Explanation in Latin of the more obscure words and sentences in Isocrates, Demosthenes, Homer' in the notebook of 1602–03. In the third and fourth classes they consisted of close-reading plus commentary, like the 'Annotations on the Acroamatic Books of Aristotle', which William Moir (1613) took down in the third class at Marischal. Alternatively, they might be complete courses on discrete subjects, like those on anatomy and mathematics recorded respectively by John Moir (1616) and James Downie (1630) in the fourth class there.[23] Students were expected to memorise the lecture on the day it was delivered, revising it through group work. At King's, all four classes are said to have assembled in the common school at 11 am to 'dispute [the lectures they had heard] amongst themselves until noon, while their professors walk about in their midst.'[24] At Marischal, under the *Statuta*, the process was prescribed in detail. Each class heard its master lecture from about 7 am to 9 am. At 10 am it had an hour of supervised or private study. At 11 am it reassembled in the classroom and, supervised by its master, divided into small groups to go over the lecture; under the *Leges* the class worked in pairs. Students who needed more time revised in private later. Then, towards the end of the afternoon, the master tested the class on the lecture for 90 minutes.

Students were also required to develop what would nowadays be called 'transferable skills'. Those prescribed in the Foundations were partly literary. The first and second classes spent an hour a day on composition, in which they were encouraged by a competition founded by Duncan Liddel: 'the haill learned men within baith the tounes as also the schollaris of the colledges and grammer schooles' were invited to compose Latin verses and orations. In 1623, when the competition was first held, William Massie (1620), a Liddel bursar, won £3 and a wreath.[25] In 1624 he shared the prize with Thomas Chalmer (1624), another Liddel bursar.[26] The compositional skills fostered at King's are illustrated in poetic tributes addressed in 1631 to a benefactor, including one by William Lauder.[27]

The skills on which students spent most time and effort were those of declamation and disputation, essential to a career in the church, teaching or public office. Under the *Statuta* Marischal students worked on them throughout the week. In the classroom they read texts selected by their masters as models of style. In private they noted maxims and aphorisms that might later give them rhetorical edge; a practice foreshadowed in the notebook of 1602–03, which contains quotations from, amongst others, Virgil, Ovid, Sallust, Euripides and Themistocles. On Saturdays they put it all into practice.[28]

Under the Foundations Saturday declamations and disputations followed the same pattern at both colleges. Students became involved halfway through their second year, when they had mastered the basics of public speaking. From March onwards the second class declaimed, while the third and fourth declaimed and disputed.

The exercises were treated as a competition; officially as a spur to effort, possibly also to legitimise the rivalry such events stimulated. The students were divided into teams and voted for the most proficient performer in each. At King's, the time and place of the exercise is not recorded; it was probably held in the common school and must have occupied the morning only, as the afternoon was used for games. At Marischal, under the *Statuta*, significant changes were made. The exercises were held from November to July: the second and third classes took part throughout; the fourth stopped in April to prepare for graduation and was replaced by the first class, which gave declamations until the end of the session. Under this arrangement, therefore, the first class joined in the Saturday exercises a year earlier than before. At the same time the organisation of the exercises was improved. The participants in each class were chosen by their master or by lot, and lists were posted in the classroom and the common school. Those chosen to declaim were excused only in extreme circumstances and had then to arrange for a substitute; those excused from disputing were replaced arbitrarily by the master. They performed in their classroom, beginning around 7 am. Declaimants spoke from memory on 'worthy, needful or useful' topics assigned by their master, who also chose the propositions to be disputed. They received feedback from him on their diction and oratorical style and were expected to incorporate it in their next performance. They had also to supply him with a written version of their speech, so that it could not be re-used. Although the competitive structure had been abandoned at Marischal, the stringent rules under which participants performed were not: 'we permit [you] to inveigh against vices not people,' they were told and were forbidden to use abusive language against fellow-students, professors, citizens or strangers.

Outsiders were included in the protected species because, as a further means of improving the standard of declamation and disputation, Marischal students gave four annual, open displays before local worthies. The fourth class performed in November, the third in February, and the second in April. In each case two students declaimed for and against a given topic, then a third extracted a set of theses (propositions) from what he had heard and defended them against all comers. The first class appeared in July: its representatives declaimed, but instead of disputing, for which they were not yet trained, they interpreted a passage of the New Testament. Like the participants from the other three years they were carefully rehearsed beforehand by their master: open displays were evidently as much about showcasing the college as they were about oratory and argument.

Students were expected to take responsibility for their own learning through private study in their rooms during meal breaks and at night. This was when they read, copied out quotations, wrote out their notes, or prepared their declamations: in 1633 when, owing to lack of rooms and beds, Marischal students were lodged in the town house, the principal claimed that it was 'to the greit hinderance of thair studies'.[30] They received assistance from several quarters. At Marischal, under the *Statuta*, they were encouraged to seek help from the master who inspected their rooms first thing in the morning, and from the master of their class before morning and evening prayers. They also had peer support: during the period of communal learning at 11 am, group leaders not only helped those who had specific difficulties with the lecture but acted as mentors; when they went over the lecture in pairs, each partner was held responsible for the other's progress. Boys from wealthy families, especially those living at a distance, were often accompanied to college by tutors, who oversaw their learning. In 1605, for example, the principal of King's corresponded with a laird, whose son was to enter the college 'vithe his pedagogue', and referred in passing to 'the Maister of Ogilvie his sonnis vithe their pedagogue'.[31]

Those who did not learn were punished. King's ordained in 1637 that bursars who made no progress were to be 'censurat and remowit.'[32] At Marischal, under the *Statuta*, any students who did not memorise the lecture were to be punished strictly; repeating offenders were taken to the principal, who made a public example of them before administering a beating. Those who played truant in teaching periods, notably in the evening session, were also punished, probably with a fine or a stroke upon the palm, the usual penalties for absence without leave. The Saturday declamations and disputations bristled with punishable offences: students who avoided declaiming, or were absent without leave from the exercises, or used abusive language, all received the same (but unspecified) punishment. The importance attached to peer support is underlined by the fate of those who failed to provide it: when students worked in pairs, both were to be punished if one failed his test.

Students had little need of printed books: dictates were, in effect, the textbooks of their day. There is little evidence from either college to show that they possessed, or had access to, other material.[33] Nathaniel Welsh (1626) is the exception: he was furnished with books – unspecified, alas – by the council of the New Town before he entered Marischal as a Liddel bursar.[34] The college libraries, notably at Marischal, were enriched at this time with handsome bequests, but there is nothing to show that arts students used them.[35]

Under the Foundations students were examined on at least three occasions in their academic career. They had a foretaste of the process, however, as entrants or as candidates for bursaries, when they were tested on their Latin. They appeared individually before a panel composed of the principal, masters and representatives of the town, and chaired by the dean of the faculty of arts, who was responsible in each college for the conduct of examinations. At Marischal, under the *Statuta*, the test comprised oral translation of Latin speeches and poetry, and translation into Latin; while a competitor for a Liddel bursary had to 'have learned his grammer with the vsuall authoris with ane beginning of his greek grammer'.[36] The testing of newcomers who applied to enter a higher class does not appear to have been regulated until the visitation of 1634, when a panel of examiners from both colleges was established. The main examinations were held at the beginning of the second, third and fourth years before students were allowed to enter the next class. They were again individual and oral, covering the previous year's coursework; the examiners are not identified but, by analogy with the practice at Glasgow, would have included at least the dean, the principal and the masters.[37] Students who were judged unsatisfactory were kept back until they reached the required standard. The importance attached to these examinations by the colleges is shown by the time devoted to them and by the severity with which attendance was enforced: at Marischal, under the *Statuta*, latecomers were fined heavily for each day of their absence and were examined more rigorously than their classmates.

For a time, at least, all four classes at King's underwent an additional annual assessment, reports of which survive from the period 1603–08.[38] The students were examined on their coursework and conduct in the classroom and were placed in one of three grades; they then 'circulated' (processed) in files and circles according to their grading. In 1603–04, for example, Thomas Burnet came first in the first grade of the first class, heading a file of three. In some cases the assessors (not identified) explained their decision: John Leslie, in the second grade of the second class, was 'first in intellect but last in probity of conduct'; John Fyfe and Matthew Lumsden, in the third grade of the third class, were placed last because they were 'deceitful, idle and disrespectful'.[39] No such fate awaited Thomas Burnet: he proceeded to come equal first in the third and fourth class.

Students in the fourth class who intended to graduate as Master of Arts faced a further examination. First, however, they had to demonstrate their eligibility. At Marischal, under the *Statuta*, they had to have completed all four years of the course and paid their tuition and other college fees. They had then to take an oath to respond in a seemly fashion during the examination and to abide by the verdict of the examiners, who would again have included the dean, the principal and the masters. The examination at King's is said to have comprised 'various disputations, first private then public'.[40] The former are presumably the 'examinatiounes and tryallis' that followed the 'repeitting' of their lectures. The public disputation usually took place on a day in July; recorded dates range from the 16th to the 26th. It was held in the common school from noon until evening in the 1620s, from dawn to midday in the 1630s.[41] At Marischal, under the *Statuta*, candidates were examined internally on their entire course.[42] The public disputation there also took place in July, in the morning; probably in the common school like the open exercises earlier in the year. With their master presiding, candidates attacked or defended theses that he had devised; from the 1620s onwards these were published in advance. The examination, to be effective, must have involved audience participation, but there is no record of this. The earliest, documented public disputation was held at Marischal in 1616. John Seton (1612) and six other students defended theses presented under the headings, General, Logic, Ethics, Physics and Spheres (astronomy). Under Ethics, for example, they defended theses which began with Aristotle's view of the relationship between the dead and the living, and went on

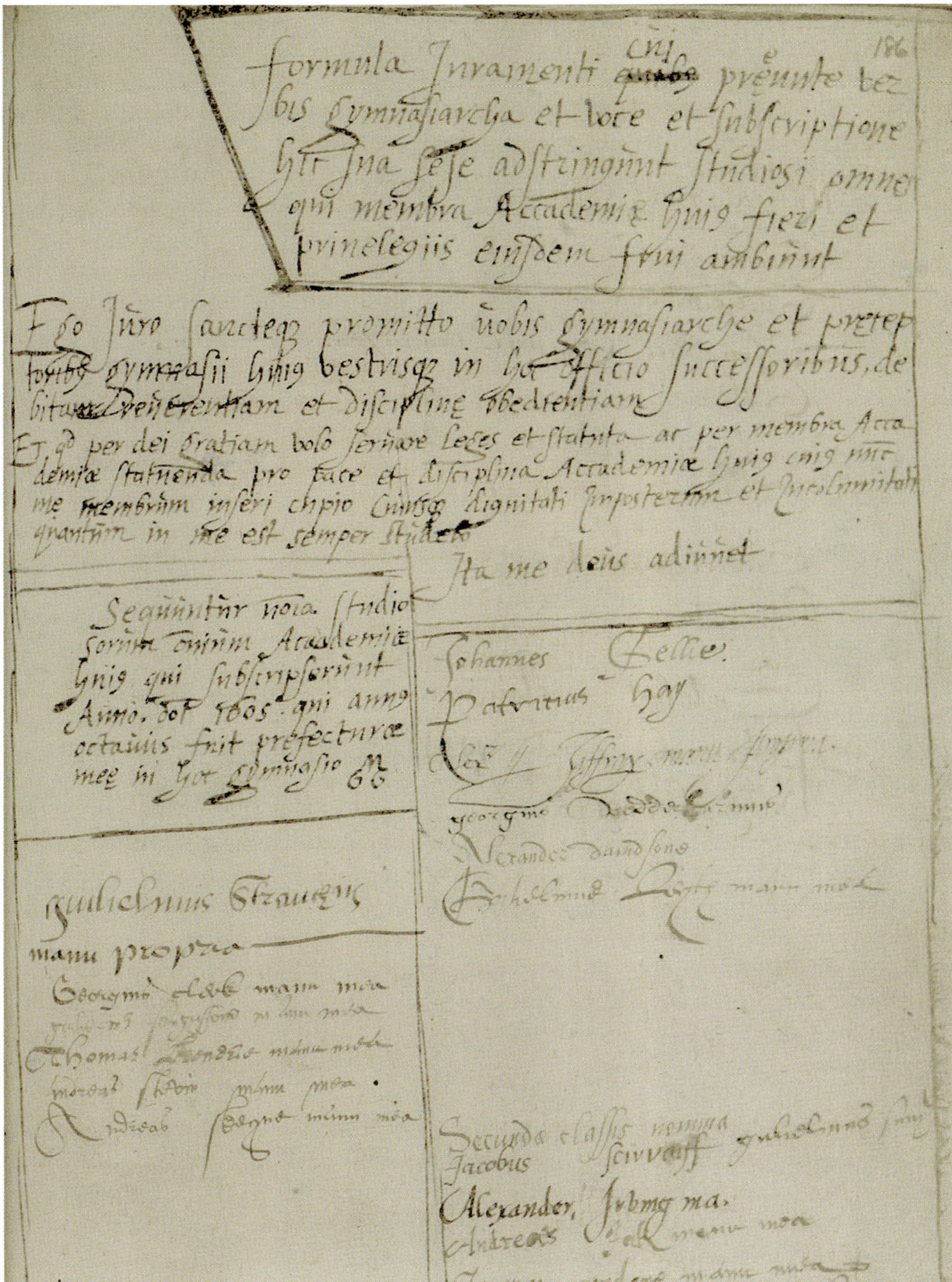

2 Alexander Jaffray, as a tertian at Marischal in 1605, subscribes Principal Gray's statutes with his own hand, 'manu propria'. AUL, MS M 2, f 186.

to deny the efficacy of requiem masses and the concept of purgatory.[43] When the disputation ended, the examiners named the candidates who merited the degree and ranked them in order of proficiency. John and the others all passed.

Students graduated as Master of Arts either on the day of the public disputation or immediately afterwards. According to the Foundations, the degree was 'the crown', 'the finishing-touch', and 'the laurel', and the graduation ceremonies at King's and Marischal reflected this sentiment. At King's, the event was said to last for at least two days and to be marked by such elaborate orations and erudite lectures 'that it exceeds all belief and cannot easily by credited by those who have not seen it'; Simon Fraser, Master of Lovat (Inverness-shire), a student there in 1636–37, stayed on simply to catch it.[44] Unfortunately, the only vestiges of the ceremony are two ornate orations made by the presiding masters and two versions of the graduation oath.[45] The ceremonial at Marischal, however, can be reconstructed from the Foundation Charter and *Statuta*. John Seton and his fellow graduands would have processed in the common school, in the order in which they had been ranked by the examiners, led by the student who was considered to be the most diligent, modest and pious among them. After taking the graduation oath before the dean of faculty, professing their faith, and promising to give in later life what support they could to the college, they would have been invested by the principal with the Master's cap.

Some students valued the degree, either as a mark of achievement or as a requirement for postgraduate study. At Marischal, according to the *Statuta*, it could not be gained either by prayers or bribes, suggesting that both had been tried; and in 1615 the fourth class there declared that 'they are most desyrous . . . to be determinat Maisters.'[46] Other students, having completed the academic courses, left without graduating (Table 1.1). Of the class of 1620 at King's, for example, 16 entered, 11 stayed on into the fourth year, three left before graduation.[47] No reasons for this are given, although they doubtless included the cost of a further four months residence and the irrelevance of the degree to those who did not intend to enter a profession. It was probably for the latter, or for family reasons, that Thomas Burnet, the best student of his class in its first, third and fourth years, did not become a Master of Arts.

Students were discouraged from celebrating their graduation or the completion of their course. Under the Foundations, they were not allowed to hold graduation feasts, a prohibition repeated at the visitation of King's in 1628 and at Marischal under the *Statuta*. Instead, they had to contribute towards the upkeep of the fabric or the library; at Kings, this was made a condition of graduation. King's did, however, permit the 'valediction', an oration that celebrated the end of teaching for the year. Accordingly, on 15 May 1632 the four classes assembled to hear William Lauder deliver his 'Panegyricus'. Buried in his flatulent Latin prose was some sound advice. '[I] urge you,' he told the first class, 'with all my heart to toil away night and day in the study of Greek.' 'The difficult beginnings of logic,' he told the second, 'yield gall to you [now], but in the end, they will furnish you with honey.' And he urged the third class not to flag: ' "Well begun is half done", is in my opinion a compliment owed . . . only to those who persevere to the end.'[48]

The profundities of the scriptures

King's and Marischal saw themselves, and were seen by others, as seminaries 'baith of the Kirk and commoun weill'.[49] Their students therefore received an education that was, according to the Foundation Charter, 'godly' as well as 'liberal'. The godly side consisted of religious instruction and regular worship. As a prerequisite, however, students had to profess their adherence to the Confession of Faith 'at least once a year';[50] at Marischal, under the *Leges*, they had to affirm their profession by participating in the Lord's Supper and were expelled if they recanted.

Students received daily instruction in religion. At King's, under the New Foundation, the third and fourth classes attended the principal's lectures on 'the profundities of the Scriptures' and 'the sacred tongue' (Hebrew). These were supposed to be delivered from Monday to Friday, with a test on Saturday. They were often neglected, however, by over-worked or under-motivated principals, with predictable results: in 1638 they were reduced to two a week, to be given 'altho [the principal] suld have but two or thrie auditouris.'[51] At Marischal, under the Foundation Charter, all four classes attended the principal's lecture on theology;[52] a weekly event because, until 1620, the principal was responsible for teaching the fourth class. In addition, under the *Statuta*, each class had a short period of bible study before the morning lecture, while the first class also read through the New Testament in Greek. Under the Foundations students at both colleges had identical instruction on Sunday. At 6 am each class read a book of the New Testament in Greek and was tested on it at 4 pm; the first and second class worked, respectively, through the narratives of Luke and Acts; the third and fourth, through the doctrinal issues of the Epistles to the Romans and the Hebrews. At Marischal, under the *Statuta*, however, the first class had to study the Catechism of Ursinus (the Heidelberg Catechism).

Students worshipped in college on weekdays, assembling in the common school for morning and evening prayers. These are said to have begun at 8 am and 5 pm at King's;[53] at Marischal, under the *Statuta*, they were held at 6 am and 6 pm; in each case they may have lasted about 30 minutes.[54] At Marischal, under the *Leges*, they were conducted by a precentor and would therefore have included psalms; they also included a reading from the New Testament or a historical work, and catechism. Although the occasion was used for roll-calls and other business, college prayers remained a solemn act of collective worship; under the *Statuta* rowdy or irreverent conduct was punished with a beating.

In addition, students heard sermons during the week and attended divine service and sermons twice on Sundays. From King's, where the chapel had been abandoned for worship since the Reformation,[55] they went to the parish church of St Machar; from Marischal, to the West Church of St Nicholas.[56] Little is known about their attendance in the week: in 1606, when the inhabitants of the Old Town had 'preichingis' on Wednesdays, King's students may have joined them; at Marischal, under the *Statuta*, students may have heard sermons on Wednesdays and Fridays.[57] Sunday attendance is better documented, especially at Marischal.[58] Under the *Statuta* students processed to the West Church in silence, with 'dignity and civility', accompanied by their masters; at King's, the procession was led by the principal.[59] Inside the church they had to settle quietly and inconspicuously: a separate loft was built to accommodate them in 1612.[60] They had to listen reverently and attentively, and were tested on the sermons afterwards. Any breach of conduct was punished by a beating but not until the following day. By 1633, however, procedure at both churches had grown lax: students no longer wore their gowns, and they mingled 'promiscuouslie' with the congregation. This scandalised Charles I when he heard of it during a visit to Scotland that year: it 'looses much of the honour and dignitie of the universities,' he wrote to the bishop of Aberdeen in 1634, insisting that 'the studentis . . . repair [to church] in decent manner with thair gouvernouris . . . and that they use the said habit of gownes . . . in schooles, universities, and streetes.' He also ordered the councils of the Old and New Towns to 'prowyd fitt and convenient places within the quires of the severall churches' where students could sit. At the visitation of 1634, King's enforced the wearing of gowns in church and elsewhere, threatening any student who disobeyed with demotion to a lower class; this was the only recorded use of that punishment for a non-academic offence, showing how seriously the college took the king's letter.[61]

Relaxation of the mind

Under the Foundations students were given time for sport. The aim, according to the *Leges*, was 'relaxation of the mind', although it also burned off excess energy. The limited space in the college courtyards, however, and the proximity of crumbling stone and breakable glass meant that ball games, in particular, had to be played beyond the walls. This, together with the violence such games could unloose, meant that sport had to be controlled. As a result, under the Foundations and the *Statuta*, it was a licensed, periodic activity, supervised by a master, in which all four classes participated together, presumably to save time.

There were games, weather permitting, between 2 and 4 pm, three days a week: at King's, on Tuesdays, Thursdays and Saturdays; at Marischal, on Mondays, Wednesdays and Fridays. Students played on the Links beside the shore, which were easily accessible from the back gates of both colleges. Every effort was made to keep them out of trouble, especially truancy and fights. They processed to and from the Links, generally accompanied by a master, and they played in designated areas from which they were not allowed to stray. Marischal students were forbidden to get into games with other, more experienced players; to play for money or drink; or to use violence on the field. The last injunction was the hardest to observe since, until the middle of May at least, they were playing football. There were two matches, the players determined by age and rank and kept well apart. Two footballs were provided by the first class, their replacement and disposal carefully regulated. At King's, a variety of other 'exercises and recreations' was open to well-born students: in 1636–37 Simon Fraser outshone his peers at 'ballown, cachpole, byars, bowles, the goffe, and artching'; he also won the silver arrow for 'bowmarks and rovers', although the competition may have been rigged to ensure that he did not lose face.[62]

Strict moral discipline

Students spent up to 90 hours a week outside their classrooms apart from college prayers and church. For those who lived in, each hour was earmarked. They rose at 5 am, wakened at King's by the bursars, who brought them lights. All students then remained in their rooms until 6 am, awaiting inspection. They had breakfast from 9 to 10 am; dinner; from noon to 1 pm;[63] six hours of sport; supper from 7 to 8 pm; and they retired for the night at 9 pm. Free time in and between these slots they spent studying in their rooms. Students who lived outside had more latitude: they did not come into college until 6 am, and when they left again, at meals and at night, their time was effectively their own.

Whether they lived in or out, students had to conduct themselves according to standards set by the colleges, maintained through close supervision and enforced by punishment. The reasons for this were given in their fullest form in the *Leges*:

> The things that others have learned . . . youth can neither understand through age nor heed through experience, but with the freedom of the unbridled, it rushes at everything that presents itself and favours only what will give it pleasure. For this reason . . . youth can be shaped not only by educating it in piety and modesty but also by holding it to its duty and controlling it by laws and discipline . . .

Under the Foundations students were to be 'shaped' both individually and communally. As individuals they were to become 'diligent in their studies and upright in morals'; as a community they were to learn to 'live peaceably among themselves with the utmost harmony'. The colleges, however, were communities within communities: under the *Statuta* Marischal students had 'to learn to live in peace and love not only with themselves but with others.'

The rigours of their timetable and the relentless ringing of the college bells would have left students in no doubt that they had to be diligent. Nevertheless, at Marischal,

3 King's College around 1640. The indistinct figures processing towards the crown tower may be staff and students. Aberdeen University Picture Collection.

the *Statuta* left nothing to chance. They were forbidden to linger around the college door at the beginning and end of the day or after church. As soon as meals were over, they had to go to their rooms and study until teaching resumed without distracting their room-mates. Similarly, the morality instilled through religious instruction and regular devotions was fortified against temptation. Students were forbidden to play games of chance, frequent taverns and other places selling drink, or wander around the town, especially in the winter darkness. These injunctions may have been intended as much to keep them safe as to keep them out of trouble; but Duncan Liddel, benefactor of Marischal, had no problem envisaging students as 'hiure-masters, theefes, breakers of yeards and sic lyk.'[64] Students were also to be 'modest' (moderate and refined), especially in their dress. They were to look clean and neat; black gowns fastened, black hats covering hair that was trimmed, not long or elaborately styled. Bursars had to dress uniformly in a distinctively subdued fashion, in long, dark gowns fastened with a white leather belt.[65] Finally, students were to behave with civility: 'he who is proficient in learning and deficient in manners lacks more than he gains.' They had to speak Latin at all times: at King's, it was said, the first words spoken on a dark winter's morning were 'Vultis lumen?' (Do you want a light?)[66] At meals they were to be circumspect in their conversation; at other times they were forbidden to talk profanely or sing vulgar songs, 'lest from licence to speak in an unseemly manner, licence to behave in a shameless fashion should follow.'

The Foundations tried as far as possible to confine students to the safe, moral haven of the college. Those who lived in were not normally allowed outside the gates. Those who lodged elsewhere were subject to the same restriction once they entered them. The emphasis within the walls was upon peace and harmony. In an age when what the Privy Council poetically called 'the weid of deidlie feid' was rampant,[67] not least in Aberdeenshire, macho behaviour and provocative acts were outlawed: under the *Statuta* students were not to attack or ridicule each other in lampoons or to utter insults; if insulted, they were not to respond with force. Violence, whether in college or on the playing field, was not tolerated: students were forbidden to wear armour or carry arms, a prohibition first issued in the Foundations and constantly renewed. When they were allowed out into the town, students were not to disgrace themselves or their college. Marischal on its city-centre site was especially sensitive to public opinion; fearful, as the *Statuta* shows, that the sight of uncivil, foppish or idle students would cause outrage, shame and disgrace. The college insisted that its students should treat the townspeople, especially ministers and magistrates, with respect, and that they should at all costs keep the peace. This was notoriously at risk when disputes among the students themselves, or with the students at King's, spilled out into the streets. Around 1600, students matriculating at Marischal had to swear that they would not carry weapons in the town and that they would not get into contention with older students, even light-heartedly, without permission from the principal;[68] under the *Statuta* they had to settle disputes with King's in the presence of the staff, 'lest [they] proceed from words to blows as has been the custom amongst them.'

Students could only meet these standards if they submitted to 'strict moral discipline'. The Foundations therefore empowered the principals of both colleges to enact 'good statutes for preserving discipline firm and secure'. The maintenance of discipline depended so much upon the principal that during a brief interregnum at Marischal in 1614–15 it broke down, and special measures (below, p. 24) were needed to restore it.[69] Statutes were to be made 'as occasion may demand and for special purposes'; they soon proliferated, affecting every aspect of students' lives from entry to graduation – quite literally at King's, where the visitation of 1634 required the fourth class 'to continue in discipline until laureation day.' These laws were regularly collected, codified and updated by the principal and masters. Although no codes survive from King's before 1641, their existence was mentioned at the visitations of 1619 and 1634. The *Statuta* shows signs of several, undated revisions. At King's, matriculating students swore to obey the statutes of the college, although the form of the oath is not recorded. At Marischal, there are three versions, in each of which students promised to obey 'the laws and statutes of the college, which have been ordained or may be ordained for securing and preserving peace and discipline.'[70] There is, however, no reference to the public reading of the laws until 1634, when the principal of King's, having neglected the duty, was ordered to read them each December in the presence of the masters and the students.

Students were constrained to obey the laws by a series of administrative procedures. Under the *Statuta*, for example, they had to have oral or written leave of absence before they could go beyond the gates. The rule was reinforced by early-morning and evening inspections to catch those who had, again literally, gone over the wall. There were also roll-calls: before morning prayers to identify absentees and latecomers; after breakfast and dinner to ensure that those who ate in town had returned; and at evening prayers. On games afternoons students were checked when they arrived at the playing fields and again when they returned, in case any had absconded on the way. The regimented columns in which they processed to games, church and sometimes a funeral, were a further precaution against surreptitious desertions. The pivotal figure in all this was the hebdomadar, a post held by each of the masters on a weekly rota. It was he who gave the students leave of absence, inspected their rooms, and usually escorted them to games;[71] at Marischal, he kept the college keys after the boarders had been locked in for the night. The hebdomadar was assisted by his fellow masters but especially by the public censor, who was appointed from among the students. At King's, the public censor is an obscure figure, who is said to have called the register at prayers and before Saturday declamations and disputations.[72] At Marischal, under the *Statuta*, he held his post for a week, taking the four main roll calls and reporting to the principal on Saturday or Monday with a list of absentees. He also reported the names of students who swore, spoke in the vernacular, or behaved in a disruptive fashion in college, at church and in the town. Under the *Leges* he took over the hebdomadar's duties at games. Marischal also had class censors, who reported to the master, daily and in private, the names of those who talked, were idle, or caused trouble in the classroom; in addition, they were empowered to give students leave to go out of the college. Open to abuse as they no doubt were, the censors' powers seem to have been taken for granted in what was, after all, an age of licensed spying and prying.[73] Students had yet another authority figure to contend with: 'our discipline,' wrote the principal of Marischal, 'rests in no small way on the integrity of a diligent and honest janitor.' He had to unlock the gates between 5 and 6 am and during the breakfast, dinner and supper hours; he had to man them at all other times; and he was to allow no student to leave without permission.[74] At King's, these duties were originally delegated to bursars, but a porter was appointed by 1604.[75] The power of the masters and the censors to report students who infringed college discipline extended beyond the college walls. In the New Town, at least, they had allies: under the *Statuta* and the *Leges* townsfolk themselves were empowered to report students seen wandering the streets.

Discipline, embodied in the codes of laws and maintained by a system of passes, checks and informers, was enforced by punishment. The principles on which this was to be administered were set out in the Foundations: penalties should be in accordance with the seriousness of the offence; the severest reserved for those who re-offended. Accordingly, students who carried weapons were to be punished on the first occasion with confiscation, on the second with a beating, and on the third with expulsion. Under the *Statuta* the same fate awaited Marischal students who, after a single warning only, gambled, drank or wandered the streets, and those who repeatedly wrote lampoons. The concept of shared guilt was also present in the *Statuta* and the *Leges*: both parties in a fight were punished, and those who circulated lampoons were penalised along with those who composed them.[76] Punishment had to fit not only the crime but the widely disparate ages and means of the offenders. Corporal punishment, which could be administered with varying degrees of severity, was common for first and second offences. Under the *Statuta* students were beaten for climbing over the walls, staying out overnight and obstructing the hebdomadar during inspections; for behaving violently or disruptively on the playing field; for composing lampoons or failing to suppress them; for gathering idly around the gates; and for defiling the college or interfering with the college bell.[77] Those who were absent without leave, swore, or spoke in the vernacular, were struck on the palm of the hand for the first offence; those who did it three times were beaten. Beatings were administered in public, presumably as a deterrent, possibly to prevent private abuse: this meant that the hebdomadar could not administer punishment for offences committed during the evening or in the course of his rounds but had to reserve it until the college assembled the next day. In some cases students received financial penalties. Those who were absent without leave, swore, or spoke in the vernacular could be fined a small sum for the first offence instead of being struck on the hand, although under the *Leges* only the fine was imposed; for the second offence the fine was doubled. Those who damaged the furnishings of their room or the fabric of the college had to pay twice the cost of the damage. The punishment of students who were idle, infringed the rules on dress, and disturbed their roommates is unspecified and may have been left to the masters' discretion. Bursars were punished more severely, facing deprivation and expulsion for offences that might otherwise have merited beating, fining or relegation. At King's in 1637, when they were examined on both their 'literatour and guid behauiour', those who 'beis fund insufficiente' could be removed directly.'[78]

The conduct and control of students was as much a matter of concern to the councils of the Old and New Town as it was to King's and Marischal. The close relationship between King's and the bailies of the Old Town, which ensured that '[their] severall juresdictions be not confoundit', also served to protect students from temptation and exploitation by the townsfolk. The bailies ordained, for example, that 'na browster gif any scholler ather meit or drink within this citie'; that 'na yeoung man within this toune that hes not ane hous or rent of his awin play at cartis tabillis or dyss'; and that no-one was to lend a student 'aboue ane merk piece vpon ane word or vtherwayis'; and they banished Margaret Duncan and her husband for, amongst other crimes, enticing students to their house and 'abstracting' them from their studies.[79] The relationship between Marischal and the New Town council over their respective jurisdictions was less comfortable; nevertheless, the issue of delinquent students does not seem to have been a problem. The magistrates worked with the college to end the breakdown of discipline during the interregnum of 1614–15, and the single recorded breach of the peace was resolved to both sides' satisfaction: in 1619 Robert Boyd (1616) assaulted one of the townsfolk and was imprisoned by the magistrates, but 'being unable to pay his fine and unlaw he was ordered to be scourged in the common school in presence of two of the Baillies.'[80] As trustees of the bursaries founded privately at Marischal, the council had the power to deprive bursars of their awards if their performance or conduct was deemed unsatisfactory by the college, or if they breached the conditions of their bursary: it deprived Robert Mercer (1631) of his Liddel bursary when he 'publictlie declairit that he will not wear a blak bonnet and gowne'.[81]

Four years of fellowship

When William Lauder had finished dispensing advice to his juniors in his 'Panegyricus' in 1632, he turned to his fellow-members of the class of 1628, those due to graduate. Their 'four years of class-fellowship', he declared, had forged 'an unbreakable bond'.[82] The same kind of bonding, 17 years previously, had prompted the class of 1611 to take what became the first recorded instance of collective action in the history of the students of Aberdeen. Following the death of Principal Gray in December 1614, William Wedderburn and the eight other students of the fourth class at Marischal, whom the principal had been teaching, approached the council of the New Town. They were, they said, 'most desyrous to pas thair course

4 King's College around 1640. This engraving, loosely based upon the original (plate 3), shows the processing figures as students, hatted and gowned. It illustrates the 1791 edition of Orem's *Description*.

and to be determinat Maisters in [Marischal] rather than in any vther college within this kingdom.' They therefore begged it to appoint 'ane learned man' as their master to teach them for the remaining six months. The council, lacking the authority to appoint a new principal, appointed the master of the town grammar school, William's brother, to teach the class until July. Discipline in the college had broken down, however, and when the new master was appointed, he was given, with the agreement of the college, the disciplinary powers of the principal and more. On 1 February all four classes swore obedience to him, acknowledging, amongst other things, his right to search their rooms for concealed weapons.[83] William and his classmates may have anticipated this Draconian move as an inevitable consequence of their act; they may even have sought it. Either way, they acted with a significant degree of cohesion and confidence.

TABLE 1.1 ENTRANTS AND GRADUATES AT KING'S, 1600–39

Years	*Average annual number entering the first class*	*Average annual number of entrants who graduated*	*Graduates as % of entrants*
1600–09	19.6	10.4	53.0
1610–19	17.1	11.1	64.9
1620–29	20.1	10.1	50.2
1630–39	16.4	7.6	46.3

Source: Anderson, *Roll*, Appendix B. Complete figures for 1600 are not available.[84] Fully comparable figures for Marischal are not available: the average number of entrants, 1620–29, was 21.5; 1630–39, 22.9. Over six years in the period 1621–33, the average number of entrants was 22.3, graduates 10.6 (47.5%).

TABLE 1.2 CLASSES OF 1614 AND 1615 AT MARISCHAL, ACADEMIC YEARS 1614–19

Class	*1614–15*	*1615–16*	*1616–17*	*1617–18*	*1618–19*	*Graduated*	*%*
1614	21	19	12	9		8	38.0
1615		22	13	13	11	8	36.3

Source: Anderson, *FAM*, 2. The number of graduates is expressed as a percentage of entrants.

Classes at both colleges were for most of the period small, therefore intimate, and more likely to cohere. Fifteen students entered the class of 1611; eight of them (53%) made it to graduation.[85] Such low numbers reflect the overall trend at King's and Marischal (Tables 1.1–1.2). Although more students stayed on in the fourth class than actually graduated, there was nevertheless a significant fall in the size of the class over each four-year period, as the comprehensive listing of two classes at Marischal shows. Classes tapered irregularly as students dropped out; those who joined late were usually insufficient in number to make up the deficit. Departing students rarely left explanations. Alexander Jaffray's son and namesake (1630) was an exception: 'having staid a short time in the College and profited as little,' he left in 1632.[86] Lack of the means, ability or need to continue, together with expulsion, would have accounted for most departures; sickness and death for a few.[87] Numbers were also affected by the migration of students from one college to another. Again no reasons are given, although discontent seems the most likely. Marischal tried at first to prevent the practice: students matriculating in and around 1600 had to swear that they would not transfer to another institution before their course was finished 'except on the authority of [their] family . . . and not on the bad advice or encouragement of other people.'[88] Nevertheless, after Robert Coutts and Alexander Reid left for King's at the end of their first year in the Marischal class of 1611, there was continuous movement, mainly in the same direction. Migration was not confined to Aberdeen: at the visitation of 1634, King's and Marischal made the first of many joint attempts to regulate the entry of disaffected students from other Scottish universities. With all this mobility it is not surprising that some students went unrecorded, especially those who attended only briefly, like Simon Fraser. He arrived at King's in January 1636, moved on to St Andrews in the winter of 1637 'to try the different methods of learning there', then returned to King's in the spring of 1638, finally leaving in July.[89] Given this variability, the aggregate number of arts students at King's can only be estimated. At Marischal, however, there are comprehensive listings of students in seven years, which show the actual, aggregate number of arts students. Overall, there was little difference: both colleges reached the mid–50s. They were, nevertheless, notably smaller than the two other Scottish universities for which figures have been published: Glasgow had over 100 arts students in the 1630s; Edinburgh over 300.[90]

TABLE 1.3 ESTIMATED AGGREGATE NUMBERS OF ARTS STUDENTS AT KING'S, 1605–36

Class	*1605–06*	*1615–16*	*1625–16*	*1635–16*
First	11	25	23	24
Second	32	20	15	17
Third	10	17	9	9
Fourth	6	17	8	6
Aggregate	59	79	55	55

Source: Estimates based on Anderson, *Roll*, Appendix B, assuming an equal annual reduction in class numbers.

TABLE 1.4 ACTUAL AGGREGATE NUMBERS OF ARTS STUDENTS AT MARISCHAL, 1605–21

Year	*1605–06*	*1614–15*	*1615–16*	*1616–17*	*1617–18*	*1618–19*	*1620–21*
Aggregate	40	50	60	50	60	63	64

Source: Anderson, *FAM*, 2.

Students' ages are hard to establish. The few that are known – mainly of the famous and infamous – vary widely. Thomas Burnet was 12 or younger when he entered King's.[91] Thomas Urquhart (1622), the author and translator, was 11; Alexander Brodie (1631), the diarist, was 15; David Barclay (1626), the Quaker, and Simon Fraser were both 16.[92] Alexander Jaffray was older, possibly 19, when he entered Marischal; his son was 16; Robert Morison (1635), the botanist, as a Liddel bursar entered at 15;[93] William Keith (1631), later Earl Marischal, was 14. Similarly, evidence of students' social origins is, at best, impressionistic. The Foundations listed the ranks of society from which they were expected to come: 'princes and the upper nobility', 'the lower rank of nobility', 'farmers, ordinary merchants and craftsmen,' and 'those who are prevented by indigence from enjoying a good education'. Of the few at King's whose family or origins are recorded, the four sons of George, second Marquis of Huntly (1630, 1638),[94] came within the first category. The second and third categories were straddled by James Sharp: his father was factor to the Earl of Findlater; his grandfather was an Aberdeen merchant. Students below that level would probably have been on foundation bursaries, no records of which survive. At Marischal, the higher nobility was represented by the Earls Marischal: William, the sixth, and George, his brother, the seventh (1635). Landed families who sent sons there, besides the Jaffrays of Kingwells, included Skene of Dyce (1606), Fraser of Finzeauch (Keig) (1627), and Erskine of Pittodrie (1635). Although Marischal's bursaries were founded for the sons of the poor, preference was given to 'poore kinred', 'puire freynds' and 'poore men . . . burgesses of new Aberdeine'.[95] As a result, the Liddel and Cargill bursars at Marischal together included the sons of seven local ministers and 15 burgesses, a surgeon, two merchants and two officials of the New Town. Among the Liddel bursars themselves, William Massie was the son of a mason; Thomas Chalmer, an advocate; Robert Mercer and Nathaniel Welsh, a minister; and Robert Morison, a merchant. These bursars may well have been poor – fatherless or from large families fallen on hard times – but most of them came from groups in society, the professions, commerce and the crafts, characterised by a strong sense of self-interest, self-protection, and self-renewal. Evidence of students' geographical origins is even harder to find. At King's, the more notable students were dignified with the name of their lands, like Thomas Burnet of Leys and his classmate, Alexander Cumming of Culter. Most were from the North East and North: in the class of 1635, for example, heading the list of matriculants in accordance with convention, were Walter Ogilvie of Boyne (Banffshire), and Robert Innes of Innes (Moray); George Gordon of Gight, Gilbert Ogilvie of Craig, and James and William Crichton of Frendraught, all from Aberdeenshire.[96] At Marischal, bursars and landed families came mostly from the New Town and its hinterland.

Veray heartlie velcome

Students in the first three of the four social categories listed in the Foundations paid full fees, according to their rank. To the cash-poor colleges, with a limited customer base, they were 'veray heartlie velcome', as Principal David Rait assured the unnamed laird, whose son and son's tutor were to enter King's in 1605. Since no suitable chamber could be found, the principal added, 'yet thocht I suld strait my self the more they salbe placed in ane of my aune'.[97]

Tuition fees at King's were set at £6 for the higher nobility; £4 for the lower; and £2 for the sons of farmers, merchants and craftsmen. At Marischal, competitive from the start, they paid less: £3, £2 and £1, respectively.[98] But not for long: in 1619 the nobility were charged £13 6s 8d and the gentry £10 at both colleges.[99] Students were encouraged to consider the fee as a gesture of gratitude; nevertheless, the gesture accounted for part of a master's income and, under the *Statuta* those who were late in making it were to be named and shamed by the principal. The ambivalent relationship between student and master, and the threat it offered to the latter's authority, explains the insistence that gratitude be accompanied by respect: a student was forbidden to treat the masters in an irreverent or familiar way, 'still less act as if he were their equal.' Under the Foundations both colleges charged the same examination fees: 6s 8d for the first examination (for promotion from the first to the second class), 13s 4d for the second, £1 for the third; and £1 10s for the examination before graduation. At King's, these had risen to £1, £1 10s, £2 and £2 10s in the 1620s.[100] At Marischal, an amendment to the *Statuta* fixed the first three at 13s 4d and raised the pre-graduation examination fee to £2. In addition, there were fees for the college officers who had ceremonial duties at events like examinations and graduation. At King's, under the New Foundation, students paid 4s to the beadle for services dating from before the Reformation; the same services, no doubt, for which they paid a sum (equal to one-tenth of their examination fee) to the sacrist in the 1620s.[101] Under the Foundation Charter Marischal students paid their beadle 2s. An additional cost at graduation was the compulsory contribution to the library, set at £4 by both colleges.

Students who lived in college had to pay an annual charge for their rooms or – more accurately – for a bed in a room. Such was the pressure of space at both colleges that it was usual for three or more students to share: in 1604 the principal of King's gave up one of his rooms to 'the Maister of Ogilvie his sonnis vith their pedagogue'; in 1634 the 'ladner chamber' there, formerly called 'Aries' or 'the pantry chamber', held 'ane new studie and a new bed within it, bothe of firre [and] wther three bedes . . . all of firre.' In 1623 George Speid (1621) paid a standard 'chamber mail' (room-rent) of 10s for accommodation of this kind.[102] At Marischal, under the *Statuta* and the *Leges*, the rent was 13s 4d; an amendment to the former, however, seems to have established a scale of rents rising to £1 for the better rooms; another required students to pledge an unspecified sum to cover any damage. Under the Foundation Charter they paid the janitor 10s, amended in the *Statuta* to 13s 4d, for 'taking a brush and shovel to their chambers each day, spreading their beds in a orderly fashion and keeping their furniture in good condition.'[103] Students had also to pay for their board, but the charges in this period are not recorded.

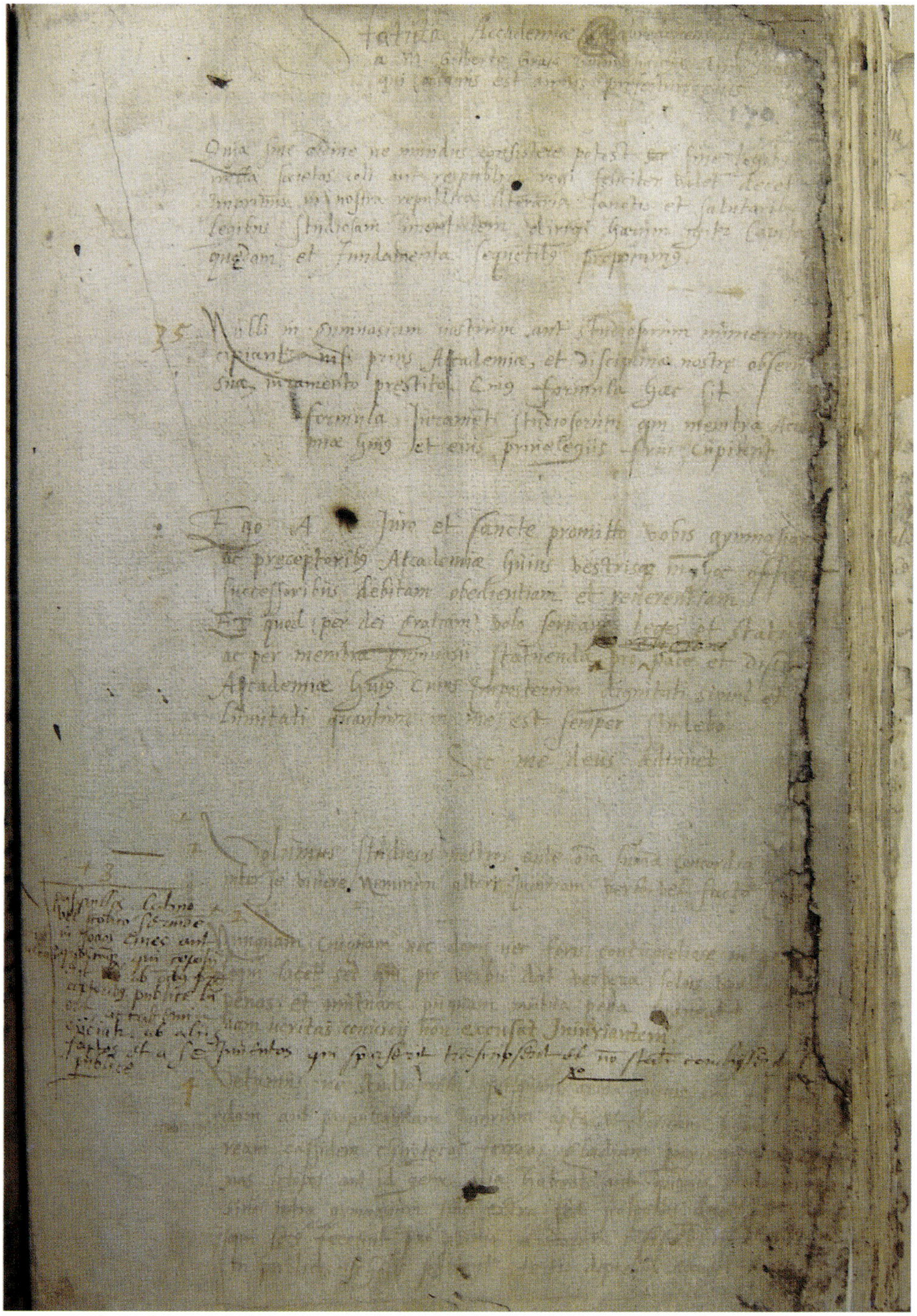

5 Gilbert Gray, Statutes, 1605, showing the heavily amended text. AUL, MS M 2, f. 170r.

At King's, they received nourishing, if monotonous, fare. In the session 1628–29, for example, fresh meat (mainly beef, mutton and fowl) and salted beef were served on all except 'fish' days (Friday and Saturday) until Lent; veal, capons, lamb and chickens appeared later. Fresh fish (whiting, trout, skate, haddock), together with 'keillen' (codlings), 'fluiks' (flounder) and 'slinks' (undersized salmon and cod), was served seasonally in the year; salted and dried cod and haddock, throughout.[104] During Lent, the fish was supplemented by fowl and eggs; and on fish days, if it was scarce, by 'cauld meat'.[105] There was college-brewed ale and college-grown vegetables. Butter, milk and white bread at 1s a loaf were bought in from the Old Town; oat bread was either baked in the college or bought in at 8d a loaf.

Puir scholaris

Students of limited means lived on bursaries, won in open competition or awarded by a patron. At King's, the New Foundation made provision for 12 'foundation' bursaries. At Marischal, the six established under the Foundation Charter were never filled. Instead, around 12 were created by Duncan Liddel and his fellow-benefactors, James Cargill and Alexander Reid; the first awards were made in 1616. Their holders lived humbly as befitted their dependent status. Originally, foundation bursars at King's were each entitled to £30. From this was deducted the cost of their bed and board. The residue was paid to them by the 'economus' (steward) in instalments at Martinmas (11 November) and Whitsunday (15 May). Around 1630 Alexander Reid, as generous to King's as he was to Marischal, gave a substantial sum 'for the help of the bursers ther table and maintainance'.[106] At Marischal, it was intended, although not specified, that foundation bursars should also receive £30. According to a sharp-penned critic of the Foundation Charter, however, this 'war not able as prycis now gois to susteine them 16 or 17 weikis':[107] the reason, presumably, why the bursaries there were never filled. The Liddel and Cargill bursaries, managed by the New Town council, were more valuable. William Cargill (1615), one of the first of Cargill's 'puir scholaris' to be appointed, received £66 13s 4d; David Rutherford (1639), £53 6s 8d. William Massie and Robert Morison, whose Liddel bursaries were linked to the sale of meal and malt, did even better.[108]

Foundation bursars at King's were exempt from tuition and examination fees, although they had to pay the beadle.[109] By 1619, however, they were required to present a silver spoon or pay £5 'spoon silver' on their entry to the college: Francis Thomson (1623) was not the only one unable to do so.[110] Graduating bursars had also to make the compulsory contribution to the library, even though this had been originally intended to curb the extravagance of wealthier students. Additionally, by the 1630s they were expected to pay something to their master. At the visitation of 1634, however, either accidentally or on investigation, the college 'fund be the fundacioune . . . that the bursars . . . aucht to be free from payment of stipends or spoones silver or aney thing . . . at thair entrie . . . or . . . outgoing according to the mynd and will of the fundator nor anie tyme during thair foire yeires course.' Spoon silver, tuition fees and, by implication, the library contribution were immediately prohibited.[111]

Bursars living in King's were accommodated in the 'wpper and nether bursars chalmer', which contained between them seven beds, sleeping two or three each; they differed only from the 'ladner chamber' in that nothing in them was new.[112] Little is known about their diet. In 1612 Duncan Liddel, planning initially to let his bursars go to either college, took note of the cost and quality of their fare at King's and stipulated that 'they sall not be buirdit with other bursers in the auld Colledge if they can be better interteanit for that same payment otherwise.'[113] In 1630, if not before, they received 'bursar aill' as opposed to 'best aill';[114] while their oatbread would have been the cheaper, college-baked kind – what was later called 'bursar bread'.

Nurseries of the commonwealth

Simon Fraser, who had experience of both King's and St Andrews, declared that 'there was more profit to be hade [at King's], where he best liked the grain of the students and the genuin temper of the masters.' Students from a different social background also spoke well of their tutelage. At King's, John Leech (1610) praised the master who not only taught him well but offered him what amounted to career guidance;[115] and William Lauder extolled the 'keen intellect, piety, love, benevolence, humility and purity of life' of David Leech, who had taught him in his first year.[116] At Marischal, William Wedderburn and the class of 1611 acknowledged 'the cairfull educatioun quhilk they hawe enjoyed thairin', but the migration of students from the New Town to the Old implies some dissatisfaction. The only dissentient on record, however, is Alexander Jaffray's son, and his attack on his master and the principal, 'both of them unfit for training up youths', was made later, from the supercritical standpoint of a Quaker. As for the fee-paying parents, the single recorded occasion on which they were moved to 'exclame and cry out against . . . the colledge', was over the cost of graduation feasts. The care with which chancellor, principal and masters sought to secure their better contentment' and to avoid a future 'grudge', suggests that this was not a common occurrence.[117] Some families were clearly content and sent more than one son to the same college. Thomas Burnet's two brothers entered King's a year after him, in 1604; while Alexander Middleton (1626) of Caldhame (Kincardineshire) was followed there by two brothers in 1628 and a third in 1629.

Students are silent on the quality of life in college. Nevertheless, living there seems to have been less than easy. The visitation of King's in 1619 revealed its defects both outside, where 'the haill place is becum ruinous', and within, where there was 'no plenisching of tyn but twa dossen of plaittis and als many trincheris, no naperie but twa buird-clothes [tablecloths] and five seruittis.' Some 20 years on, the hall was still letting in water, and work was needed to make the common school 'more lightsome, pleasant and commodious.'[118] Marischal was equally dilapidated and had to be repaired in 1622.[119] Moreover, injunctions in the *Statuta* and *Leges* against defiling the approaches with urine or filth, urinating in doorways, and (in both texts) emptying chamber-pots through the windows, suggest a degree of squalor around the college that would have defeated the once-daily ministrations of the janitor. The biggest problem was space: 'all oure Chalmers ar alredie occupied,' wrote Principal Rait in 1605; and in 1633 Principal Dun at Marischal complained to the magistrates of 'scairstie of chamberis and want of beddis', pressure that was only relieved when the privately-occupied 'backhouse' (house to the rear) of the college was vacated and partitioned for 'chamberis and beddis.'[120] Damp walls, smelly doorways and overcrowded rooms would have been familiar enough, but they could not have helped the conscientious student, intent on serious learning; still less fostered the good health he needed to cope with his four years of endeavour.

To the framers of the Foundations, those years had a single purpose. The colleges were intended to be nurseries of the commonwealth: their graduates were to go forth 'to spread the preaching of God's word in the churches or better to instruct the young, or to administer the government . . . .' The evidence for the years 1600–40 is uneven in quantity and quality: of the 37 students mentioned by name in this chapter, for example, only 24 can be traced in later life.[121] Nevertheless, it suggests that the colleges fulfilled their purpose: 19 of these students dedicated their careers, in part at least, to their town, their church or their country. Among students at King's, William Lauder became minister of Avoch in the Black Isle. George Speid was first a schoolmaster then a minister. Alexander Middleton taught at King's and was eventually its principal. John Leech became a Latin scholar and poet. Despite his poor showing in the assessment of 1603–04, Matthew Lumsden went on to graduate and became a merchant and bailie of the New Town. Robert Coutts, who migrated to King's from Marischal, became a burgess there. Alexander Reid, who accompanied him, became an advocate. Thomas Burnet's younger brother, Robert, also became an advocate, but in Edinburgh, where he was eventually made a Lord of Session, as was Alexander Brodie. James Sharp became a churchman and scholar and, as archbishop of St Andrews, was murdered by covenanters in 1679. At Marischal, Alexander Jaffray became provost of Aberdeen; John Seton, who returned to the college as master of the fourth class, dedicated a set of graduation theses to him in that capacity in 1637.[122] Alexander's son also became provost, and at a critical time in the in the town's history. William Wedderburn and Thomas Chalmer, the bursar-poet, taught in the New Town grammar school; William later returned to Marischal as a master and subsequently became a minister. William Moir was Marischal's second professor of mathematics and later principal; Robert Morison, a professor at Oxford. Robert Dunn became a physician. The others, the Keiths, Simon Fraser, Master of Lovat, Robert Innes of Innes and James Crichton of Frendraught, all succeeded to their family titles; Thomas Burnet's other brother, George, to the lairdship of Craigmyle. Thomas himself succeeded his father in 1619. As Sir Thomas Burnett of Leys, 'a sober, grave man',[123] he amply fulfilled the obligations that his education had placed upon him, taking an active part in the administration of his shire and serving as a Member of Parliament. Nor did he forget the institution that had provided his education. At his death, in 1648, he founded three bursaries, 'out of the speciall love favour and respect that he carreis to the said kingis colledge'.[124]

Chapter 2

The great decay of discipline, 1640–1717

In 1640 John Spalding entered King's College as a first-year student, or bajan.[1] It could not have been an easy decision: his father, commissary clerk in the Old Town, had twice been punished publicly for adultery, and it is unlikely that the story had been forgotten. Nevertheless, John was developing into a royalist and an Episcopalian – signing the King's Covenant 'glaydly', the National Covenant 'not willingly' – and the moderate regime at King's must have seemed congenial.[2] In the same year Andrew Cant entered Marischal College. It was the obvious choice for 'the son', as he proudly described himself in his lecture notes, 'of Andrew Cant, minister and preacher of Aberdeen'.[3] In fact, he already had friends among the pro-covenant students there and was with them when they staged a demonstration in 1639.[4]

John and Andrew entered colleges that remained dilapidated and seriously short of space. At King's, where money was still tight, 20 years passed before the 'New Work' was built, giving additional teaching and living accommodation at the north-east corner of the quadrangle; it survives today as the Cromwell Tower. Between it and the east end of the chapel were the 'Timber Muses', a new block of study-bedrooms that stood for almost 200 years. The college meanwhile did what it could to maintain the 'Old Work', including the crumbling capitols; in 1715, however, when the spire of the south-east capitol was blown down, it was not rebuilt, leaving what is now the Round (or Ivy) Tower. Not all the improvements were well received: in the 1640s students hostile to Principal William Guild boycotted his newly roofed-over privies. At Marischal, Principal Dun replaced the fire-damaged part of the college with a new classroom, completed in 1642; a new common school and library were built in 1662; and work on a residential block, also called 'the New Work', went on spasmodically from 1682 until the 1700s.[5]

For their second (semi), third (tertian) and fourth (magistrand) years John and Andrew were students of 'the Caroline University', which was formed by the union of King's and Marischal in 1641 and lasted for 20 years.[6] They received a common education, one of a predominantly spiritual character.[7] 'The chief end of study,' according to laws issued by Principal William Guild at King's in 1641, 'should be the religion of God . . . and a knowledge of His divine works and favours.'[8] In the 1680s, when the laws were re-issued, the pre-eminence of religion was unchanged, although it was not pursued with the same intensity. By the early 1700s, however, spirituality was no longer the defining force. Verses such as 'The Students Litany' and the 'Description of the useless, needless, headless, Defective, elective Masters of The King's Colledge' reveal cynicism among the students and hypocrisy among the staff.[9]

John and Andrew were diligent students;[10] the kind, said William Douglas, professor of divinity at King's, who 'take on the pallor of their papers'.[11] Others were not. The masters at both colleges needed big classes if they were to augment their small stipends, and when they exerted themselves each summer in 'the busy seeking of scholares',[12] they were ready to compromise on quality. For every Kenneth Gordon (1691) – 'begins to do much better then first promised' – they recruited a George Mackenzie (1702) – 'more of a vicious temper than ever'.[13] Their exertions, it was said, raised 'animosities betuixt the maisters of the tuo colledges, yea, and in that same colledge among themselves', which led to 'the great decay of discipline'.[14]

Not surprisingly, then, student delinquency featured prominently in the period, involving a wider range of jurisdictions than before. Andrew himself is alleged to have robbed a master at Marischal and was probably tried in the college court.[15] One of John's classmates was among several who appeared before the kirk session of Old Machar (Old Aberdeen) for fornication and related offences.[16] But a 'ryot' involving the colleges in 1659 was handled by the newly-introduced justices of the peace; while another, in 1668–69, came before the Privy Council, which also dealt with other student affrays and assaults.[17] Diligent or delinquent, students retained their constitutional role, although they exercised it on only two recorded occasions, both at Marischal. In 1664 each class, acting 'in the name' of a student nation, chose 'procurators for electing of ane Rector'. In 1674 the nations themselves seem to have voted.[18]

Orderlie through the classes

In July 1673 the Earl of Moray enrolled his sons at King's as bajans in the class of 1672. The first year of the class, devoted to Greek, was effectively over, but the earl explained that the boys had 'learned much of their greek already at home'.[19] The incident highlights a recurrent problem with the gradation of the arts degree in this period. Students arrived towards the end of the first year, or 'overleapt' it altogether, thereby saving time and money. The universities, out of pocket as a result, called the practice 'not onlie prejudiciall but destructive.' In 1644 the General Assembly insisted that '[scholleris] sall enter to the lowest classe . . . and proceid orderlie through the rest of the classes'. The universities tried to enforce this principle but without success. In the 1670s 'some of the southern colledges' accepted the situation, but King's and Marischal stood firm, convinced that first-year Greek was essential, given the limitations of their entrants:[20] 'Gramer schools in the North,' wrote Subprincipal George Fraser in 1690, 'are so farre degenerit that I would think it myself very happie if wee could get good Latinists from them. But the Grecians we gett are naught.'[21] Eventually, however, King's and Marischal gave way, fearing to lose potential recruits: 'any student,' wrote one of Fraser's more cynical colleagues in 1708,

> is permitted to enter Semie, without being obleidged to enter Bajan, if he understands the Latine tongue, and have a competencie of the Greek . . . and have allowance and approbation of the Greek Regent so to do: which a small compliment for his consent does never and nowhere fail to procure.[22]

At both colleges, the length of the session fell from ten months to eight. Examinations were held in October; teaching began in November and ended, for the magistrands in March, for the other classes in May. There is no formal record of the change, and it may simply have been dictated by the intransigence of the students and their families as they tried to economise. In practice the eight months slipped to seven or less. Students skipped the examinations, arrived after teaching began and departed before it finished.[23] At King's, for example, Hugh Rose (1655), laird of Kilravock (Nairnshire), began his second year on 24 November and returned home on 21 May.[24] But there were others who, 'by reason of the poverty of some, and parsimoney of others of their parents', came as late as December and left even earlier in May. The commissioners and the colleges tried to discourage, or at least moderate, this practice.[25] Their efforts peaked in 1676, when new starting and finishing dates were phased in over a period of three years; students had to register their arrival and departure; offenders were charged their board for the days they missed.[26] Nevertheless, irregularities continued and were tacitly accommodated: in 1695 Subprincipal Fraser's class left in March 'as is customary become.'[27] The commissioners intervened again but without lasting success:[28] In December 1712 the tutor of Robert Duff (1711) wrote from Marischal of 'so late comeing in'; while William Duff (1711), Robert's cousin and classfellow, referred to 'the riseing of our Coledge' in April 1713.[29]

For students who arrived late and left early, the summer vacation could extend from two months to four. Other breaks were few. At King's, in the years 1642–44, the students defied their masters and the local ministers, and insisted on their 'aucht days play' at 'Yooll day', possibly as a gesture against the covenanters' efforts to ignore the festival; at Marischal, by 1667 if not before, they had 'Christmas vacances'.[30] They may also have had time off to accompany the bonfires and bells with which both colleges marked royal occasions and military successes after 1660; certainly, they had a holiday at King's on the accession of 'James the 7th' in 1685.[31]

The way in which students were taught changed yet again. Following the establishment of the Caroline University, regenting was re-established at King's after a

13-year interval and introduced at Marischal for the first time.[32] In 1700, however, to raise the standard of Greek throughout the universities, the commissioners partly reversed the process, requiring bajans to be taught each year by the same master.[33] There were also attempts to make better provision for the teaching of other subjects in the arts course. King's created chairs of Hebrew (1673) and mathematics (1703).[34] Marischal made short-lived arrangements for the teaching of Hebrew in 1642 and made fresh, but equally short-lived, provision for the teaching of Latin in 1651.[35]

Students continued to work an eight-hour day, starting at dawn when, wrote Duncan Liddel and Principal Dun, 'the mind is readiest for study of any kind'.[36] At King's, the timetable was reconstructed in the 1680s. What had been called 'the laudable custom' of communal learning in the common school in the forenoon was abandoned,[37] probably because of trouble among the classes when they assembled there (below, p. 47), and teaching was confined to the classroom. The revised timetable was still in use when Subprincipal Fraser taught his semis in 1704:

> besides our meeting in the morning to give out the lessons in the ordinary courses, we meet betwixt ten and twelve, a part of which is examining repetitions, part in the teaching and examining something in the mathematics and sometime dictating notes . . . on the play days we do not meet till five hours but on unplay days we go in at four and continue till six, the first of these hours spent in disputes or declaiming orations and the other in examining the ordinary task prescribed in the morning.[38]

The 'ordinary courses' of the curriculum changed in sequence and, more importantly, in content as the period advanced. In the 1640s, at King's, John Spalding would have done Greek with some Latin and Hebrew in his first year; logic and metaphysics with some arithmetic and geometry in his second; ethics and general physics in his third; and special physics in his fourth. Fifty years later, at Marischal, Ludovic Reid (1693) would have studied arithmetic with his languages in the first year; while his courses in logic and general physics would have been 'conforme to the principles of old and new Philosophie'.[39] The 'new Philosophie' was introduced after decades of what Gilbert Burnet (1653) at Marischal called 'the Aristotelian way, as it is now managed by some schoolmen'.[40] The manner of introduction varied from class to class. At King's, for example, William Anderson (1676) would have heard the ideas of Descartes condemned as 'deceptive, novel and heterodox';[41] Alexander Campbell (1677) would have heard a more tolerant view.[42] In the 1690s, however, Kenneth Gordon would have heard both sides from Subprincipal Fraser, who declared the scepticism of Descartes 'both useful and legitimate, without any stain of impiety', adding that 'we do not consider it . . . to be necessary.'[43]

At first students continued to take down lectures from dictation. Andrew Cant's logic dictates of 1641–42 fill 106 pages in minute script, with 'Arguments',

'Questions' and 'Objections'; 'adversions', 'syllogisms' and 'resolutions' are noted in the margin. Dictation, however, was no longer considered best practice. In 1648 the university commissioners condemned it as 'a hinderance not only to other necessarie studies but also to the knowledge of the text it selff'.[44] At King's, in the 1650s, only bursars had to write everything down;[45] others were free to use second-, third- or fourth-hand dictates, like Hugh Rose, who bought 'a third yeares course' in 1657. At Marischal, in the 1690s, even bursars acquired copies: among them was Ludovic Reid, who used notes written three years earlier.[46] As courses at both colleges became uniform, the practice spread: in 1698, when the commissioners planned to replace dictates with a printed text, Marischal claimed that 'few are obliged to write.'[47] Nevertheless, in 1704 Subprincipal Fraser was still dictating notes 'to such as cannot attain to the buying of copies.'[48]

Students were still required to declaim and dispute in Latin, Greek or Hebrew on Saturdays. What they declaimed and disputed, however, was – inevitably, in an age of religious and political controversy – more rigorously policed than before. At King's, Principal Row prohibited declamations on 'difficult theological points or politics'; the hebdomadar vetted the list of theses to be disputed;[49] and it was only with the connivance of like-minded masters that Jacobite students were able to declaim against the king in 1715 (below, p. 52). At King's, the role of the common school as a forum was again diminished: in the 1680s only tertians and magistrands were allowed to perform there; the semis disputed in their classroom.[50] At Marischal, in the 1670s, 'the inferior classes' attended the event but the semis, again, were relegated to their room, 'which [the masters] find by experience profitable for the students.'[51] Nevertheless, the spirit of the Saturday-morning show lives on in verbatim reports of a public debate held between students of divinity and the Quakers of Aberdeen in 1675.[52]

Students' learning methods changed, with increasing emphasis on private study. Not only was communal revision abandoned, there was no longer any insistence on peer support. Classes had still to 'mandate' (memorise) the morning lecture nonetheless. Some found it easy: 'I was,' recalled Gilbert Burnet, 'so quick at learning that, as soone as our Regent had explained the Task we were to have for that day, I presently got it exactly, and never lookt on a book all day long.' Others lacked his facility: from Marischal, James Ogilvy (1675), son of the Earl of Findlater, assured his mother, 'I shal through Gods assistance . . . give pains to my book.'[53] Repetitions, or tests, continued, although at Marischal, in James's day, 'too short tyme [was] taken be maisters for examinatioune of the lessons at night'.[54] The practice helped to focus the mind of an easily-distracted student like George Mackenzie, who did best at 'the tasks he gives daily accounts of'; at the same time, it left him with 'a laziness . . . to prosecute anything by himself'.

Language learning was also a matter of 'memory and diligence'.[55] Students were expected to memorise the rules of grammar and syntax, consolidating them by

6 A gowned student, 1677. New, the red gown could cost over £16 Scots. Aberdeen University Picture Collection.

close-reading set texts, and applying them by declaiming, disputing and conversing in Latin or, if they were up to it, French, Greek and Hebrew.[56] Principal Row explained the technique:

> Let each and every student guard against using the vernacular and take care to speak Latin; but also, by praiseworthy emulation, one with another, speak Latin in good Latin style, nay, in the best Latin style; to this end let the rules of ornament, precision, selection, word order, and agreement be observed; and in order to banish from this place barbarism, solecism, discordance and mispronunciation, the four plagues of Latinity, a lists of barbarisms and solecisms shall be kept by each student, to be checked with regard to all four.[57]

Eventually the system broke down. As teaching in philosophy changed, so did the need for close-reading: in 1676 the commissioners complained that 'the knowledge of [Greek] doth much decay . . . since they left off to interpret Aristotle's text'. Students persistently refused to converse in Latin, and in the laws of the 1680s the requirement was dropped;[58] at Marischal, however, a Latinised slang was used, mainly by former pupils of the grammar school, as late as the 1830s (below, p. 119). Standards fell, and competent classicists like Thomas Ruddiman (1690) from King's were few;[59] by 1700, Marischal students who wished to progress beyond the rudiments of Greek did so by 'after industry'.[60]

Students from wealthy or distant families continued to work with private tutors. In 1642 one escorted a son of the Marquis of Huntly to King's. In 1655 Hugh Rose was accompanied by William Geddes, who had styled himself 'pedagoug' while Hugh was at school but now called himself Hugh's 'governour'. In 1712 Robert Duff's tutor resolved that his charge should apply himself 'assiduously closely and sedulously' to his work, 'which (God willing) I shall see to.' Masters at both colleges often recommended poor but worthy graduates for tutors' posts: 'the young man ye recommend,' Subprincipal Fraser assured a correspondent, 'whom I know to be most deserving . . . will not be forgotten by me if any occasion of a pedagogie fit for him fall in my hands'.[61]

More students are now known to have owned, or had access to, printed textbooks. Hugh Rose bought 'Pareus on Ursin', the works of Horace, Virgil, Juvenal and Persius, 'Buchanan's Psalms' and the 'Confession of Faith'.[62] Printed books were thought to have their limitations, however: students, it was said in 1676, could not be instructed in religion 'simplie be prescriving a parcell of the respective books to them.'[63] Nevertheless, by the end of the period use and ownership had increased: at King's, in March 1704, Subprincipal Fraser prepared to try 'print logick books' on George Mackenzie; and at Marischal, in 1711, William Duff was ready to buy books if his father did not send them. John Fraser (1687), a Marischal graduate who went on to study divinity, owned books valued at over £100 when he died in 1695.[64] The college libraries were for the most part irrelevant to the needs of students in arts. At King's, they did not use the library until late in the century;[65] and although the management – and mismanagement – of the library at Marischal is well-documented, they are not mentioned among the readers.[66] Around 1676 both colleges agreed to place an authorised version of their courses in each college library;[67] probably more for the record than for reference.

Students who could afford it were permitted, and ultimately encouraged, to acquire other skills. As a tertian at King's in 1657, Hugh Rose bought a 'musicke-book' and took lessons from the master of the Old Town music school. In 1683–84 Subprincipal Fraser arranged music, dancing and writing lessons for one of his students,[68] and in February 1704 he was busy on behalf of George Mackenzie:

> 'I have lately begun him for one hour . . . [on] Wednesday and Saturday . . . for attaining some smatterings in the French . . . [not] to attain to a true pronunciation in it but to be enabled to peruse books write in that language which may be of use to him afterward if he were in a place where he might come to the true pronunciation.'

George was taught by the professor of Hebrew and, when he was away, by Fraser himself: '[George] and I will meet the hours appointed for it and go on the best we may with the little I have.'

Learning did not stop at the end of the session: students were expected to continue in the vacation. At King's, in the 1650s, Principal Row required them not only to go over what they had learned, but to compose their declamation for the following year.[69] Around the same time Gilbert Burnet, having mastered his coursework effortlessly at Marischal, 'was held to hard duty' in the vacation by his father. Those who were slow learners or simply idle were encouraged to stay on for extra tuition during the summer. 'It would be exceding good and usefull for your sones breading,' Alexander Campbell's father was told in 1679, that '[he] should stay here a good pairt of the vacance, for we can mak recreations to him without diverting his thoughts from his studies.' Through this sort of summer-schooling, in July 1704, Subprincipal Fraser tried to improve George Mackenzie's learning skills: '[I] put him first to tasks of eight days or a fortnights mandating and at these periods to give an account of it as I touched any part of it and in process of time give him half a book more or lesse and then a whole book after reading it to give account of it briefly.'

Extended learning, rigorously assessed, should have compensated for the irregular observance of the session, but both colleges allowed examination standards to slip. The examination in Latin for candidates in the bursary competition and non-bursars lost its force. In 1644, candidates had been required 'after tryall [to] be abill to mak a congruous theame in Latine, or at leist being admonisched of [their] error can reddilie schow how to correct the same'; this was the translation of an English text into Latin later known as 'the Version'. By the 1670s, however, a schoolmaster's testimonial often sufficed. In 1676 the colleges agreed that the test should be reimposed, 'in regaird many are admitted to the colledges who have not learned thair Latine grammar'. They went further, requiring that boys arriving late in the first year 'be examined . . . whither they can read the Greek, and have learned at least the simple declinations.'[70] But the situation did not improve: in 1695 Subprincipal Fraser wrote of a student, 'his great defect was, as of many, that he had not a stocke of Latin before he came'.[71] Evidently the problem was endemic: in the same year the university commissioners imposed on all the universities discrete tests in Latin for bajans and in Greek for semis.[72] The October examinations for entry to the second, third and fourth classes were also less than rigorous. Worse, at King's they were abandoned: in 1665 the college noted that they had been neglected 'for some few yeires bygone' and insisted that 'immediatlie after the returne of evry student . . . every on shall be examined upon his preceiding yeirs course'. In 1676 both colleges agreed that latecomers should not be exempt, and the commissioners took the same line in 1695.[73] Robert Duff, entering Marischal late in December 1712, faced being 'publickly examined all alone'.[74]

The examination that preceded graduation was taken more seriously. In 1644 the General Assembly insisted that 'such tryall be takin of studentis, speciallie of magistrandis, as these quho are fund wnworthie be not admitted to the degrie and honour of masteris.' A similar determination was expressed by both colleges.[75] The public disputation attracted both the interest and participation of local worthies: at King's, in 1662, nearly 300 copies of the theses were distributed; and in 1673, when the event had to be re-scheduled, the college had immediately to alert 'persons of quality, lest they should meet with any disappointment theranent'.[76] Regular attenders included Professor Douglas, said to have been 'a great disputer in the schools at graduations', although he was no admirer of extravagant rhetoric.[77] Theses had to be checked before publication for anything 'contraire to the true Religion and good maners'.[78] Some got through: in 1659, when Hugh Rose's class assembled in the common school at King's to defend the theses of its master, John Strachan, it heard them denounced for their 'popish positions' by 'young Mr Andrew Cant', now a master at Marischal; the event was re-staged at St Machar's, where the students' graduation took second place to a vituperative debate between Strachan and his opponents.[79]

The graduation ceremony was for a time simplified: possibly a concession to prevailing puritan values. In 1675, however, when the colleges complained that 'the circulation of scollars is become now out of custome and practise', a visitation ordered it to be reintroduced immediately. By 1677 the spectacle had been restored: magistrands, dressed in black clothes and wearing black gowns instead of the usual red (below, p. 47), disputed from 10 am to 4 or 5 pm. Then, after a break for refreshments, they returned to the common school, where each graduand took the graduation oath, '[ascended] the Desk' to be capped and, after a short speech to the audience, was received with 'clapping of hands, sounding of trumpets, shouting etc.'[80] There are no other references to trumpets at either college but several testify to the size of the audiences. Graduations at Marischal, for example, were so well-attended that in 1664 the college persuaded the town to let it use Greyfriars Church, paying £1 4s for 'thrie dealls cutt for dressing the pulpit and seatts to the students ther being considerable students as young Gordonstoune and Cragivarrs sonne and Baylyie Allexanders.' In 1665, however, it was forced to return to the common school where, because of 'the multitude of people and throng and severalls running out and in the second schoole . . . the dore and seatts were sumwhat broken'.[81] Although graduation continued to be held in July until the 1690s,[82] the date was not immutable: in 1644, when Old Town and New were caught up in national affairs, John Spalding and Andrew Cant graduated in June; in 1673 the event was re-scheduled at the Earl of Moray's request; and at the time of the Jacobite Rising in 1715 special arrangements were made at King's,[83] while the ceremony was abandoned at Marischal (below, p. 54).

Graduation was still no more than an option. At King's, in particular, a surge in entrants after 1660 was accompanied by a marked downturn in those who wanted to take it (Table 2.1). In February 1695 Kenneth Gordon refused to graduate, apparently with his family's approval, and he was not the only one of Subprincipal Fraser's students to see no value in it. An increasing number of students, however, chose a third way, private graduation. At King's, for example, five graduated privately in the period 1640–59; 40 in 1660–69; 13 in 1670–79; and 12 in 1680–89.[84] For some, it was a means to evade the public oath of conformity to the prevailing regime; for others, a matter of convenience; for others still, a way to avoid disputing in front of an audience. The authorities tried to suppress the practice: in 1664 and 1675 visitations of King's forbade 'privat laureatione, nor any without examinatione [except] wpon reasonable and weighty considderationes'; and in 1695 a similar prohibition was issued to all universities by the commissioners.[85] The last had some effect: when Murdoch Morison (1714) asked to graduate early from King's, 'being obliged to go off by reason of the great distance from his country the Lewes', his request was discussed and finally approved at a full meeting of the masters.[86]

Graduation feasts returned. At King's, the ban against them had been renewed in 1641 and 1653: such extravagance was shameful, said Principal Row, in times when money was short. He failed, however, to shame Hugh Rose, who spent over £2 10s 'with masters and other friends' on an 'away coming' party in May 1657. The ban on feasts was dropped from the laws of the 1680s, and by the end of the century they were accompanied by a graduation ball. At Marischal, there were 'multitudes of people at the Laureation feasts' in 1673.[87] This did not stop the colleges from collecting the 'library money' formerly levied in place of banquets. The magistrands of King's also defended the right to their valediction. According to Subprincipal Fraser, 'some classes fell into great heats who should be the man and factions grew yearly to such a height that the masters were obliged to discharge that innocent parade . . . but in process of time they began to make their orations like the former. . . . The masters do connive but not fully authorise for fear of former disorders.' At Marischal, there is a single reference to 'the Valedictorie', in 1689.[88]

Prayer and reading a pairt of the scripture

In August 1640, the triumphant covenanters of the General Assembly carried out a visitation of King's and Marischal. At King's, they dealt with the last vestiges of resistance. At Marischal, where opposition had subsided, 'it was ordanit that the Nationall Covenant . . . be subscryvit be the studentis within this college . . . . And befoir the schoolleris be requyrit to subscryve . . . the maisters ar to explaine it aucht dayes befoir.'[89] When King's students subscribed is not certain: they may have been among the 'bairns of 15 or 16 years of age' who had signed with John Spalding in May. In 1650, however, their successors were summoned to St Machar's to 'subscryve the solemn league and covenant who had not subscryved it formerlie'.[90]

These were decades in which religious instruction and worship were imposed upon students with particular rigour. In the 1640s students at both colleges were instructed systematically in the Heidelberg Cathechism.[91] At King's, on Sundays, they combined study and worship as before, continuing to give an account of the sermons 'according to the old and most praiseworthy custom'.[92] Every day, at dinner and supper, they had readings from the Scriptures and suitable works of history given by such bursars as were not serving dishes and pouring water.[93] Under Principal Row the lectures in Hebrew (Wednesday) and theology (Friday), and the test upon them (Saturday), assumed a new importance; his students had also to write out 'the foundations of the Christian religion in 50 chapters' and study them, together with texts in Latin and Hebrew; in the vacations, they had to revise and meditate upon the Scriptures they had heard during the year.[94] Instruction at both colleges in the 1660s and 1670s was perceived to be less rigorous: inadequate to withstand the twin threats of Catholicism and Dissent. In 1676, 'considering the necessitie that the students be carefullie instructed in the grounds of religion', visitors of both colleges prescribed a syllabus of texts for use by each class.[95] Bajans were to be taught from 'some approvin catechism', possibly Thomas Vincent's *Explicatory Catechism or, An Explanation of the [Westminster] Assemblie's Shorter Catechism* (1673), used in 1690.[96]

Daily and Sunday worship proceeded much as before. At King's, however, under Principal Guild's laws, each student had to provide himself with a bible and book of psalms, and psalms were repeated regularly at mealtimes. Under Principal Row's laws, daily worship was brought forward by half an hour in the morning, and the order of procession to St Machar's on Sunday was prescribed with schoolmasterly exactitude. Alms, collected from the students by the masters in advance, were delivered by the hedomadar to the deacon at the church door. By 1660 the college

7 James Fraser, polymath, was commemorated in the Wardlaw Mausoleum, Kirkhill, Inverness, 200 years after his death.

loft there could no longer accommodate the students, and they overflowed into the 'common loft', where they were railed off from the rest of the congregation. In 1679 there were plans to build 'a round seat for the convenience of some gentlemens sons in the Colledg who take up other seats in the church', but seating arrangements in the loft, recorded around 1686, do not mention it.[97] Marischal's loft in the West Church also needed work: in 1640 the General Assembly had to instruct the town council 'that the scholleris be set so in the kirk that they may here the minister commodiouslie'; in 1662 the seats were extended and a back was put 'to the Maisters seatt to hold off the students feete'; in 1697 the loft was enlarged.[98] Students were expected to attend their local church during the vacation. Inevitably, this exposed them at close quarters to sectarian infighting. James Anderson (1694), for example, had just begun his final year at Marischal, when he was summoned before the presbytery of Aberdeen to testify against one minister whom he had heard in the summer rubbishing another.[99]

Students were also required to worship regularly in private. No doubt they had been expected to do so earlier, but the form of their devotions was now regulated. At King's, under the laws of the 1640s, they were to retire at night to their rooms where, after reading a chapter of the bible, they were to pray in turn, using the standard forms of the liturgy for the benefit of younger students, 'who are not yet able to pray in public without some help from books'.[100] The injunction was repeated in the 1680s without any reference to the liturgy. Under Principal Row they went through a similar routine after waking in the morning and were encouraged to sing psalms, especially at night. The hebdomadar was made responsible for enforcing these rules: in 1690 he was required to ask on his nightly inspection 'if prayer and reading a pairt of the scripture be gone about'.[101]

Play days

'By excessive mental effort,' wrote Doctors Liddel and Dun, 'our brain becomes drier than normal . . . or our innate heat is stifled by a mass of crude humours . . . Exercises are especially appropriate, since they activate every part of the body alike.'[102] Students at both colleges continued to revive their bodies as well as their minds with two hours of football on the Links, three afternoons a week,[103] on what Subprincipal Fraser called 'play days'. At Marischal, bajans still provided the balls: the one exception to an order of the town council in 1659 abolishing the 'servitude' of junior to senior classes.[104] Students with money to spend enjoyed other sports and facilities, some of them provided by the colleges. At King's, in the 1650s, they played 'handball or hand tennis',[105] endangering the windows to Principal Row's evident concern. In 1658 he incorporated a 'billiard house' in the New Work.[106] It was still in use in the 1670s and 1680s, and in 1703 it was illuminated with candles for the queen's birthday.[107] From the 1660s onwards, if not before, students played bowls and similar games, probably at the front of the college. Overthrows and ricochets, however, were evidently a hazard: in 1663 the kirk session asked the college 'to restraine their students from playing at the bullets because . . . there had been skaith gottin that way'; in 1668 the bailies forbade the townsfolk to 'play at the bulleis' and requested the college to co-operate 'in respect of . . . sundrie inconvenients that have fallen out therby.'[108] By 1675, however, the college had its own bowling-green: 'the pryce of every man playeing' there was 3s, payable to John Ross, the janitor, who managed the green and the 'bulziard table' on the college's behalf. In 1689 the green was used for drilling 24 townsmen 'in the discipline of war'; it survived and was still in use in 1702.[109] Students who could not afford the green fee evidently carried on as before: in the 1680s they were forbidden 'to throw iron bowls'.[110] Archery continued to be a student sport, and in this period, if not before, the college had its own butts; the silver arrow was hung on display in 1672–73.[111] Archery was also practised at Marischal but, like bowls, presented some risk to the townsfolk living nearby: in 1656, on the order of the town council, proper butts were set up; in 1663 they were moved from 'the great guairden' to the site of 'the old latrons [privies]', 'some having gott preyjudice with arrowes . . . and the Counsell having maid ane act against [them]'.[112] Swordplay combined exercise with self-defence: at King's, Hugh Rose's brother, John (1663), took lessons from a fencing master.[113]

Grosser crymes

In 1641 Principal Guild ruled that 'none shall be admitted to [King's], none maintained there, in whom there is no sign of modesty and diligence'; he later excluded, specifically, 'those of a profligate or idle nature'.[114] It was an aspiration impossible to fulfil. Nearly 20 years later Professor Douglas found alongside good students 'who grow thin from study not sex; to whom town is a prison and a university, paradise', those who were ignorant or affected ignorance, who swaggered around arrogantly, with powdered, scented hair – hard drinkers, high rollers and heavy smokers.[115] The result was that at King's the laws grew longer at each revision, as successive principals sought to protect the conscientious and control the irresponsible. They restated the absolutes: diligence, morality, modesty, civility, harmony and non-violence. They required students returning from vacation to bring a testimonial of good conduct from the local kirk session. They extended the list of prohibited weapons. They set out the case against vices such as gambling, which fostered the desire for money, did not exercise the mind, was more a matter of luck than skill, and fomented trouble. They were especially hard on profligacy, blasphemy and obscenity. Finally, to secure compliance, they reinforced the authority of the hebdomadar, the censors and the janitor. Censors were now appointed, by turn and for short periods only, from among the bursars: a measure, perhaps, of the unpopularity of the job. The colleges also legislated to reduce offences beyond the walls. King's continued to warn its students against bad company and 'vaging' (wandering) around the Old or New Towns. Both insisted that gowns should be worn in public: they specified 'black, dark or some sober colour' for bursars, and red for the rest – the first documentary reference to the red gown at Aberdeen.[116] Bursars at Marischal received a separate injunction from the town council to adopt the black gown and hat hitherto specified only in the Liddel foundation.[117] This insistence upon gowns was not simply to promote corporate distinction; it was a means to identify those who misbehaved in the town; as such, the rule was reinforced by the university commissioners.[118]

Offences were for the most part punished as before: 'corporallie, by pecuniall mulct, and grosser crymes by extrusion'. At Marischal, by the 1660s, there was at least one 'penitentiall chamber'.[119] The bursars, as usual, were treated with greater severity. In 1659 a revised code of laws governing their conduct in college and during vacation was drawn up by Principal Row at his most sententious. It required them to wear their belts as a mark of punishment for speaking in the vernacular and other minor offences. For much of the period, in fact, the bursars were suitably docile. At King's, in 1700, however, the masters complained of 'the many abuses of which [they] are guilty': these included 'not weareing their gownes', '[not] keeping publick prayers', arriving late at the beginning of the year, and absenteeism.[120] It was a hint of bursar power to come (below, p. 53).

Student delinquency in this period went far beyond casual or wilful disregard for college laws. At its most innocent – and to the masters most irksome – it took the form of 'classicall tumults': turf wars over classrooms and class seating in the common school.[121] These climaxed each year, when teaching ended, in what Principal Leslie at Marischal called 'that damnable custome of chalking the schooles', covering doors and walls with graffiti. In 1666 he had to pay

> for a ratle of Iron to the comon schoole dore and a bolt therto, and a new slott to the utter dores they being all broken up and locks and slotts broken at the chalking of the schooles . . . for repairing the whole schooles particularly the second schoole windows and formes desperatly brocken and the stensions broken out and all the brodes of the windows and hinggers or cuisses of the broades both of the second and third schoole brocken pitifullie by the students that yeare and the back dore of the first transe and muse miserablie broken be the furie of the students at that chalking of the schooles.[122]

At King's, as at Marischal, chalking spread from 'the schools private or publick, gates doores stairs' to 'the doores and gates of . . . houses within [the] town'. Eventually, in the early 1670s, both colleges made students sign undertakings to abandon the practice on pain of expulsion. The formality of these acts had an effect: at Marischal, for example, James Lumsden (1670), a regular offender, who had once gone to ground in his room, forcing a master to break the lock 'taking him out to punish him', signed the undertaking of 1673 and sinned no more. At King's, however, there was a resurgence of vandalism around 1686.[123]

'We shall not', promised James and his fellow signatories, 'nor incite nor provoke students . . . to abuse the college'. Chalking involved concerted action, a source of serious concern to both colleges in the period. At King's, students were forbidden to gather in their chambers at night, as a precaution against rowdiness and 'immodesty',[124] or to meet in the porter's lodge. More significantly, they were not allowed to form organised groups. In 1646 the college forbade them 'wpon any pretence whatsomever, [to] enter in a band or combinatioune for supplicating or obtaining of any thing that way'; in 1653 Principal Row threatened the ringleader of any 'sect, faction, rebellion or conspiracy' with expulsion; and in 1671–72 all four classes had to promise not to enter into 'conspiracies, associations or compacts' against other students, much less against their masters.[125] The masters had other ways of foiling student plots: 'I was,' wrote Gilbert Burnet, of his classmates at Marischal, 'too young to be infected with their disorders, and too talkative and too much in our Regent's favour to be much trusted by those that drew the rest into vice, for they suspected me to be his spye, and so I was indeed.'

Students committed other, more serious, crimes: singly, in small groups, and in large bands. Individually, they got drunk and fornicated. Some 20 students appeared on these charges before the kirk session of Old Machar in the period, nine of them in the 1670s. In 1643, for example, John Spalding's classmate was denounced for fornication at the end of his third year and appeared before the session on 1 October, when he returned for his fourth. He got off lightly, as students often did, performing a single act of repentance 'upon the stole'; the woman not only did penance but also paid a fine.[126]

Groups of students committed affrays and assaults. In 1665 a party from King's, 'drawing their swords and shooting their pistolls', helped the son of a local laird to abduct a woman one Sunday from St Machar's, then fled. They were sentenced in their absence at a visitation of the college: they were not to be re-admitted until they had been punished by the masters and by the kirk session 'for profanation of the lord's day'; in the event, only one complied.[127] Early in 1685 there were two group assaults on masters. The first, at King's, involved the sons (otherwise unidentified) of the lairds of Cawdor and Innes (in the counties of Nairn and Moray), although the main offender was the 'servitor' of one of the boys, who committed 'ane abuse . . . upon the masters.' The college complained to the Privy Council: the council, obstructed by Innes in its efforts to arrest the servitor, issued an act requiring civil authorities to bring students guilty of 'tumult, abuse, or insolence' to 'condigne punishmennt, as the masters of the universities . . . shall impose.'[128] In the second incident, at Marischal, three students 'struck, reproached and disobeyed' a master. They were sentenced by the college to be publicly whipped in the common school.[129] The causes of these assaults are unknown but may have been religious or political.[130] Finally, in 1705, Thomas Reid (1703) was one of four King's students who freed an inmate of the tolbooth in the Old Town: they 'broke the floore . . . and helped the prisoner up through the hole they had made'. They were handed over by the town to the college for punishment and were fined 50 merks

(£33 6s 8d) each, to be paid or pledged before they could return. Early in 1706 Reid sought readmission, explaining

> that he was content instantly to pay twenty Merks . . . that he had used all meanes, tho in vaine, to prevaile with his father to come in and finde surety for his fine, that in short it is with vast difficulty that he could get this money beg'd and borrowed and that he could not possibly get any more.'

Noting that he 'was both studious and very well inclin'd', the college agreed.[131]

Bands of students fought on behalf of their colleges on the streets. Although such 'riots' had occurred before, the first on record was in 1659. 'Students of New aberdene in Number about Twentye or Thirtye, all armed with Battones full of Iron pyckes [spikes], with Iron Clubbes, Durkes and other Murthering weapons, and wnder silence of the Night, breake in wpon the students and Inhabitants of Old aberdene'.[132] They were searching for classmates who had been enticed, they believed, to enrol at King's. Failing to find them, they 'did dangerouslye wound and hurt diverse Gentle Mens sones of the best qualitye in this Countie, and many Townes people also.' King's complained to the Aberdeen magistrates, who ordered the culprits to be arrested, depriving two of their bursaries. The affair was also reported to General Monck, the departing military governor of Scotland, who appointed a committee of justices of the peace to settle the dispute. The committee found nine students guilty but refrained from imposing 'civill punishments' upon them; instead, they were to seek pardon at King's and compensate the townsfolk, while the ringleaders were to be expelled.

The second encounter was in 1667, outside Marischal. The cause is unknown, but the occasion was a funeral. The Earl Marischal, who witnessed the affray, arranged a reconciliation between the colleges; in doing so, however, he offended some of the Marischal staff; their students took advantage of the breach to break the principal's windows. The affray itself prompted the magistrates to ban students, especially of King's, from attending funerals in the town.[133]

The third encounter went to three rounds between December 1668 and January 1669.[134] In the first, some 30 King's students, convinced that their classmates had been enticed to Marischal, descended on Aberdeen and abducted two Marischal students from their lodgings. In the second, Marischal students retaliated, ambushing a band from King's on a victory parade around Aberdeen. In the third, they attacked other King's students rash enough to come to town: they grabbed one of them and having 'belted him from the street to their public school . . . loused down his breeches and . . . did exercise base and horrid barbarities upon him.' The Aberdeen magistrates, having failed to get satisfaction from King's after round one, complained to the Privy Council; King's lodged a counter-complaint after rounds two and three. The council again kept things at college level: it remitted the magistrates' complaint to the bishop 'as only proper judge thereto'; it recommended

8 The Old and New Towns of Aberdeen, from James Gordon's plan, around 1660. The inset picture of King's shows the unfinished Cromwell Tower and Timber Muses, built to accommodate its increasing numbers.

the Earl Marischal 'to consider of the complaint [of King's]'; and it counselled the magistrates that 'hereafter . . . incaice any ryot or abuse fall out they apprehend the persons guiltie and present them to their respective masters.' Noting, however, that 'there have severall abuses creipit in which hes occasioned these ryots and may occasion more if not prevented', it also appointed a visitation of both colleges, directing the visitors' attention especially to the methods by which the masters competed for recruits. The visitors, wistfully invoking an earlier age 'when discipline was in vigour', reinforced the college laws and imposed a code of practice for recruitment.

Battle was joined again in 1677. 'Their has been a pley in the Marischal Colledge Leatly,' James Ogilvy informed his mother, 'and when the Masters were going to punish them that were fighting, the old town colledginers came over to the new town with swirds and pistols and did take the Lads that should have been punisched over to the old town with them'. Some of the King's students eventually tried to apologise:

> we did goe ower both to your Colledge, and principall and Rectors houses to have made an acknowledgement, and to have intreated the favoure of your mediatioune for our regresse. And seing we had noe acceptance, then we have now put this lyne to intreat that ye would yet doe us this courtesie, quhich will be ane lasting obligatioune putte upon us to walk more orderlie for the future, and to acquite our selves one all occasiones.[135]

Finally, in 1700–01, a band from King's, accompanied by a mob of townsfolk, invaded the lodgings of a student in the New Town, forcing Marischal to set up a watch at night. After abortive meetings between the colleges and with the New Town magistrates, the dispute was eventually settled by an intermediary.[136]

Bands of students also staged religious or political demonstrations. Of the three on record, only the first passed off without trouble. Soon after the Revolution of 1688, Marischal students advertised a spectacle entitled *The Pope's Procession*. The pope, having come 'to Congratulate the good Success the Roman-Catholicks had in this Kingdom, and more particularly in Aberdene', was to be carried from the college gate to the market cross; then '*Babylon* falls', and he is tried and executed. The show was to feature a large cast, the college mace, fifes, trumpets, tapers, flambeaux, fireworks and the ringing of the Trinity Church bell; but it would not, the students assured the magistrates, be 'Tumultuary'. Later, answering allegations that the show had not taken place, the bookish John Fraser, then a semi, attested with 98 other students that it had and that 'severall Persons of Honor, Gentlemen and others were Spectators.'[137]

In 1692, following the re-establishment of Presbyterianism, students of both colleges targeted Aberdeen's over-zealous Presbyterian magistrates. They began in 1692 at a burial, when a King's student, Simon Fraser (1691) of Beaufort (Inverness-shire), assaulted a civic dignitary. As a result, in 1693, when the magistrates overrode the objections of their ministers and appointed a Presbyterian to preach in St Nicholas, they warned the students, heavy-handedly, to stay away. Naturally, the students took this as a challenge: over 70 of them, Simon again prominent, entered the church and vandalised the magistrates' pews. Expelling the Presbyterian congregation, they 'Caried a Chair in procession round the pillars of the church crying behold the presbyterian pulpit, and singing Carle and the King come and beat ane old man to sing Glory to the father whill they at the same time most Blasphemeously did sing Lilli Bullero'. Soon afterwards there was another confrontation at yet another funeral, prompting Marischal students to shout 'Cammies or Cameronians' after the townsfolk and hiss them. The magistrates went to the Privy Council, warning that 'the peace of the place and the securitie of their Maiesties government' were threatened. The council summoned Simon and several others to appear but, as Subprincipal Fraser reported, 'the boyes [had] skampered of here and theire' and citations were served haphazardly 'as a montebanke were delivering his billets [handbills].' This time the council ordered the colleges to report on the punishments they had imposed; it talked of interviewing the students and their parents; and it empowered the magistrates henceforth 'not only to seaze upon . . . but also to punish [students] guilty of any Ryot Tumult or dysorders within . . . their jurisdiction'.[138] Clearly, the council had lost patience with, and confidence in, college discipline; as unrest spread throughout the other universities that year, it issued an act setting a scale of penalties for student offenders.[139]

Finally, there was Jacobitism. Its prevalence among the staff of King's and Marischal is well-documented; less is known about its manifestation among the students. What were probably Jacobite demonstrations were staged against the magistrates by Marischal students in 1714 and by students from both colleges in January and May 1715.[140] Some time after September King's students disrupted services at St Machar's, where prayers were dutifully said for King George. In October the masters at Marischal abandoned their posts and their students, and the college doors were closed for two years. After this the only events recorded were at King's and followed the Pretender's arrival in Scotland in December. Celebrating with 'Ringing of Bells, a huge Bonfire at the Colledge gate and illuminations', students attacked the manse and the house of a merchant, where they acquired weapons, and went out to Fetteresso 'to waite upon the pretender'. Some also made 'publick declamations . . . against his Majesties Title and Government' in the common school, 'which Harangues were stuffed with scurilous Reflections upon His Majestie and his Generall.' Finally,

> so high run the Madness of these Students . . . that at the last Solemnity Observed by the Rebells they burned His Majestie (under the name of the Duke of Brunswick) . . . in a Bonfire at the Mercat cross assisted by the College servants and a Rable in arms. To which Treasonable spectacle they with Drum beating required the attendance of honest people who still refused all their threats.

It is something of an anticlimax to find that only eight students seem to have been active. As observers noted, however, most of them were bursars. Ever mindful of the threat of expulsion, bursars usually stayed out of trouble.[141] In 1700, however, they had been restive. Now, allegedly dominated by one of their number who was also the servant of one of the Jacobite masters, they briefly took the centre of the stage. They were tried and punished by the college in April. James Gatt (1713), heard making a 'harangue' (declamation) by Thomas Ragg, his classmate, was expelled; Aeneas Sage, also a classmate, and the remaining six demonstrators were expelled and fined the standard 50 merks each.[142] The civilist (professor of law), another of the college Jacobites, participated in most of the hearings; this may have led to an otherwise unexplained attack on his house and family by Thomas Ragg and a second student witness in May.[143] In 1717 King's was purged of its Jacobite staff. Their successors were commendably magnanimous towards the culprits: in 1718 James Gatt, having been of a 'loyal and discreet carriage ever since' and 'of a promising genius', was allowed to graduate with the class of 1714; Aeneas was admitted to his final year with the class of 1719.

Most of the students involved in the affrays, assaults and riots were tertians or magistrands.[144] If they were not all built like Aeneas – six feet-two 'with more than ordinary strength' – they were well armed with guns, blades and blunt instruments. Not surprisingly, they were regarded with fear and handled with care. In 1680, for example, a man from the Old Town, found in a married woman's house, under her bed and behind locked doors, claimed that he had been 'troubled by the way with some students of the Colledge' and had taken refuge there. No-one actually believed him; but no-one questioned the plausibility of his excuse. In 1690, according to Subprincipal Fraser, when troops of cavalry were quartered in King's, 'a little commotion' with the students 'occasioned the other [the cavalry] to stand under armes all night'.[145]

Bad students, said Professor Douglas, were often the prey of 'evilly idle meddlers, scurrying from place to place', and the most serious affrays in the period were inevitably attributed to agitators. 'This Grosse outbreaking', General Monck was told in 1659, 'hath beene wpon ane designe to perturb the peace of the nation'; the 'insolencies' of 1693, according to the Aberdeen magistrates, were at 'the instigation of the Secret abaitters disaffected to his majesties government.'[146] There is no corroborative evidence of these assertions. Furthermore, the Jacobite masters apart, there is little to support the other common accusation that the incidents were caused or connived at by the college staff. It was openly acknowledged, however, that masters contributed to a volatile atmosphere by their 'emulatione and jealousies' and their 'unhandsome wayes of Sollicitationes for Schollars'. Beyond that, their culpability lay rather in their inability to enforce their own laws against 'vaging' and violence, and their complacency: 'I could have ventured anything,' wrote Subprincipal Fraser after the demonstration at St Nicholas, '[that] none I was concerned in would go and had their parol on it. I will not be so readie to believe again.'[147]

Condiscipiles

Turf wars in college, especially the common school, were the most obvious – if least edifying – manifestations of class identity in the period. James Lumsden, for example, was involved in a 'great tumult of semies and bajans fighting' and was later one of a number of 'furious tertians'.[148] Riots, too, involved class loyalty: at least six of the Marischal band in 1658 and five of the King's band in 1669 were classmates of the supposedly enticed students. The reclamation of the valediction ceremony at King's, however, shows class spirit in a better light; and two initiatives at Marischal demonstrate group, if not class, solidarity of a more positive kind. In 1716, when teaching was suspended, tertians and magistrands successfully applied to King's to finish their course and graduate there; and in 1717, seven students who had been bajans and bursars in 1715, having claimed that '[their] Regents deserted them', successfully petitioned the Aberdeen council to renew their bursaries and allow them to re-enter as semis.[149] There is, in addition, the first clear evidence of relationships within a class based on kinship, school, or place of origin. James Fraser (1651) went to King's from Moray with his cousin and compatriot, Hugh Fraser, and a schoolmate, Arthur Stratton. After they graduated together, James and Hugh planned a Continental tour together and it was to James's 'greefe and resentment' that Hugh had to pull out.[150]

TABLE 2.1 ENTRANTS AND GRADUATES AT KING'S, 1640–79

Years	*Average annual number entering the first class*	*Average annual number of entrants who graduated*	*Graduates as % of entrants*
1640–49	24.0	12.5	52.0
1650–59	24.8	13.0	52.4
1660–69	58.8	27.7	47.1
1670–79	51.6	19.3	37.4

Source: Anderson, *Roll*, Appendix B. Complete figures for 1660 and 1667 and after 1680 are not available. Nor are figures for Marischal: however, the average number of entrants there for 1640–49, was 12.6; the average numbers of entrants and graduates for 1652–56, were 25.4 and 13.6 (53.5%); the average numbers for 1665–68, 20.7 and 10.2 (49%).

In the first half of the period – there are no comparable figures for the second – the size of classes at King's rose dramatically; at Marischal, there was a modest gain (Table 2.1). The average number of entrants at King's in the 1640s was 46% higher than that in the previous decade, despite the uncertainty of the times, not least an outbreak of the plague in 1647–48. According to Sir Thomas Urquhart, this expansion was the personal achievement of Principal Guild;[151] certainly, it was not replicated at Marischal, where there was an almost identical percentage decrease. In the 1650s the gap between the colleges closed; but in the next two decades, when university entrance expanded nationwide,[152] King's surged ahead. The growth can be attributed in the first instance to the more settled state of the North and North East, allowing students to set off for the Old Town with some hope of a safe arrival. It may also reflect an increased take-up by urban, professional and commercial families, although this cannot be clearly demonstrated from the college records as they stand. On top of this, the masters themselves made a contribution, 'soliciting for and seeking in of schollars throw the countrey' and 'intyseing the schooleris from the one [college] to the tother.' They operated through direct approaches to students and their families, and indirect approaches through friends, misrepresenting 'their neighboures and especially those of their own professions'. In the end, their practices were blamed for the riot of 1669 and were outlawed by the visitation that followed it: thereafter, students could only move to another college if their families had relocated or if they qualified for a bursary there. Despite this, solicitation, enticement and slander continued into the 1670s, the masters unable to agree on a protocol to eliminate them.[153] Enticement seems eventually to have waned, but solicitation and slander persisted: in 1701 a master from King's accused the staff of Marischal of spreading false rumours about the college; in 1702, however, he persuaded a former student to recruit for him amongst families and schools in the north, assuring him that 'you will do a kindness both to your Alma Mater and old Master'.[154] What these efforts lacked in propriety, they made up in persistence; but the results remain unquantifiable.

The foundation of new bursaries at both colleges also contributed steadily to the numbers of entrants – and graduates. At King's, in the first documented bursary competition on 10 October 1676, William Anderson was one of nine candidates and became one of five bursars among the 44 entrants to the class; in 1680 he was one of four bursars among its 12 graduates.[155] At Marischal, in Gilbert Burnet's class of 1653 there were three bursars among the 19 entrants and 15 graduates; in James Ogilvy's class of 1675 there were six among the 30 entrants; Ludovic Reid was one of five bursars among the 18 graduands of 1693; and in the Duffs' class of 1711 there were nine bursars among some 50 students.

TABLE 2.2 MIGRATION BETWEEN KING'S AND MARISCHAL, 1640–79

Sessions	*Marischal to King's*	*King's to Marischal*
1640–49	6	13
1650–59	14	10 [18]
1660–69	13	11
1670–79	30	0

Source: Anderson, *Roll*. Four migrants from the King's class 1650–54 are recorded, although additional evidence suggests a further eight (below, p. 191).

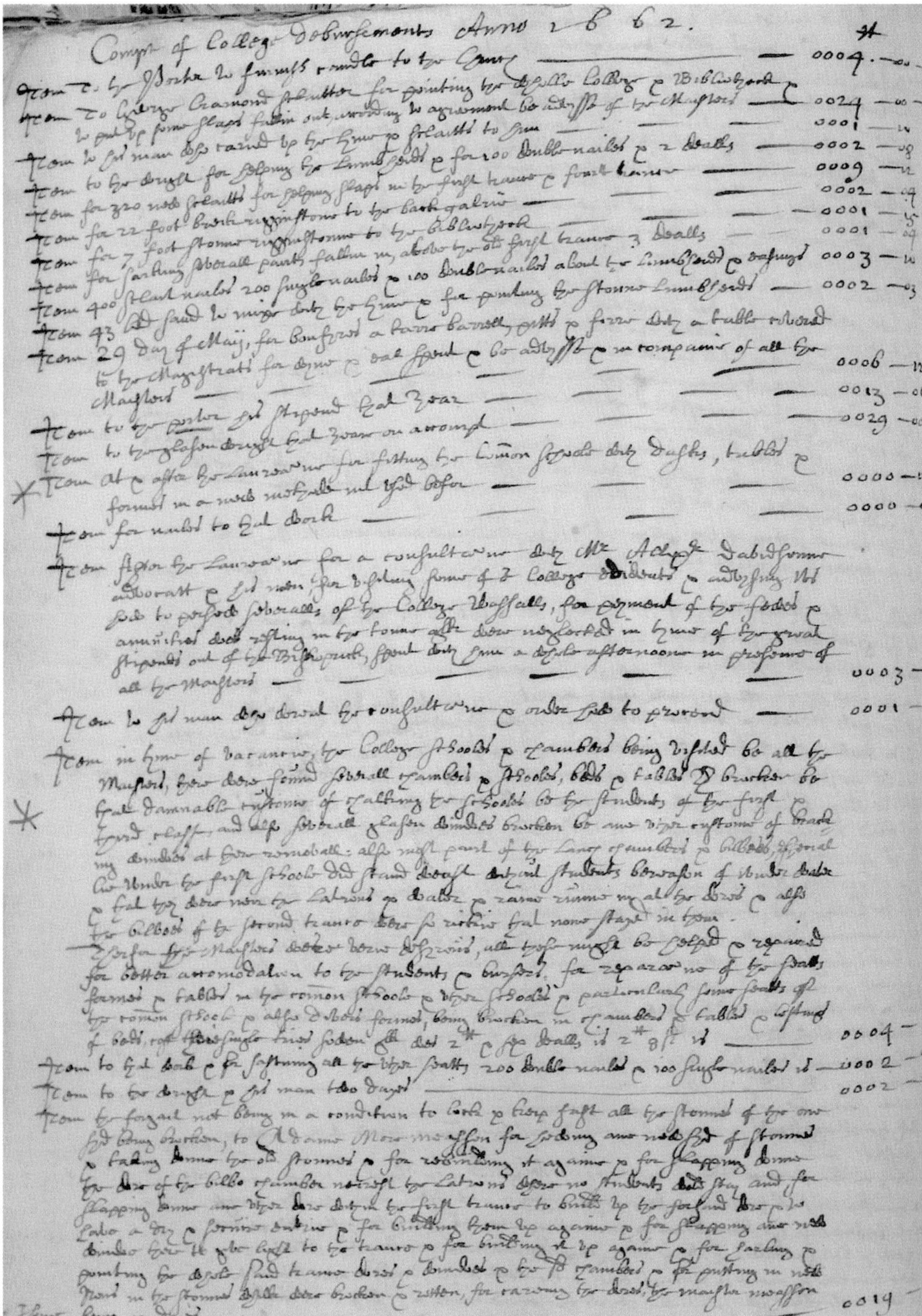

9 The Marischal College accounts are enriched by comments: here, in 1662, on the 'damnable custome of chalking the schooles'. AUL, MS M 57, f. 37v.

Migration between classes rose to new, and dramatic, heights. James Fraser recalled how, in 1654, Robert Ferguson (1650), another of his schoolmates, 'kendled a flam in Our Kings Colledge . . . and led twelve students oute off the 4th classe with him to the new Colledge . . . and were graduat in Mr Cants Classe there . . . And all of them acknowledged it was by his instigation, and pettish humore.'[156] Some ten years later, Andrew Cant's nephews migrated from the Marischal classes of 1663 and 1665, apparently with parental approval.[157] Others switched colleges 'on accompt of discipline exercised or to be exercised'; enough to prompt measures against the practice.[158] In the majority of cases it is hard to distinguish between this kind of migration and enticement; the overall numbers, however, show that King's came out well ahead.

TABLE 2.3 ESTIMATED AGGREGATE NUMBERS OF ARTS STUDENTS AT KING'S, 1645–76

Class	*1645–46*	*1655–56*	*1665–66*	*1675–76*
First	20	22	35	40
Second	16	14	53	56
Third	14	11	39	21
Fourth	14	9	39	26
Aggregate	64	56	166	143

Source: Estimates based on Anderson, *Roll*, Appendix B, assuming an equal annual reduction in class numbers.

TABLE 2.4 ACTUAL AND ESTIMATED AGGREGATE NUMBERS OF ARTS STUDENTS AT MARISCHAL, 1649–75

Class	*1649–50*	*1655–56*	*1668–69*	*1674–75*
First	16	20	26	–
Second	19	28	18	–
Third	8	13	14	–
Fourth	7	13	8	–
Aggregate	50	74	66	108

Source: Figures for 1649–50 (admissions) and 1674–75 (rectorial election, recorded by nation): Anderson, *FAM*, 2. Estimates for 1655–56 and 1668–69, based on Anderson, *Roll*, Appendix B, assuming an equal annual reduction in class numbers.

The aggregate number of arts students had doubled at both colleges by the mid-1670s (Tables 2.3–2.4). Assuming even minimal growth after that, it was more than the new and refurbished college buildings could accommodate. The number of students living in is not known. At King's, however, the average attendance at the college table in May 1650 was nearly half the estimated aggregate;[159] and lists of students in college on 18 February 1714 show that of 22 known bajans, at least seven, including Aeneas Sage and James Gatt, lived in; at least ten, including Thomas Ragg, did not.[160] At Marischal, the number of arts students paying chamber mails is first recorded in 1669: 50 paid, not far below the nearest estimated aggregate of 66 in 1668–69. In 1688–89, however, fewer than 30 paid, although there was an aggregate of at least 99. The college was in the middle of rebuilding at that time, however, and the number of rooms available may have been affected; numbers rose again from around 37 in 1694–95 to a peak of 74 in 1709–10.[161] Those who could not live in had to lodge in town – possibly more cheaply, certainly unsupervised. Some, at least, must have welcomed the opportunity.

Students' ages at entry continued to vary widely. The precocious Gilbert Burnet entered at ten; the prodigious Thomas Ruddiman at 16; big Aeneas Sage at 19. Nevertheless, in 1704 Subprincipal Fraser considered that 'a great many of them that come [to King's] are two young'.[162] Their social origins – regularly recorded for the landed, accidentally revealed in a few other cases – similarly show no change. James Fraser at King's and Ludovic Reid at Marischal were, like Andrew Cant, sons of the manse. George Mackenzie at King's and Gilbert Burnet at Marischal were, like John Spalding, sons of lawyers. And there was 'Baylyie Allexander's son', who entered Marischal in 1660. New bursaries at Marischal extended the trend of the previous period. Beneficiaries continued to be, largely, from 'the middling sort': either genuinely in need, or fortunate in their connections. Their fathers (where occupations are specified) were mainly ministers, merchants, craftsmen, or civic officers. A significant number of applicants were fatherless; in contrast, a much smaller number gave poverty as the reason for their application.[163]

TABLE 2.5 KING'S COLLEGE, GEOGRAPHICAL ORIGINS OF ARTS STUDENTS EXPRESSED AS A PERCENTAGE OF THE NUMBER IN THE CLASS, 1646–77

Class	*1646*	*1658*	*1663*	*1677*
Aberdeen	0	0	0	0
Aberdeenshire & North East	54.8	66.7	62.3	39.0
Highlands & North	29.0	23.5	13.0	30.5
Rest of Scotland	9.7	7.8	13.0	15.2
England, Wales, Ireland	0	2.0	0	1.7
Overseas	0	0	0	0
Not known	6.5	0	11.7	13.6
No. in class	31	51	77	59

Source: Anderson, *Roll*. The classes selected are those in which origins are given for 98–100% of the students. Definitions of the categories are given below, Appendix 4.

TABLE 2.6 DISTRIBUTION OF ARTS STUDENTS AT MARISCHAL IN 'NATIONS', 1674–75

Mar	*Buchan*	*Moray*	*Angus*	*Total*
64 (59.2%)	11 (10.1%)	24 (22.2%)	9 (8.3%)	108

Source: Anderson, *FAM*, 2, 244–6. Mar: Aberdeen, south and central Aberdeenshire. Buchan: north Aberdeenshire. Moray: northern counties. Angus: counties south of the Dee; anywhere else in Scotland or beyond.

More is known than before about the geographical origins of students. Table 2.5 shows that the surge in numbers at King's came from the northern counties, principally from Moray, which provided almost 30% of the class in 1663; Ross-shire, in contrast, sent a smaller, steadier stream,[164] but accounted for the largest number of highland-born students in the college.[165] Table 2.6 shows the predominance at Marischal of students from Aberdeen and its hinterland, mainly in a rectangle formed by Aberdeen, Ellon, Insch and Alford.[166] Of the 21 English students at King's in the period, 17 entered after the Restoration, probably from the stream of nonconformists who sought a university education in Scotland then. Surprisingly, in view of the strong connexions between the North East, the Baltic coast and beyond, only a few students entered either college from the Continent.

The rigours of travel to and from the colleges, especially for students from the northern counties, should not be underestimated. James Ogilvy had simply to ask his mother, Lady Findlater, to 'send in the horses for us', when he was ready to return to Cullen House in Banffshire. But Hugh Rose, his tutor and 'page' spent some £20: 'by the waye coming home', 'for a horse hyre to Keith', for carrying the baggage, part by sea, and part by land' and 'at Speye'. As for Thomas Ruddiman, he had to walk from Boyndie (Banffshire) and is said to have been attacked and stripped by gypsies on the way.

Not aniewise extravagant

In an era of economic, as well as political, instability, the cost of a university education for those who paid full fees stretched all but the wealthiest families. In October 1691, for example, Kenneth Gordon had to delay his entry to King's 'seing what should maintaine him in these circumstances could not be called for [then]'. Those who put up the money – parents, or kinsmen – expected it to be managed properly by those to whom they entrusted it, whether masters, tutors or other kin: when Kenneth eventually arrived in November 1692, Subprincipal Fraser reported regularly on his finances; while William Duff himself assured his father that he had not been 'aniewise extravagant in my pocatmony.' The laws of King's encouraged students to be thrifty, and at both colleges they were required to be scrupulous in paying their dues and settling their arrears.[167] Some masters helped with credit and advice: at King's, Subprincipal Fraser promised that Kenneth should 'not want what is needfull till [his money] come'; at Marischal, the Duffs' master advised on 'quartering' (lodging) in town. Sometimes the students helped themselves: John Spalding earned extra cash writing documents for the kirk session; William Jack (1666), also of King's, did the same for the college.[168]

Tution fees at King's rose in the 1640s to a minimum of £20 for the sons of the nobility, £13 6s 8d for lesser ranks, and £10 for the sons of farmers and tradesmen.[169] Hugh Rose paid £30 in 1655–57 and 1657–58, covering the cost not only of his own tuition but that of the 'page' who accompanied him. In the laws of the 1680s, however, the cheapest rate is no longer mentioned. Examination fees are not listed, but Hugh paid £1 2s for his first exam and £1 13s for his second, suggesting that they had risen only slightly. At graduation, from at least the 1650s onwards, students paid the sum of £4 12s in 'book and staff money' (to the library and for the ceremony). Those unable to pay, like William Jack in 1670, left a 'ticket' (pledge) and redeemed it later.[170] At Marischal, neither tuition nor examination fees are recorded; by 1712, however, according to Robert Duff's tutor, 'lairds' were said to give the masters '3 or 4 guineas' (£37 16s, £50 8s). Graduation fees were the same: John Gentleman (1684) paid £4 12s in 'bibliotheck' and 'mace' money.[171] The cost of private graduation, unstated at King's, started around £8 at Marischal.[172] Little is known about other college charges. At King's, in 1641, students were required to pay 6s to the beadle, and between 6 and 10s to the printer.[173] Hugh Rose also gave the janitor sums of over £4. At Marischal, in the years 1702–10, graduates were encouraged, if not actually required, to contribute to the cost of finishing and furnishing the new hall, begun during the building programme of the 1680s.[174]

Students paying chamber mails at King's faced a hike in charges in 1646: 'a bed in a chamber' was £1; a muse, £2; 'muses only within chambers that wants beds', £1 6s 8d.[175] Not that there was much on offer. There were chambers with integral or adjoining muses in the 'west quarter'; off the 'trances' (passages) and stairs of the dilapidated 'south quarter'; and in at least one of the capitols.[176] In 1658, however, only nine in all were habitable. The New Work, begun that year, provided 13 new chambers by the following winter, rising to 24 when it was finished,[177] and there were studies on at least three floors of the Timber Muses.[178] By the 1700s rents evidently varied according to location and size: a single student paid £1 10s for 'the first chamber in the low stair' of the Old Work; two paid £3 each for 'the first chamber in the high stair' there; a chamber without a muse in the New Work cost £6; a 'north' muse on the first floor there cost £4; as did 'the uppermost timber muse'.[179] At Marischal, in 1650, a chamber cost £3 6s 8d per person; a muse, £1 10s. From the 1670s onwards there seems to have been a unitary rent of £1 10s.[180] Well-born or wealthy students generally rented single chambers. Hugh Rose took one for himself, his tutor and his page. He spent £20 bringing in 'twa bedis, with curtaines, a table cloth, chaires etc.', a hired 'kist' (storage chest), straw for the beds; and over £12 on candles and fuel. Most students 'chambered' with each other: Kenneth Gordon, in November 1692, with four others, two of them his kinsmen, two from the same county. They also shared muses: Thomas Ragg, having lived out as a bajan, moved in as a magistrand to a 'north' muse on the sixth floor of the New Work, which he shared with a tertian; while Murdoch Morison and five other islanders and highlanders occupied a 'south' chamber and muse on the third floor.[181]

'A quarter's buird' for Hugh Rose and his retinue cost just under £80: about all that is known of subsistence costs at either college. Under the laws of precedence enforced by Principal Row, Hugh would have sat at the high table; his tutor and page at one of the long tables lower down. Under the principal's equally stringent rules of etiquette, they would have taken their food in three fingers and turned their backs when they belched. What they ate is not known. Some years earlier, however, on Tuesday, 21 May 1650, breakfast consisted of bread and saps (bread soaked in ale); for dinner, there was mutton, lamb and meat broth, salmon and haddock, with plumdames (damsons, possibly prunes) to follow; for supper, lamb, salmon and plumdames. On Tuesday, 25 November 1651, dinner and supper were both of beef, mutton and haddock. On Tuesday, 23 March 1652, there was beef, haddock and codlings, eggs, rice, and plumdames.[182] Whatever his fare, Hugh seems to have enjoyed it: he contributed handsomely to 'a collection to the cooke'.

Meat, at least, may have been plentiful for James Fraser, who lived out, lodging and boarding with a 'flesher' (butcher) in the Old Town.[183] Other students lodged with John Ross, the janitor, whose widow was still putting them up in 1704.[184] Marischal students likewise lodged with their janitor;[185] and with tradesmen living near the college. The cost of lodging in Old Aberdeen is not known; in the New Town, however, Robert Duff's tutor reported in 1712, 'private Gentlemen' were charging 'forty pounds Scots or three pounds Sterling'. William and Robert, lodging with a kinsman, paid £33 6s 8d each: the same sum Robert's father had paid 'at the college table' in his student days and as much as he would allow his son.

Fees, board and lodging apart, the heaviest item of expenditure was clothing; this despite repeated laws imposing sobriety in dress. At Marischal, according to Robert Duff's tutor, 'the Lairds [did] not look as Lairds but as Little Princes', and Robert had to have 'gold mounting' on his coat or at least 'a fashionable wig . . . for he must be something honestlike.' Gowns themselves did not come cheap: John Rose paid £16 7s for one in the 1660s; Subprincipal Fraser had to help with the purchase of Kenneth Gordon's in November 1692; while the Duffs' kinsman bought Robert a gown of 'a very fine Scarlet' at a price which shocked his tutor.[186]

10 Gilbert Burnet, 1723. Marischal honoured the memory of its graduate and benefactor with this posthumous portrait, probably by Andrew McIlvraith; it cost over £69 Scots. Aberdeen University Picture Collection.

Honestlie manteinit

The number of bursaries grew at both colleges. At King's, Sir Thomas Burnett's bequest in 1648 for three 'poore scollers' to be 'honestlie mainteinit' was the first of nine providing up to 36 bursaries. At Marischal, 17 benefactions provided over 40 bursaries, although not all of them proved viable. As important as their number, however, was their value. At King's, each foundation bursar now received £40, barely enough for his subsistence: even when the amount was increased in 1652, a master noted with concern that 'they have but 70 Merkis [£46 13s 4d] for ten moneths and nothing for cloaths, books . . . in the tyme of vacancie'.[187] By the 1670s they were on £40 again and remained at that level for the rest of the period; some later, privately-founded bursaries were worth even less. Thomas Ruddiman, grateful for the guinea (£12 12s) that his sister had put in his pocket before he left home, would have been one of many who relied on supplementary funding. The little that bursars there received, they often received late. In his first year, 1676–77, William Anderson's money was paid on time: it came in three equal 'quarters' (instalments) on 28 October, 29 March and 1 June. As a semi, however, his first instalment was not paid until 15 December and his third in two payments on 4 June and 2 July. As a tertian, he received only half of his third instalment. Finally, as a magistrand, he had to wait until four days before graduation to receive his third instalment and the half-instalment owing from his third year; the money was paid on the orders of an embarrassed principal, 'out of the verie first and readiest of the Colledge rentis'.[188] At Marischal, awards were higher to begin with but were reduced by a combination of fluctuating prices, falling interest rates and mismanagement: a Cargill bursar received £53 6s 8d in 1640, £40 in 1660 and £30 in 1690.[189]

Despite the prohibition of 1634, foundation bursars at King's continued to pay spoon silver, while all bursars paid the beadle's fee and the printer's. In the 1650s and 1660s they had to find a lump sum of £5 12s; in William Anderson's day, spoon silver was deducted at source.[190] Furthermore, while the principle of free tuition for bursars at both colleges was confirmed on more than one occasion during the period, a charge was levied nevertheless. In 1669 it was 'recommendit to the maisters of both colledges to be favourable to the poore bursers as to ther sallaries and stipends'; and in 1677 a benefactor of Marischal conceded that his bursars might pay up to £6 13s 4d for 'stipend or colledge fee'. In 1710 charging was declared by both colleges to be 'constant practice', although done on a discretionary basis.[191] Discretion was also shown to bursars who could not afford the full graduation fee: at Marischal, for example, Francis Milne, a Crombie bursar, graduated with John Gentleman in 1688 but paid only his bibliotheck money of £4.

Bursars at King's spread beyond the rooms traditionally allocated to them in the Old Work. Around 1715, for example, they occupied all but one of the muses on the second floor of the New.[192] Some shared with wealthier students, acting as their servants in lieu of rent. In November 1704 Subprincipal Fraser arranged for a bursar to share with George Mackenzie, describing him as 'very fit to wait on a young man'; the lad was removed in April, however, having failed to keep George out of trouble. At Marischal, despite the pressure on space at the time, Francis Milne lived in for all four of his years: as a bajan, he paid the basic rent of £1 10s; as a semi and tertian, he roomed with classmates and fellow-bursars; as a magistrand, he shared with John Gentleman, a classmate but not a bursar.[193] The austerity imposed on foundation bursars at King's remained in force. At meal-times those who were not reading, passing dishes or pouring water, sat at their own table, laid with a 'harden' (coarse) table cloth instead of linen, where they ate 'bursar bread' and, on one occasion, were served codling while the other students had spring lamb.[194]

All weill bestowd

Responding to a 'very angry letter' from the laird of Dipple, the Duffs' kinsman assured him that 'you shall vow all weill bestowd'. In fact, judgements on the quality of the King's and Marischal experience, by students or parents, are few but generally favourable. James Fraser praised his 'deare and indulgent Master', John Strachan, but had little good to say about the rest of the staff, least of all the 'vain and ostentive' Principal Row. Hugh Rose was less ambivalent: in 1664, 'in testimoniall of the love he [bore] . . . towards the Colledge', he spent £144 furnishing 'Kilravock's chamber' in the New Work.[195] Gilbert Burnet said cryptically of his time at Marischal that he 'did escape out of it very little the better, and not much the worse for it'; nevertheless, he called his master 'a very pious good natured man, and considerably learned' and later founded bursaries 'in remembrance of my Education there'. John Fraser founded his bursary at Marischal only four years after he had graduated in 1691 – an unequivocal expression of confidence in the college. Among parents, the lairds of Cawdor and Innes, apologising for their sons' conduct in 1685, acknowledged 'the great caire and paynes' that the college had 'bestowed on our children and our selffes'.[196] Other families, like Burnett of Leys and Gordon of Straloch at King's, and Forbes of Pitsligo at Marischal, demonstrated tacit approval by sending more than one generation to the same college. The Roses of Kilravock, who did likewise, may have been equally attracted by free accommodation in the fourteenth laird's chamber.

The church, education, the law and its administration, and the land continued to be the principal occupations of most graduates from King's and Marischal. Among those who entered the church was James Fraser; he officiated in Kirkhill (Inverness-shire) – Fraser country – and wrote prolifically, notably his 'Chronicles of the Frasers'. Others included John Rose, William Anderson and Murdoch Morrison, who served a parish on the island of Lewis. John Fraser would no doubt have joined them, had he not died in the middle of his divinity course. James Gatt, his affiliations in the 'Fifteen' well behind him, was not only a minister but also a poet, writing pro-government verse at the time of the 'Forty-five'. Aeneas Sage became a missionary, then minister, to what his grandson called the 'near-pagans' of Ross-shire. And it was in the manse at Strachan, Kincardineshire, that Ludovic Reid, from Marischal, raised his son Thomas, the Enlightenment philosopher. Hugh Fraser, having missed out on a grand tour with James, became a schoolmaster and later a minister at Croy, not far from his cousin. It was common for those studying divinity, or having studied it, waiting for a pulpit, to teach in a parish school. Thomas Ragg was one of many others who did so. Thomas Ruddiman started out as a schoolmaster but fulfilled his prodigious potential as a scholar in Edinburgh, although *Rudiments of the Latin Tongue* (1714) ensured that his name lived on in the schoolrooms of the North East. James Ogilvy studied law before entering politics and becoming, as Earl of Seafield, Lord High Chancellor of Scotland. Hugh Rose represents those students from landed families who subsequently immersed themselves in county business. Of students who made their way in England, Gilbert Burnet, as his precocity portended, won the greatest renown, as bishop of Salisbury, counsellor of William and Mary, and historian of his own times; James Anderson, alerted to the perils of sectarian strife, became a presbyterian minister in London, author of *The Constitutions of the Free-Masons* (London, 1723) and compiler of *Royal Genealogies* (London, 1732). More typical were the friends James Fraser looked up in London: 'Mr Arthur Straton who commenct Master of arts with me . . . in a Chaplancy at Oxford [and] Mr Ludovic Burnet, Usher to a School . . .'. Also in London at the time was Robert Ferguson, 'The Plotter', whose notoriety as an intriguer was to be rivalled by Simon Fraser of Beaufort, later Lord Lovat. Andrew Cant, having returned to Marischal as a master, then became a minister and, re-entering academic life, was appointed principal of the University of Edinburgh. John Spalding, in contrast, compiled his *Memorialls of the Trubles* in comparative obscurity, where he remained until 1839, when the founders of the Spalding Club redeemed him.

Chapter 3

A great deal of useful knowledge, 1718–1825

Pryse Gordon entered King's College in 1776. Fatherless from the age of two, he had been raised by his grandfather, a Banffshire minister. Grandfather was a friend of the earl of Seafield, patron of the Redhyth bursaries, and Pryse was duly presented to one, like his three uncles and three brothers before him.[1] James Bentley entered Marischal College in 1787. Fatherless from the age of four, he had been raised by his mother in the New Town and was accordingly entered in the Marischal bursary competition.[2] He came only thirteenth but, as the son of a merchant burgess, received a Liddel bursary worth more than those awarded to boys with better marks.[3] Pryse always maintained that bursars came off better than students who paid their own way, 'libertines' as they were now called:[4] '[they have] the pleasure of paying for every thing *double*; but I suspect they do not acquire an ounce more learning.'

By the time Pryse entered, King's had extended its buildings again. Around 1725 it replaced the ruined, residential south block with a new mixed-purpose building, fronted by a colonnade, or piazza. Part of the top floor of this block eventually became 'the Lobby' – social space used by the students for dances (below, p. 78). The library was also rebuilt, but the new structure proved inadequate, and its contents were re-housed at the west end of the chapel in 1772. The east end of the chapel functioned as the common school and only resumed its original role in 1825. In the same year the college rebuilt its west front, losing what remained of the southwest capitol, and remodelled the Cromwell Tower. At Marischal, in 1741, a four-storey south wing was added to the existing two blocks.[5]

For much of the period King's and Marischal sought to survive in an increasingly competitive academic market by providing the polite learning required by a Hanoverian-Whig-Presbyterian establishment, together with the skills and knowledge needed in commerce and industry.[6] Fundamental to the survival strategy of both colleges was the reform of the philosophy curriculum. At King's, this was carried out in 1753–54 on the incentive of the philosopher, Thomas Reid. At the same time other changes were introduced, going further than most students and their families were willing or able to follow. They were soon rescinded, but the ensuing recriminations inaugurated years of internal strife. At Marischal, innovations in the teaching of mathematics and experimental science preceded the reform of the curriculum itself in 1752. Refraining from any other changes, the college gained in both numbers and support at its rival's expense.

Pryse and James followed the reformed curriculum. Their education, 'put upon a more rational and useful footing', dealt with 'those parts of Philosophy, which may qualify Men for the more useful and important Offices of Society' and '[rendered] the study of the Sciences more advantageous in life, than it is generally thought to be'.[7] Spirituality was not neglected: 'our minds were improved,' recalled one of James's classmates, 'in observing the beauty, order, harmony, variety and utility of the works of our Creator.'[8] Nevertheless, the colleges accepted that some of their students, at least, had aspirations beyond the pulpit or the classroom: '[they] do attend the Universities with many different Views', said Principal John Chalmers in 1760; 'their plans and schemes for Life do not depend upon the knowledge of [Latin or Greek], and yet by attending the other classes, they may learn a great deal of useful knowledge'.[9] By the end of the period, however, the system was under fire. Students were said to be complacent, believing they could get a degree 'because [they] had dosed for three hours daily in the class-room for twenty months' and had undergone 'a matter of form examination for three minutes'.[10] Against a growing public perception of inertia within the Scottish universities as a whole,[11] both colleges had to address the lack of rigour in their courses and procedures.

By the time Pryse and James entered, students had long forsaken their role in the constitution of the college, limited as it was. At King's, their part in the election of the rector was ignored; at Marischal, they retained the right of electing procurators but left the choice of rector to the staff. They attached little importance to their loss, or to the rector himself for that matter, appealing to him on only one recorded occasion, at King's in 1763 over the quality of college food (below, p. 94). In the 1820s, however, advocates of university reform encouraged Marischal students to reclaim their right of choice, declaring that 'defects and corruption . . . have been the consequence of [some universities] possessing inactive, and merely nominal Rectors'. They recommended Joseph Hume, the local, radical MP and 'the declared enemy of corruption and sinecure.' Hume had been a candidate in 1823, but the professors had engineered his defeat; they could not prevent his election in 1824, however, and again in 1825.[12] During these years Hume received a number of complaints about the college: in November 1825, therefore, in the name of what would nowadays be called transparency and in defiance of the professors, he held a rectorial court, declaring it 'to be more especially his duty to ascertain the rights of the Students, and see justice done them.'[13] In real terms the court achieved little; but it reminded students that they had a voice and, through rectorial elections, a legitimate means of projecting it.

I think I have enough to do

For much of the period the academic year lasted only five months. Beginning around 1 November and petering out in March, with graduation early in April, it was barely long enough to support the old curriculum, let alone the reformed version. In 1753, therefore, King's revived the seven-month session of the late seventeenth century, running from October to May. Prospective students, however, were either unable or unwilling to pay the extra costs involved, and the experiment was abandoned after six years.[14] The session was later lengthened by a few days,[15] but according to Pryse Gordon's nephew, Abercromby (1817), even the students wanted more.[16] Nevertheless, by 1825 it lasted only 21 weeks. Marischal, presciently, did not extend its session in the 1750s, although in 1773 more teaching time was released by reducing the Christmas vacation from a fortnight to three days. Although subsequent calls for extension were 'from prejudice . . . never carried into effect', Marischal gained further time by paring the Christmas break to a single day and in 1825 offered ten days more than King's. This was still not long enough for the reformers, however, and was among the grievances raised that year with the rector.[17]

Both colleges retained regenting for the second, third and fourth classes (the first being taught by the professor of Greek) long after the other Scottish universities had abandoned or modified the system. They considered changing to the professorial regime when they reformed the curriculum. Marischal, keen to keep up with the competition, adopted it. King's, producing a nine-point argument in favour of the three-year relationship between student and master, rejected the idea and did not go professorial until 1799.[18]

Following the reform of the curriculum, students spent less time in the classroom than before. At King's, bajans had a six-day week of 16 to 18 hours; semis, tertians and magistrands, one of up to 25. These were 'hours' in name only: of the three main teaching times, 8–9 am, 11–12 am and 3–4 pm, the first followed morning prayers and could last less than 30 minutes, while the others were sometimes prolonged for practical exercises.[19] At Marischal, the hours were much the same: William Knight (1798) spent 18 in class as a bajan and a magistrand; 24 as a semi and tertian.[20] At both colleges, students put in additional time on optional courses: for William Knight, in his third and fourth years, this meant an extra three hours a week. Finally, weaker students had a further hour or more of private tuition from individual masters: 'Mr Leslie [professor of Greek]', wrote James Urquhart (1772), a tertian at King's, 'proposes I should attend him once a Week together with two others. A Scheme which I think will be much to my advantage.'[21] The 'private college' was now carefully regulated to protect the 'publick class':[22] 'I have entered no other Class this winter than the Greek,' wrote Alexander Watt (1788) from Marischal, 'in which I think I have enough to do and Professor Stewart desired me not to do it.'[23]

Pryse Gordon's uncle, Walter Morison (1752), was among the last students to follow the unreformed curriculum at King's. By the time Pryse and his brothers entered, the reformed version was not only embedded but its courses already close to overload. In their first year they studied Greek with 'exercises' in English literature; and Latin with lectures on classical history and antiquities. In their second they had elementary mathematics combined with civil and natural history; in their third, advanced mathematics combined with natural philosophy; and in their fourth, moral philosophy and logic. By the time Pryse's son, George, entered the class of 1807, mathematics had been detached from the overburdened courses and was taught separately in the second and third years; ten years later, however, chemistry was added to natural history in the second year.[24] At Marischal, where courses multiplied in the same way, William Knight recorded the unrelenting pace and pressure of the expanded second year.

> [1799] Nov. [2] The first lectures were on Versification . . . Then Chronology, and (Nov. 20) a short view of Ancient Geography, Lectures on the States of Society, the forms of government, and the histories of Ancient Egypt, Persia and Greece. Nov. 30 Comparison of the Institutions of Athens and Sparta. Dec. 11 History of Rome commenced – ended 3 January [1800]. January 4 [the professor] began Natural History.
>
> The same day (Nov. 2) we repaired to the adjoining mathematical classroom. [We] spent the first three meetings in Arithmetic, then went through the Six books of Euclid, with the interruption of a few lessons on Algebra at Christmas – then ended with Trigonometry, Surveying, Levelling, and the use of the Globes.

By the time Abercromby Gordon entered King's there had been another major change. Under the reformed curriculum, students at both colleges had been expected to take Latin and Greek beyond their first, elementary year. For much of the period this was optional, but in 1817 at King's, and 1818 at Marischal, it was made a requirement of graduation.[25] The problem was that students entered with, at best, a modest knowledge of Latin: 'about three-fourths of them', complained the professor of humanity (formerly the humanist) at King's, 'are totally ignorant of Prosody.' At Marischal, where there was no chair in the subject, the redoubtable James Melvin was drafted in from the grammar school to help.[26] If students' Latin was modest, their Greek was minimal: Pryse Gordon arrived at King's with 'a smattering', but the majority had to start, like William Knight, with the alphabet. The colleges had therefore to underpin their advanced courses in the classics with private tuition.

By the 1770s most lectures were in English, although the practice does not appear to have been imposed formally at either college; Greek, however, was taught through the medium of Latin. In 1825, 50 minutes was reckoned 'sufficiently long to keep the attention of large classes'.[27] Masters generally read their lectures; some extemporised; while James Beattie, at Marischal, favoured the Socratic approach.[28] Students' notes of some courses read like a spontaneous record; however, some are clearly old-fashioned dictates.[29] Beattie, for one, made his students 'take down in writing an abstract of the lectures and conversations [discussion]'; and in the 1820s the professor of moral philosophy at Marischal dictated the 'heads' of his lectures, because 'the subjects I have to discuss are so very abstract'.[30] From the 1750s onwards lectures on historical and scientific subjects might be illustrated from

'Collections of natural and artificial Bodies', which the masters amassed and curated.[31] At King's, the humanist's 'little museum' was admired by Pryse Gordon. At Marischal, Patrick Copland's air pump, electrical machine and 'hydro-pneumatic trough for gases' enraptured William Knight. William was less impressed, however, by provision in the mathematical classroom: 'Senex's old globes were perched on brackets, and rattled as they turned round', and '[the professor] used a slate, French chalk, and a sponge.'[32]

Disputation and declamation continued into the first decades of the period.[33] Following the reform of the curriculum, however, disputing was deemed unnecessary and was dropped; declamations survived but were eventually replaced by Latin essays read aloud. At King's, students performed on Mondays; at Marischal, on Fridays; in both cases at 11 am in the common school.[34] The event was combined – inelegantly but presumably it saved time – with the weekly meeting for discipline (below, p. 82). William Malcolm (1808), as a magistrand at King's, made a speech on 'The ancient systems of philosophy'. William Knight and Alexander Thomson (1812), as magistrands at Marischal, read essays 'on Taste' and 'the Ionic School of Philosophy'.[35]

Students, whether they lived in or out of college, were free to learn in whatever way they pleased. They did, however, receive some guidance: at Marischal, for example, the college laws of 1741 advised them to spend one hour away from their books before settling to them again. Unsupervised learning best suited those who, like Alexander Watt at Marischal, were not bright but capable of 'deligence and application'. Some preferred to learn alone, notably Charles Burney (1777) at King's, who lived 'like a hermit'.[36] Others were more gregarious: at King's, James Mackintosh (1780) was one of a group who rose at 5 am one winter to read Greek;[37] at Marischal, William Knight studied Latin in 'a little smoky closet' with one of his classmates and repeated some of Patrick Copland's experiments with another. However and whatever they learned, students at both colleges faced frequent oral tests: at Marischal, for example, in the session 1787–88, James Bentley's magistrand contemporaries were tested on three or four days out of six, often in the short 8 am slot.[38] These tests were eventually supplemented with written work: again at Marischal, William Knight, as professor of natural philosophy, introduced first voluntary then compulsory weekly exercises between 1823 and 1825. There were, inevitably, students who could not keep up. Charles MacEver (1752), 'being sensible that he was not well founded in Greek and Latin, and finding the Mathematicks a little too hard for his age', repeated his first year at King's.[39] The majority opted for private tuition: the diligent Alexander Watt, having been discouraged from it in his first year, 'attended a master for mathematics and arithmetick' in his second, in preparation for the natural philosophy course. The better off, like John Leith (1772) at Marischal, continued to bring along their own tutors. John's 'preceptor' was evidently short on social skills but, according to John's mother, not easy to replace:

11 Pryse Gordon as he appears in the frontispiece to his *Memoirs* (1830).

> Here there is not one, that can in any degree answer . . . And as the time of leaving the Town for the Summer is at hand, I shall certainly be obliged to ask Mr Donaldson to continue during it, as without one we can not do and I understand from every one of the Regents of this college that they think John in good hands as to learning; and the Peadentry of his [Donaldson's] Address, and appearance, I'm of Opinion, can not do much hurt.[40]

Lectures were now regularly supplemented by required or recommended reading. This was no problem for Lord George Hay (1725), a bajan at King's: having built up a solid collection of classical texts, grammars and dictionaries at school, he simply had some of them sent from the family seat at Yester (East Lothian) and then bought more.[41] John Rose (1791), another bajan, bought 'a Horace', 'a greek delectus', 'a [Greek] new Testament', 'a Homer', and the works of James Thomson and Allan Ramsay; together with 'one Volum of Sections', presumably in anticipation of his mathematics courses.[42] At Marischal, James Leith, John's brother, bought four volumes of Livy before entering in 1775 and 'Homeri Ilias Greek and Latin' afterwards;[43] while William Knight, bookseller's son and boy-bibliophile, entered his third year there with at least two of the recommended natural philosophy texts already on his shelves.[44]

Additionally, students could now borrow books from their college libraries on production of a line from a master and payment of a returnable deposit.[45] At King's, where the library was regularly augmented by new stock from Stationers' Hall, London, a number did. George Colman (1781), for example, having idled his way through school and university in England, had been sent there by his father 'as to an academical Penitentiary'.[46] Borrowing books 'out of boredom', he embarked on a course of self-instruction that 'more than made up my time lost at Westminster and Oxford'. At Marischal, it was different: 'I made no great use of the Library,' recalled one graduate;[47] neither, it seems, did many others. One reason was the deposit, by then, a minimum of £1;[48] it was among the grievances raised at the rectorial court in 1825, but to no avail.[49] An alternative to the college libraries were the circulating libraries in the New Town: John Rose used one, and William Knight subscribed to Brown's and Burnett's.

Students continued to acquire subjects 'which are not commonly reckoned Academical'.[50] At King's, John Munro (1719) learned French, dancing, and the flute.[51] In 1753 the college institutionalised the practice, recommending suitable teachers and allowing them to teach on the premises, ensuring in this way that students did not lose out by living in the Old Town. By 1763 a teacher of drawing had a room in the college; he also taught French – so well, that in 1767 the chancellor, Lord Deskford, encouraged students to benefit from his presence by offering to pay for their lessons.[52] At Marischal, students were able to attend teachers in the town: 'according to your desire,' Alexander Watt informed his father in 1788, 'I have begune to learn the Spinet'; William Knight had lessons 'in China ink drawing' in the Netherkirkgate.

Some students stayed on after the session ended in order to take such classes. Others stayed on for private tuition in their weaker subjects: John Munro, for example, spent his first vacation at King's doing Greek. In 1754 the college insisted that a sufficient number of masters should stay to supervise summer students.[53] Supervision was, if anything, more necessary in the New Town: in 1744, when a Marischal bajan planned to spend his first vacation there, the principal warned his father to 'think of close Business for him: For a Spark of his Cast, Idleness is the Mother of Mischief.'[54] William Knight, in contrast, passed his entire first and second vacations at a 'mathematical school' in Correction Wynd, preparing himself for the following sessions. Students who went home in the summer were expected to digest the learning crammed into them during the short session. Often, a King's professor recalled, they went over their course with their local schoolmaster.[55] Many did not bother, however, least of all in the lax years around 1820: 'it was common', said Abercromby Gordon, 'on going home for seven months, and returning again to the second Greek class for instance, [that] we brought back very little Greek with us.'

An effective system of examinations might have concentrated their minds, but neither college had one. In fact, for much of the period and for most of the students, the stiffest examination they faced was the bursary competition.[56] It was not just the Version that taxed them: when James Bentley dropped seven marks in the Marischal competition in 1787, it may have been the setting as much as his syntax that was to blame. William Knight described it ten years later.

> Some fear and trembling attended my steps, as the city clerk put questions respecting my parentage, before ushering the collection of candidates into the Great Hall, in which were assembled the heads of learning and science, clad in black gowns, the Provost and magistrates of the city, and their attendants in scarlet coats, more terrible than their superiors in our estimation. After taking our seats at a long table, Professor Stuart, in a calm and distinct manner, dictated a piece of English to be changed into Latin, and we were left to ourselves, watched by the men in red. I did what I could, but sat uneasily, discouraged by observing that there were difficulties in the task which my knowledge of Latin was insufficient to master; I was besides chilled by cold, and distracted by the grandeur of the apartment and the paintings as they then appeared to me.

George Abercromby Young (1818), explaining the unexpected failure of two fellow-candidates at King's, claimed that 'the nature of the competition had made them nervous and unhinged their wonted composure'.[57] Such vicissitudes made success sweeter. William Knight entered the competition again in 1798, tormented by fear of failure, and justifiably felt 'great satisfaction' when he came first.[58] James

McGrigor (1784), another first bursar at Marischal, recalled that he ran home 'at a quicker pace than ever I ran in the course of my life, to announce my success'.[59] To John Macdonald (1820) at King's, it was 'the first overpowering, the first delicious moment of life.'[60] Presentation bursars at both colleges were also examined on their knowledge of Latin, but the process is not recorded.[61]

The October examinations were less traumatic. At the very beginning of the period they were limited to the bursars and, at King's anyway, seem to have weeded out the work-shy. In 1720, however, the college considered holding a second examination towards the end of the session itself.[62] What happened next is uncertain, but in the course of the century the October examinations at both colleges were replaced by 'Black-stone' examinations, in February or March. These were held in the 'Public Hall': at King's, 'before the whole University; at Marischal, before the principal and professors 'and of all the students and public who choose to attend.'[64] As a bajan, in his Greek examination, William Knight was questioned on 'one verse of Matthew's Gospel'; as a semi, in natural history, on 'the Blowpipe and Theory of Combustion'; and as a tertian, in natural philosophy, on 'The Pendulum'. In second-year mathematics he had 'the Second Book of Euclid'; in third-year, 'Hadly's Quadrant'.[65] By the 1820s, however, these end-of-session examinations were acknowledged to be lax and ineffective. At King's, they were blamed when bright bursars failed to fulfil their promise; at Marischal, they were condemned as 'an annual farce'. In 1825 both colleges decided to reintroduce the October examinations (called 'entrance', preliminary', or 'initiatory') to ensure that the bursars had consolidated the work of the previous session. These were also oral, but only the principal and professors were present.[66]

The fourth-year examination for magistrands who intended to graduate changed at both colleges in the course of the period. Again, the circumstances are uncertain but were most probably linked to the reform of the curriculum. Candidates no longer had to display their knowledge and skills in a public disputation but simply underwent an oral examination. By the end of the century, however, this had become a mere formality – a scandal according to some. At King's, while regenting was in force, the magistrands were examined by the master of the tertian class, on the ground that their own master, after three years with them, might not be impartial. After regenting was abandoned, however, the procedure remained unchanged, and the professor of natural philosophy examined a class that he had himself taught in its third year. Not that it mattered: 'the examination,' said one professor, 'to be sure, is not long, nor is it very difficult'.[67] At Marischal, meanwhile, James Beattie introduced what one critic called a 'humbug [examination] . . . when the promoter kindly furbished the young gentlemen with both question and answer.'[68]

Marischal was the first to change its ways. In 1825, belatedly concerned for its 'interest and character', the college resolved to introduce examinations on the work of all four years conducted by the appropriate professors. And did so immediately. The magistrands were informed of the change only 12 days before they were due to be examined, although they were assured that allowance would be made for the short notice. Nevertheless, five candidates were failed. Three took their case to Joseph Hume's rectorial court, arguing that they would have passed under the old system but had been given inadequate time to prepare for the new. They also claimed – inconsequentially – that professors came late to lectures, and hinted – injudiciously – that the record of their examination might have been 'got up' for the occasion. The professors replied that 'no student within the walls of the College should have been ignorant of the questions . . . proposed to these candidates'. They refuted the second charge with ease and the third with outrage. The rector, however, agreed that the notice given was inadequate; he maintained that the students' case 'was a hard one' and recommended that it be remitted to the professors for reconsideration.[69] But the professors, refusing to recognise the legality of the court, took no further action.

Masters sometimes offered prizes to stimulate competition among their students and reward progress.[70] Towards the end of the period, however, class prizes were introduced on a regular basis. The first to be established, at Marischal, in 1782, went to the most proficient among the bajans, sometimes with unexpected results: the winner in James Bentley's class of 1787, for example, had previously come only fifth in the bursary list.[71] The first at King's was founded by George Hutton, along with his bursaries in 1801, for the best scholar among the magistrands.[72] Candidates sat written examinations on their four years' work in what could be a four-day ordeal: when John Macdonald competed, three of the examinations began in the afternoon and lasted until dawn the next day; while the fourth ran from 8 pm on Friday to 9 pm on Saturday for John, and to 4 am on Sunday for his fellow candidates, both of whom collapsed. King's institutionalised class prizes in 1819. At a loss how to award them, it allowed each class to vote for its best student.[73] Additional prizes were likewise established at Marischal in the 1820s, some of them also awarded by a class vote.[74] Verdicts on the practice varied. 'I have never seen an instance of an undeserving person getting a prize,' said a professor at King's, 'but I have certainly seen instances of [well-qualified] young men left out'. But a professor at Marischal, asked if the prizes had excited greater emulation among the students than had existed in his own, prize-less time, replied, 'Much greater.'[75]

Graduation, ostensibly the ultimate prize, was still seen by students as an optional extra. At King's (Table 3.1), the number of entrants who went on to graduate was, on average, less than 60% of the class and sometimes under 40%. To Abercromby Gordon's contemporaries there, around 1820, graduating was 'a matter of ridicule'. At Marischal (Table 3.2), the proportion graduating, where known, was even lower. William Knight, as a bajan, was impressed by the ceremony – 'there was a band of military music, a great crowd, and much essayfication' – and three years later participated in it as a graduand. In contrast, Donald Sage (1804) rubbished the proceedings as 'a mere literary farce', where the principal dubbed the graduands with 'an old dusty piece of scarlet cloth.'[76] The public disputations were replaced at both colleges by orations – 'essayfication' – in Latin or English. At King's, in 1812, William Malcom's topic was 'whether a public or private education be most to be preferred'. At Marichal, in 1772, subjects included 'Cultura Animi' and 'Happiness'.[77] Private graduations, sometimes for an entire class, were common;[78] too common for William Malcolm, who was 'not a little rejoiced' to hear that his class was going to graduate in public.

Students and staff alike now took end-of-session celebrations for granted. Only at King's, in the 1720s, when meetings to raise money for 'Treats at Valedictories and Graduations' got out of hand, did the college intervene.[79] Graduation balls at both colleges are said to have been held in the common school.[80] In 1802, however, the newly-graduated William Knight preferred to walk through the streets, 'which were illuminated for the Peace of Amiens', and to sup with his classmates 'in the Old Ship Tavern . . . on St Catherine's Hill'.

The more important duties of religion

Religious instruction, in an era of moderation, was reduced at both colleges to a single hour for each class on Sundays. At King's, in the 1780s and probably earlier, classes met on Sunday morning before church to study subjects like natural history and anatomy in a religious context. These were possibly the lectures 'on some subject connected with natural theology' mentioned in 1799.[81] At Marischal, according to the laws of 1741, students still assembled after church to study what they heard. This may have led to the 'discourses on . . . subjects of Natural and Revealed Religion' referred to, and retained, when the curriculum was reformed some ten years later.[82] In 1793, Alexander Murray (1742) bequeathed funds to King's for a weekly lecture intended 'to tincture [the] students with just and liberal notions of pure undefiled religion and virtue, without descending to party distinctions and controversy.' Problems, logistical, doctrinal and constitutional, dogged the bequest, however, and it was not implemented until 1824.[83] In the meantime a local philanthropist, John Gordon of Murtle, considering it 'a matter of regret that so little provision is made for the Instruction of our youth in the more important duties of religion', founded courses of lectures on 'practical religion' – the Murtle lectures – at both King's and Marischal.[84]

Students at both colleges had morning prayers daily at 8 am. At King's, these were led by the hebdomadar in the common school.[85] At Marischal, under the laws of 1741 and 1799, they were held in the common school by each of the masters in turn; from 1814 onwards, they were held in the classrooms.[86] Evening prayers were

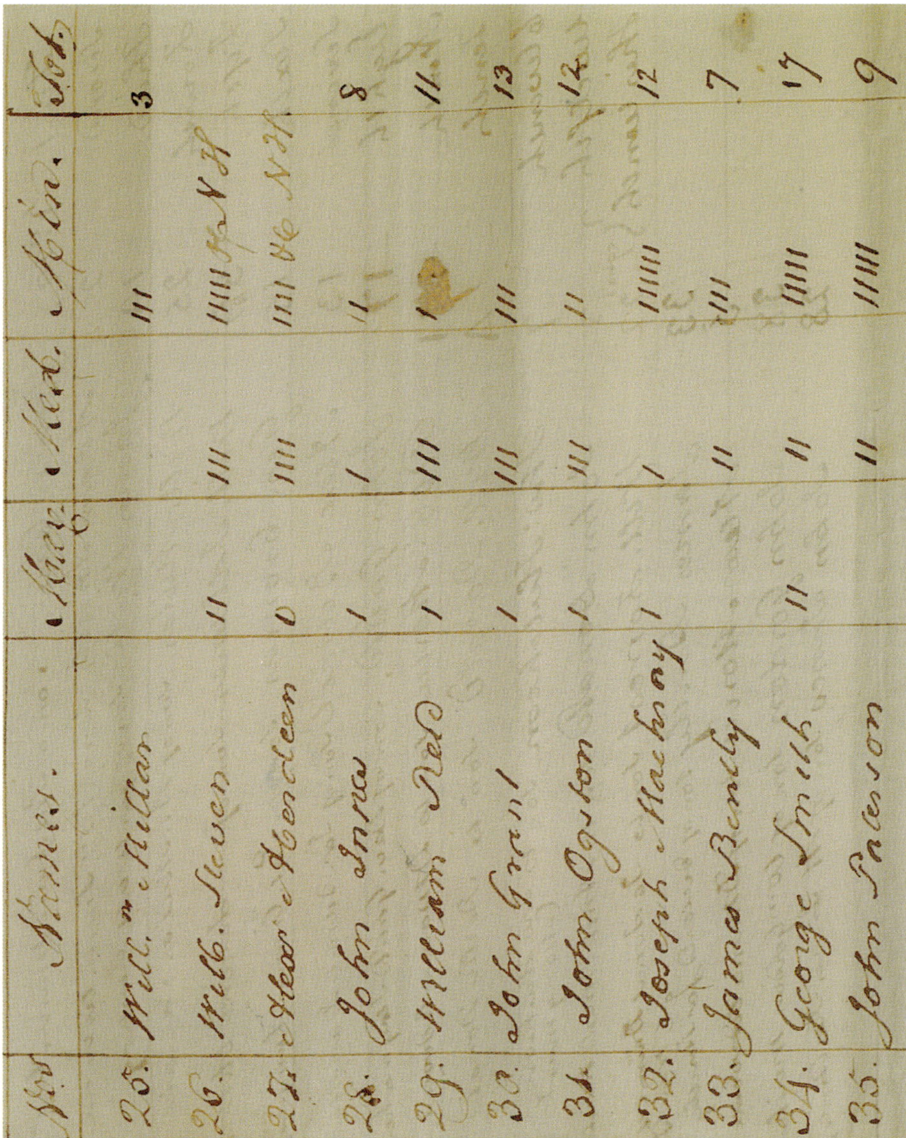

No.	Names.	Maj.	Mod.	Min.	Tot.
25.	Will.m Millar			111	3
26.	Will. Steven	11	111	11111 NB	
27.	Alexr Henderson	0	1111	1111 NB	
28.	John Innes	1	1	11	8
29.	William Reid	1	111	1	11
30.	John Grant	1	111	111	13
31.	John Ogston	1	111	11	12
32.	Joseph Mackay	1	1	11111	12
33.	James Bentley		11	111	7
34.	George Smith	11	11	11111	17
35.	John Paterson		11	11111	9

12 James Bentley, competing for a bursary in 1787, made no major errors in his 'version', but his two moderate and three minor ones cost him seven marks; he came thirteenth. AUL, MS M 366.

abandoned, presumably because of the shorter teaching day. The pattern of Sunday worship also changed. At first, students at King's continued to process to morning and afternoon services at St Machar's; an occasion, Alexander Murray was to recall, of 'uncommon grievance and indecorum . . . in an inclement and dangerous season'.[87] The college loft there was enlarged in 1743, 'whereby [they] might be in View of the Masters and many of them brought nearer the Pulpit and thereby hear the better'.[88] By 1799, however, King's permitted students, on request, to worship however and wherever their parents wished. This was as much a pragmatic as a liberal gesture, since the college loft was filled to capacity.[89] Attendance at St Machar's fell further than anticipated, however; this decline, together with a desire to eliminate disorderly processions, prompted Alexander Murray to leave additional funds to restore the college chapel for divine service. At Marischal, students went to St Nicholas West until 1769, when they moved to a gallery in Greyfriars. Under the laws of 1741 they were forbidden to attend 'fanatical meetings of Quakers and superstitious meetings of papists';[90] by 1799, however, members of other, more acceptable, denominations could apply to attend churches of their own. As at King's, numbers at collegiate worship fell: in 1799 William Knight 'went to the College Church, where [the minister] preached to a small audience', and by 1814 attendance was so low that the college procession was discontinued.[91]

Softening the severity of study

'Our business is easier for us than it was last Winter,' wrote James Urquhart in 1774, at the start of his third year at King's; 'we have more time to soften the Severity of Study with Relaxation.' By then most students lived out and relaxed in their own way, in their own time. There are no further references to organised games or play days at either college, although Saturday afternoon may have been left free purposely for privately organised sports. At King's, John Munro fenced, played golf and rode. Pryse Gordon played battledore and shuttlecock, skated and, a military career before him, took lessons in broadsword and singlestick from 'a Highland serjeant'. George Colman also fenced and made 'excursions on horseback', although 'none but boys could find pleasure galloping over a scotch road, in a scotch winter'.[92] At Marischal, the delicate John Leith rode but not when 'the Snow rendered [it] improper'; Alexander Watt, again with soldiering in view, took up fencing.

Dancing, whether at 'shines' (parties), to a fiddle in the Lobby, or more formally at balls, was an alternative form of relaxation. At King's, three bajans made the most of it: John Munro at a 'shane dance' in 1720; Pryse Gordon at 'dancing balls', 'college balls' and the graduation ball in 1777; and John Rose at 'the students dance' early in the session 1791–92 and two shines at the end. At Marischal, in 1760, students are said to have used the common school for dancing on Saturday afternoon; later, they used a room in Broad Street.[93]

Some students socialised in a more sophisticated fashion. At King's, Charles Burney betrayed his reputation as a recluse and 'took several frisks . . . to Gordon Castle',[94] while George Colman drank wine with the provost of the New Town. Marischal students, according to the staff, 'had better opportunities of seeing company, at their spare hours'.[95] Not John Leith, however: in 1772 his mother would 'not allow him to accept of one invitation to dine all the Christmas holly days – Except one day at my Uncles.' Students also socialised with staff: at King's in the 1770s, for example, James Urquhart 'drank tea with Professor Gordon . . . a very easy Good humoured man'.

In an age when clubs and societies thrived, Aberdeen students were notably slow to form their own. In other universities, observed two masters at Marischal in 1786, 'the establishing of societies among the elder students, where the various objects of their studies are freely discussed, has proved highly useful . . . Nothing of this kind has been attempted here, unless in the Branch of Divinity'.[96] There was, however, at least one 'little debating society' at King's, founded around 1781 by James Mackintosh and his early-rising coterie; topics for discussion included 'the Duration of future Punishments.' By 1795 an official college debating society existed.[97] An outbreak of hooliganism there at Christmas 1811 led to the expulsion of Alexander Tawse (1808), who threatened the officers, including William Malcolm, with 'a damnable leathering'. At Marischal, a 'Disputing Society' was founded in 1795, taking as its first topic 'Has the Norman Conquest been of advantage to Britain?' A later incarnation met weekly from 7 to 9 pm; it was open to all except bajans, but its officers were mainly magistrands. Around 1802, however, under William Knight's presidency, it antagonised Principal William Brown, a refugee from the turmoil on the Continent. He abolished it 'in an angry speech, in which we were classed with the Illuminati of Germany and the Clubs of France.' A new literary and debating society was established in 1815 by Alexander Thomson, who pronounced it 'a source of much innocent enjoyment'.[98]

There's magistrand conduct for you!

Commending the 'unexceptionable' conduct of John and James Leith at Marischal in the 1770s, their granduncle contrasted it with 'the Idle dissipate life of others about their Age.' For these, the trend towards non-residence had obvious implications. 'While the students were scattered over the town in private quarters, and might dispose of themselves as they pleased but at school hours', wrote Thomas Reid, 'we found it impossible to keep them from low or bad company, if they were so disposed.' It was partly to counter this that King's had re-introduced compulsory residence in 1754 and with it round-the-clock control. As Reid later admitted, however, college supervision was 'so strict, that when managed in the most prudent and impartial Manner, it must be grievous to those who are not very regular or very diligent'.[99] In fact, even the regular and diligent were daunted by it and went elsewhere. Thereafter, the laws of King's, like those of Marischal, focused mainly on the students' conduct 'at school hours'.

Their behaviour, inside the classroom and beyond the walls, was much the same as before.[100] At King's, students were involved in riots in 1728 and 1781;[101] at Marischal, 'challenges' between individuals[102] and scuffles between classes had repeatedly to be banned. In addition, groups from both colleges tangled with the tougher elements of the New Town. Around 1770, following a 'bicker' there with some sailors, King's students are said to have been pursued to their own college gates.[103] In 1781, after dining in Aberdeen, George Colman and some other English students 'were several times annoy'd by a party of Choice Spirits who paraded the streets at night'; they retaliated 'arm'd with bludgeons'. In 1790 Alexander Watt and others were attacked outside their New Town lodgings: 'I never heard of a place so infested with such a set of banditty as this,' Alexander wrote; 'we are in great danger to go out after it turns dark.' Nevertheless, the only reputed fatality in the period was 'Downie', an unpopular college sacrist, said to have died of fright as a result of a student hoax. The story, which features masked men, armed guards, a mock trial, and a headsman with a glittering axe, adds a frisson to Aberdeen's otherwise unexceptional student lore but is without any hard foundation.[104] None of these outbreaks appears to have been political or religious in origin. Both colleges steered clear of the second Jacobite rising; and the republican spirit that James McGrigor encountered at Marischal around 1789 did not manifest itself on the streets.

Some offences displayed new – or, at least, previously unrecorded – features. Alexander Tawse's Christmas revels in the Old Town led to broken windows and street lights; 'there's Magistrand conduct for you!' wrote William Malcolm smugly. Sex was no longer confined to houses and closes beyond the college walls: according to William, the incorrigible Alexander 'took in some wenches to some private room in college'; and students are said to have had sex with girls who attended the dances in the Lobby.[105] At Marischal, the laws of 1741 forbade them to frequent coffee-houses; those of 1816, plays.[106]

Certain offences acquired more significance than they had in the past. Snowballs, for example, were no longer merely a threat to college windows. According to Pryse Gordon, bursars used them against libertines; Pryse himself threw one at the sacrist of King's and accidentally hit a master. At Marischal, according to the college laws, they were filled with stones and used against townsfolk. Classroom misbehaviour, too, was taken more seriously than before, especially at Marischal. There, from the 1790s onwards, outbreaks of what William Knight called 'merriment and row' and 'much ruffing' (foot-stamping) occurred in the first mathematics class, where the professor, Robert Hamilton, was unable to keep order among the semis. The trouble peaked in 1803, when George Mortimer (1802), who had been accused of 'making [a] noise with a slate pencil, like a knocking at the Door of the Class', was expelled. 'You have been convicted,' he was told, 'of . . . habitually disturbing [the] class, and preventing your fellow students from receiving benefit therefrom, and of thus doing the greatest injury to the University of which you are capable.'[107] A new offence – unrecorded, at least, in previous periods – was the cutting of gowns. It is first mentioned in the Marischal laws of 1741 and was repeatedly prohibited: possibly because gowns were expensive; probably because of the knives. As late as 1825 a committee was formed to deal with the problem: a semi who had been 'cut severely with a pen-knife, which was pushed through his gown sleeve', appeared before it and showed his scar.[108]

The traditional modes of maintaining discipline were retained at King's throughout the period. The hedomadar was now described as 'the more special superintendent of morals of students' and in this capacity 'perlustrated' (inspected) the chambers of students who lived in, and took morning prayers.[109] The duties of the public and class censors, all bursars, remained much as before but under the laws of 1765 were more stringently enforced. The public censor, for example, 'for any wilful imposition on the Masters or breach of the trust reposed in him by them . . . shall for the first offence be fined in one half of his Burse and for the second be deprived, and expelled.' At non-residential Marischal, the post of hebdomadar is not mentioned. Discipline was maintained by the staff individually and, when this failed, collectively. In 1803, for example, the embattled Robert Hamilton remitted George Mortimer's case to his colleagues in the faculty of arts 'on account of the enormity of the offence, and the difficulty of fixing it on individuals'. Hamilton sought the faculty's support on other occasions with embarrassing consequences (below, p. 82). The public censor survived but, under the college laws, reported directly to the principal. Both colleges continued to combat absenteeism with roll-calls at morning prayers and, in the early nineteenth century, issued certificates of attendance.[110]

Punishment was now mainly by fines. At King's, in the 1760s and 1770s, these ranged from 1d to, more commonly, 6d for offences such as snowballing. Under the laws of 1794, however, rates had doubled and snowballers paid 1s. Fines were also levied for acts of violence and breaches of the peace: Pryse Gordon was ordered to pay 5s for his misdirected snowball; his professorial victim, however, 'by no means approved of such heavy mulcts' and gave him the money. In the early nineteenth century serious fines were reckoned in guineas: at King's, in 1812, one of Alexander Tawse's associates was fined 10s 6d. (half a guinea) for carrying a bludgeon and uttering threats. At Marischal, statutory fines remained unchanged for much of the period. Students paid 6d for snowballing; 1s for damaging the fabric, plus twice the cost of the damage; and 2s 6d for profanity. Beating, not mentioned at King's, was still in use at Marischal in 1741, usually for repeated offences; by 1799, however, it had been replaced by doubled fines or expulsion. Expulsion hurt in its own way. When George Mortimer was expelled for clowning at Marischal, his father protested that the sentence would expose George 'to the displeasure of a friend', meaning a patron. George was readmitted but left for good at the end of the session: according to William Knight, '[he] used to lament the stigma of this expulsion greatly.'[111] At both colleges, punishments were imposed each week in the common school. The routine was well-established by 1799 and continued throughout the period, although the meetings at Marischal became fortnightly in 1814.[113] 'Public schools', as these occasions were known, combined the traditions of public punishment and weekly declamations and were an important fixture in college life: in the Marischal laws of 1816 the occasion received a paragraph to itself, replacing the one on Sunday worship.

Both colleges continued to apply a double standard of discipline to bursars. At King's, under the laws of 1765, they were fined twice the amount imposed on libertines, 'because [they] ought to set an Example of good order and Diligence to the rest.' Those who repeated offences or committed crimes of violence were punished by deprivation and expulsion without the option of a fine. Such serious penalties, however, were carefully considered. Alexander Tawse was deprived of his ten-guinea bursary for his roistering, womanising and threatening behaviour; he would have been expelled, had not a professor – in William Malcolm's view, wrongly – defended him. At Marischal, however, lack of such consideration drove the bursars to rebel. In 1814, following more trouble in Robert Hamilton's mathematics class, second-year bursars were ordered by the faculty to inform on the offender, sentenced to a fine when they protested their ignorance, and threatened with the loss of their bursaries. Eight of them challenged the order, claiming that it breached the principles of the bursary system and impugned their honour. Their petition was rejected but evidently made an impact: the matter was quietly dropped.[112]

The habit of friendship and intimacy

The solidarity of the class was unaffected by the changes of the period. The growing number of students who lived out often shared their lodgings with classmates: Donald Sage, for example, lodged with a friend, compatriot and classmate in the house of yet another classmate. Even the home-based William Knight had a circle of nine 'to whom a more or less degree of attachment existed'. Nevertheless, at King's, social status and geography could be divisive. 'The sons of the richer lairds, or private gentlemen', claimed Pryse Gordon, 'look down on the poor bursars, who in return . . . treat them with contempt'; and in 1812 William Malcolm wrote that Alexander Tawse's case had split the class, 'the Highlanders taking one party, the Low country lads another.' The *praeses* (president) of the class, as Lord George Hay is described in 1727, was presumably a peacekeeper as well as a spokesman. No such tensions are recorded at Marischal. In fact, among the libertines in William Knight's circle was the son of the landlord of the Knights' bookshop. Even the rebel bursars of 1814 took the class and its ethos seriously, fearing that they might 'become the indignation of all their associates' and that 'strife and

13 'West front of King's College . . . As Rebuilt in 1826'. Not popular with the purists, it provided much-needed new space. Aberdeen University Picture Collection.

discord will ensue in early Life, which through future years may separate those who would otherwise have associated in the habit of friendship and Intimacy'.

TABLE 3.1 ENTRANTS AND GRADUATES AT KING'S, 1720–1825

Years	*Average annual number entering the first class*	*Average annual number of entrants who graduated*	*Graduates as % of entrants*
1720–29	27.4	11.4	41.6
1730–39	23.9	8.9	37.2
1740–49	21.8	8.5	38.9
1750–59	17.3	8.0	46.2
1760–69	27.6	16.1	58.3
1770–79	32.9	17.3	52.5
1780–89	29.9	15.3	51.1
1790–99	28.8	16.2	56.2
1800–09	41.0	22.5	54.8
1810–19	60.1	23.1	38.4
1820–25	76.6	27.8	36.2

Source: Anderson, *Roll*, Appendix B.

TABLE 3.2 ENTRANTS AND GRADUATES AT MARISCHAL, 1770–1825

Years	*Average annual number entering the first class*	*Average annual number of entrants who graduated*	*Graduates as % of entrants*
1770–79	34.5	15.9	46.1
1780–89	38.9	12.6	32.3
1790–99	38.9	15.7	23.2
1800–09	47.0	24.0	51.1
1810–19	65.3	32.4	49.6
1820–25	67.0	22.5	33.5

Source: Anderson, *Roll*, Appendix B. Comparable figures are not available earlier.

Admissions at King's were at first well below the highs of the previous century (Table 3.1). Nor did the changes of the 1750s produce the growth that the college looked for. 'The Number of Students', declared disillusioned masters in 1759, 'has greatly diminished . . . chiefly owing to the two following causes, 1st. The expence and length of the Session, 2d. The uniting of the Bursaries in the Gift of the College.'[114] Once the changes had been rescinded, however, the masters' efforts to 'beat up' the North for recruits were rewarded by a steady increase. After

1800, as the population of the region rose, the entry-rate climbed steeply for the rest of the period. At Marischal, during the 1750s, admissions were high compared to those of King's: 39 in 1755, 25 in 1756 and 70 in 1758. By the 1780s, however, '[the college] thought from 30 to 40 a good class'.[115] Only in the early 1800s did the intake again rise sharply (Table 3.2).

The relative number of bursars and libertines at King's changed markedly in the 1750s and subsequently varied widely. When Pryse Gordon's uncle entered the class of 1752 at King's, there were 17 bursars (68% of the class) and eight libertines. In 1758, however, there were 'but thirteen or fourteen [in the first class] whereof two or three only were Libertines.' In Pryse Gordon's own class of 1776 there were 18 bursars (39.2%) to 28 libertines. In his son's class of 1807, however, they numbered 20 (54.1%) to the libertines' 17.[116] At Marischal, the mix was more consistent: in the classes of 1780, 1790, 1800, 1810 and 1820, bursars comprised between 40 to 45%; James Bentley's fellow-entrants of 1787 fitted roughly into this pattern with 20 bursars (38.5%) to 32 libertines.[117]

TABLE 3.3 FLUCTUATION IN CLASS SIZES AT KING'S, 1812, 1820

Class	*First year*	*Second year*	*Third year*	*Fourth year*
1812–16	54	51	33	27
1820–24	76	68	52	44

Source: Evidence (1826), 216–17.

At both colleges, the size of the class continued to fluctuate over its four-year life. Poverty, sickness and death remained the predominant causes.[118] Migration, however, was less significant: the most notable instance involved the King's class of 1752, seven members of which, unwilling to accept the extended session, enrolled at Marischal.[119] The practice persisted, however, to the end of the period.[120] Three other factors were specific to the times. Thomas Reid identified one in 1759. In the New Town, he wrote,

> their children being too young when they leave the Grammar School to be put to business, they put them a year or two to the College [Marischal], tho they have no intention that they should follow learning. This is the reason why their first class is commonly for some years past more numerous than all the rest put together. But there is no such disproportion in ours [King's] where the highest class is often more numerous than the lowest.[121]

No figures survive, however, to support his claims. Then there was the Militia Act for Scotland of 1802, under which older students were liable to be conscripted by ballot for home defence. As an 18-year-old magistrand at Marischal, James Melvin (1809) 'was drawn as a militia-man', recalled his professor, 'and would have been obliged to serve . . . if he had not connected himself with a society, by which a substitute was provided.' The number of those less fortunate than James is not known but was sufficient to impel both King's and Marischal, along with the other Scottish universities, to campaign for their students to be exempt as English students were.[122] Finally, figures from King's, first recorded in 1812 (Table 3.3), show a significant drop in numbers in the third year, as those who lacked either the motivation or the mathematics for natural philosophy abandoned the course at that point. At Marischal, numbers also fell in the third year, though not as sharply. By 1820, however, the utility of the subject and the reputation of the Marischal professors had turned things around: 'There has always been,' said Professor William Knight in 1827, 'both in the time of my predecessor [Patrick Copland], and in my own, a considerable number of students in that class, quite unconnected with the other classes in the College, the Mathematical classes excepted'.[123] These were mainly private students and their numbers inflated the size of the class, making the rate of fluctuation difficult to determine precisely.

TABLE 3.4 ESTIMATED AND ACTUAL AGGREGATE NUMBERS OF ARTS STUDENTS AT KING'S, 1735–1826

Class	*1735–36*[e]	*1755–56*[e]	*1775–76*[e]	*1795–96*[e]	*1815–16*	*1825–26*
First	17	16	27	37	56	77
Second	15	15	24	24.4	58	62
Third	13.8	5.8	22	15.7	41	52
Fourth	11	10	18	15	27	45
Aggregate	56.8	46.8	91	92.1	182	236

Source: Anderson, *Roll*, Appendix B; *Evidence* (1826), 216–17. A figure of 100 to 130 was given by the college in the *OSA* (1799).

TABLE 3.5 ACTUAL AGGREGATE NUMBERS OF ARTS STUDENTS AT MARISCHAL, 1785–1825

Class	*1785–86*	*1795–96*	*1805–06*	*1815–16*	*1825–26*
First	38	36	54	68	54
Second	35	36	40	66	67
Third	39	30	50	58	69
Fourth	21	18	17	41	33
Aggregate	133	120	161	233	223

Source: Anderson, *Roll*, Appendix B; *Evidence* (1826), 291–2. A figure of 120 to 140 was given by the college in the *OSA* (1799). Later figures include significant numbers of private students, who are not differentiated in *FAM* at this time.

In overall numbers of arts students, even allowing for its significant numbers of private students, Marischal was ahead in the middle and later decades of the period, although King's nosed in front at the end (Tables 3.4–3.5). Both colleges, however, were outstripped by Edinburgh and Glasgow, with only the dismal performance of St Andrews to comfort them.[124] Almost all the students of both colleges lived out. At King's, the diaspora took time. It was well under way in the 1720s; in 1730, however, evidently alarmed as much by the disciplinary as the economic implications of the trend, the college insisted that the 24 bursars 'who wear black gowns' (were presented by the college) should live in.[125] Residence was made compulsory in 1753, and by 1757 the entire complement of bursars, albeit reduced by the amalgamation of bursaries, occupied chambers together with those libertines who had not sought a dispensation to do otherwise.[126] Ten years later, when the bursary system was back to normal, 56 bursars lived in the college, together with around 20 libertines.[127] By 1780, however, the Old Town was one big boarding-house: 'most of the Inhabitants live by letting Rooms to the Students', said the college and claimed that 'one hundred students lodged there'.[128] By 1799 only 'the more opulent' remained in college: in the 1820s they numbered 'twenty, less or more'.[129] At Marischal, in contrast, residence seems to have been abandoned when, or soon after, the college reopened in 1718. The circumstances are neither recorded nor explained.

The ages of students at entry were as disparate as before. There was the usual scattering of 12-year-olds, including William Knight; while an unnamed ditcher from Ross-shire is said by George Young to have attended King's in 1819 aged 43. Their social origins, as far as they are known, were also much the same. At King's, Lord George Hay came from the nobility: his father was the Marquis of Tweeddale. John Munro of Newmore (Ross-shire), James Urquhart of Meldrum (Aberdeenshire) and John Rose of Montcoffer (Banffshire) were from landed families. Many, like Pryse Gordon, his uncles and his nephew, were sons of the manse. Charles MacEver was the son of a Lewis tacksman; Charles Burney, the son of an English scholar. At Marischal, however, 45 of the 62 members of James Bentley's class of 1787 present a unique sample (Table 3.8), in which the professions, commerce and trade, and the land (including farming),[130] were equally represented. Information from Marischal for the period 1810–25 is tabulated in Appendix IV (Table 1). It shows a marked decline in students from landed families (from 35.0% to 15.1%),[131] some of whom were educated in England, and a gradual rise in students from the professions, notably teachers (from 2.6% to a peak of 9.6%). In contrast, there are rising numbers from industry and commerce (from 13.0% to 24.4%) and agriculture (from 3.9% to 15.1%); and a small but steady stream (averaging around 10%) from the 'Intermediate' and 'Working class' categories (officials, clerks, craftsmen, tradesmen, semi-skilled and unskilled labourers). These rises may reflect local confidence, prosperity and stability, or represent a drive for self-betterment via the professions; there is at present not enough evidence of motive to be certain.

TABLE 3.6 ARTS STUDENTS FROM ABERDEEN, ABERDEENSHIRE AND THE NORTH EAST, 1776, 1787

Class	*Aggregate*	*Old and New Aberdeen*	*Aberdeenshire*	*Banffshire*	*Other Northern counties*
King's 1776	52	2	11	16	23
Marischal 1787	62	11	30	0	21

Source: Anderson, *Roll*, *FAM*, 2.

The geographical origins of students at King's (from 1720) and at Marischal (from 1770) are tabulated in Appendix IV (Tables 2–4). They conform to the patterns of previous periods: King's drawing strongly on the northern counties; Marischal, mainly on Aberdeen and its immediate hinterland. Marischal was also home to students from expatriate northeastern families sweating it out in the West Indies and other colonies. The contrast between the two is heightened by a comparison of Pryse Gordon's class of 1776 at King's, and James Bentley's class of 1787 at Marischal (Table 3.6). Just over 30% of Pryse's class came, as he and all his relatives did, from Banffshire, compared to 25% from Aberdeen and Aberdeenshire together. In contrast, students from Aberdeen (17.7%) and Aberdeenshire (48.3%) made up two-thirds of James's class. At the other extreme, there was a single overseas student, from Kingston, Jamaica; he would have found at least one compatriot shivering in the college when he arrived.

There were new and easier ways to travel to college, but most students chose the cheapest. Pryse Gordon teamed up with a classmate on the 50-mile, two-day hike from Deskford to King's. In 1804 Donald Sage walked with his 'man' from Kildonan (Sutherland) to Marischal: 'within two miles of Inverury, I fairly broke down, and fell prostrate upon the roadside'. Later in the century those who could afford wheels used them: George Colman travelled up from London in a post-chaise and pair; George Young travelled down from Banff for the bursary competition at King's in the mail coach, along with four fellow-competitors. Among those who came by boat was the Orcadian, Alexander Watt, crossing back and forth from Kirkwall to Peterhead or Aberdeen: 'I was verry sick on the passage so much so that it has loused all my teeth, it was owing to the dirtiness of the Vessall which was insufferabel.'

Yellow with blue dots

In 1795 Alexander Watt nearly missed the boat. 'I have only six shillings over to carry me to Orkney', he wrote to his father, 'which cannot do it unless you order a vessal to call at the bay for me on her way from Leith.' Other libertines

14 Marischal College, 1822. This view, one of an Aberdeen series by G Smith and J Swan, gave undeserved dignity to the decaying blocks. Aberdeen University Picture Collection.

managed their finances better. Some did not try: instead of paying their fees, they 'mispent the Money . . . in a way equally prejudicial to their morals, and inconsistent with their Proficiency', forcing both colleges to insist repeatedly upon payment on entry.[132] Shrewd fathers took no chances. Lord George Hay's money – £102 over the period 1726–28 – was disbursed by a local agent; while George Colman's allowance was doled out by the subprincipal of King's, who suspected him, not unjustifiably, of being the kind of young Englishman who 'breeds muckle harm to our lads frae the highlands . . . and sets unco' bad examples of *economy*.' Economy itself was sometimes not enough. In his first two years at King's, 1752–54, Charles MacEver 'spent so little, that [my father] could easily keep me for four years here.' Then the session was extended:

> [This] made me be at such charges, as made my father give over all hopes of sending me to the College . . . At last I asked of my father, if it was possible for him to spare any small sum. I obtained my demand, but I'm afraid, may make him be in Debt ere long . . . My uncle got the Debursement of it, and bestowes so sparingly upon me, that betwixt this and the two former years, I fell in Debt about £5 sterling . . . Tis impossible to stay here upon the allowances he makes.

For much of the period libertines continued to pay for public tuition according to their social status or means. At King's, in 1726, Lord George Hay paid four guineas (£4 4s); in 1755 a student of the middling sort might expect to pay two. At Marischal, in the 1780s, James Bentley's contemporaries paid three guineas, two, or one and a half. In 1799 the college declared, 'fees . . . have not been raised for many years';[133] in 1813, however, considering 'the great increase in the expence of living and the fall in the value of money', it set a new, basic rate of three guineas, which lasted until the end of the period. King's did likewise.[134] Libertines at both colleges also paid for additional courses in Latin, Greek and (at Marischal) mathematics. On top of that there were matriculation and examination fees, servants' dues, sums for candles and fire in classrooms, and (at Marischal) a contribution to the buildings fund. The largest additional expense was graduation. Libertines graduating from James Bentley's class paid between £2 4s and £1 18s 10d for the examination, the ceremony and library money.[135] In 1806, however, concerned at 'the low rate of fees', the college raised the total to £2 14s for Scottish students, £8 for others.[136] Lord George Hay also incurred costs as president of his class, dipping deep into his pocket when required: in 1727 he gave £1 10s to a collection on behalf of the graduands of that session. Textbooks were a further significant expense. At King's, Lord George Hay spent £2 15s 5d in 1726–28; and John Rose, 18s 1d in 1791–92. At Marischal, James Leith spent over 13s in 1775–76, some of it at the New Town book auctions.[137] In 1765 King's had forbidden its students to attend these, partly to keep them out of trouble, partly to stop them from 'purchasing unnecessary Books . . . thereafter stating it to their Parents and Friends as money necessarily expended on their Education', thus 'tending to raise unreasonable clamour as if the Education were expensive.'[138]

Libertines who lived in King's occupied chambers in the new south block and the Cromwell Tower. In 1730 the most expensive rooms, at 12s for the session, were in the new block facing south; the cheapest, at 5s, were garrets there and 'closets' – probably the former 'muses' – in the tower.[139] In 1753, with the introduction of compulsory residence, all the chambers were refurbished, and libertines paid 16s or 12s for a 'room with a closet'.[140] In the period 1761–71 some 30 chambers were still in use: the most expensive rented by a single libertine was Number 14, off the central stair of the south block, at £1 12s; the rest went for between 16s and 12s and were generally shared.[141] In 1781 George Colman occupied 'a small sitting room, and a light closet to sleep in . . . with an adjoining room and closet, for my servant'. He paid around £2, which he dismissed as 'inconsiderable'. By 1799, however, the few students living in were accommodated in a 'boarding-house', paying £6 a quarter, all found.[142] Chambers came with bare, whitewashed walls and 'bedstead, tables, chimney grate, and fender'. Everything else – 'feather bed, bed cloaths, chairs, tongs, and bed-hangings' – had to be hired, or bought and sold on.[143] George Colman had his sitting-room papered 'yellow with blue dots'; his second-hand furniture, in walnut, mahogany and 'stain'd wood', later fetched almost £9 at auction.

Libertines who lived in usually ate in college, along with those who lived out but came in for meals. Most of them would have eaten at the first table, paying 50 merks (£2 15s 6¾d). Dinners are not described, but suppers consisted of 'any of the Two following things . . . Eggs, Sowens, Roots, Pancakes, bread and Butter, Oxcheek, Finnen haddocks . . . and a Mutchkin of Ale.'[144] Students are said to have eaten in the hall, but there several references to the use of a 'dining room'. In 1781 George Colman ate in his room, and by 1799 the 'public table' was said to have been abolished 'for some time'.[145] A 'college table' mentioned in 1812 was probably associated with the boarding-house; it had been unused for some years before it was abolished in 1836.[146]

In the 1750s, when King's was promoting compulsory residence, health care was an important part of the package. Students with infectious diseases would be excluded from the college; the sick would be nursed in 'two of the best-aired and commodious rooms' or in the town; and special diets would be ordered by the professor of medicine. Libertines bore the cost of treatment, however, either by their physician of choice or one employed by the college.[147]

Of the libertines who lived out, some occupied houses with a parent or relative. In 1772, for example, when John Leith entered Marischal, his mother rented a house on the Green nearby and in 1773 took one opposite the college gate. Others lodged with masters: Lord George Hay, for example, stayed with the professor of Greek at King's, paying £6 13s 4d a quarter for himself and his servant; in 1744 Thomas Gordon had room for 20 boarders. In 1754, after consulting leading families in the region, King's approved the arrangement as an alternative to compulsory residence for 'Gentlemens Sons'. Little is heard of the practice after that, although it continued into the 1820s. At Marischal, according to James Beattie in 1780, no professors took in boarders. In the 1790s, however, Principal Brown, supporting a large family on a small salary, lodged and boarded 'a few young gentlemen'.[148] The majority found their own digs. In 1759 Thomas Reid observed that in the Old Town, 'there are no boarding houses which Gentlemens Sons would now put up with'.[149] Twenty years later George Colman would have agreed: lodged temporarily in the best room of a 'cabin, one story high, opposite to the college gate', he contemplated whitewashed walls, a truckle-bed, a smouldering peat fire with no grate, and an uncurtained, rattling window. Others were less fastidious, however: in 1791, probably but not certainly in the Old Town, John Rose was pleased with the 'apartment' for which he paid £1 7s for the session, and satisfied with his board at £6 7s 6d. John was lucky: in 1799 the college estimated town rents at £3–£4 a quarter.[150] 'The town of New Aberdeen' – Thomas Reid again – 'has greatly increased in a few years in populousness and Riches.' Inevitably, for students at Marischal, the cost of lodgings increased too. In 1788 Alexander Watt found that a furnished 'flat' of two rooms and a kitchen cost £3 10s a quarter: 'its verry dear but is as cheap as I have heard of'. In 1799 the college admitted that rents had risen but claimed that 'young men of the best families' could still be boarded and lodged at under £30 a year'; others at well under £15. Two students sharing a room in Queen Street together paid 13s a week for bed and board (around £6 10s each for the year); 'boarding', wrote one, 'is very high in this place.'[151]

Libertines who fell sick in their lodgings, whether in the Old or New Town, procured their own treatment. John Rose paid 1s for 'stuff for my ears' and gave 6d to 'a man for carrying over a mixture.' The delicate John Leith had a mother to look after him; a luxury denied Alexander Watt, who was 'verry poorly' in the winter of 1788–89.

Early in the period, at least, a libertine's gown was still a sizeable item in his accounts. At King's, John Munro bought six yards of red frieze (coarse wool) for his, for around £10 Scots (16s 8d); while Lord George Hay paid £2 16s 8d for the finished article. Gowns there had a 'close sleeve, below the entry for the arm';[152] richer libertines, according to Pryse Gordon, were allowed to wear 'a scarlet cape to [theirs]'. None of which mattered to George Colman: after a few outings he had his gown 'of superfine scarlet cloth' made into a coat. Marischal gowns had long open sleeves and by mid-period, if not before, collars: in October 1775 James Leith paid 2s 8d to have a gown cleaned and repaired, and 'a coler' put on it, possibly from the '¼ Yard of Crimson velvet' he bought around the same time.

Beef and broth

At King's, 16 foundations provided 41 bursaries. The number would have been higher if George Hutton's ambitious plan, in 1801, for 48 new bursars had worked, but it ultimately produced no more than eight. At Marischal, 20 foundations provided 32. It was size, however, that mattered. In 1732 a bright lad from Lord Braco's estate was awarded a foundation bursary at King's, worth £3 6s 8d. 'If we could have provided him with a better Burse,' the principal told his lordship, 'He should have obtained it.'[153] Throughout the period both colleges were embarrassed by the smallness of some of their bursaries, particularly the older ones. King's tried to remove the problem when it extended its session: 'that the Bursars may be better enabled to support themselves . . . the Masters have resolved to unite the small Bursaries in their gift . . . in such manner as none of them shall be under Six Pounds thirteen Shillings and four pence Sterling.'[154] The strategy failed: 'the expence brought on by the late Alterations is so great,' said opponents of the scheme, 'that Students could scarce be found to accept of Bursaries at first, and after they had accepted of them, they were obliged to desert them'.[155] The problem seemed intractable: in 1782 both colleges were said to have 'a great many bursaries . . . some of them under three pounds a-year, and by much the greater number, not exceeding six.'[156] Gray's bursaries, founded at Marischal in 1768, were worth double that but were awarded by examination in a specific subject, mathematics, for a limited period, two years.[157] There was another problem. Pryse Gordon was presented privately to a bursary worth £9; James Bentley had to compete publicly for one of half that amount. Competition bursaries, complained one father in 1807, 'are so small that they are scarcely worth one's while'; he wanted a presentation bursary for his son and begged a well-connected kinsman 'to ask . . . in a passing way' about one'.[158] By the end of the period the disparities had not been resolved, and bursaries at both colleges ranged from well over £12 to under £5. Competitors were undeterred, however, and between 1800 and 1825 the number of competitors more than doubled (Table 3.7).

TABLE 3.7 MARISCHAL COLLEGE BURSARY COMPETITIONS, 1780–1825

Competitions	*1780–89*	*1790–99*	*1800–9*	*1810–19*	*1820–25*
Average no. of competitors	32.2	25.0	29.6	51.0	72.5

Source: AUL, MS M 16, 17. The figure for 1781 not is available. Averages for 1790–99 and 1800–09 are affected by the uncharacteristically low candidatures of 14 in 1798 and 16 in 1800.

Pryse Gordon's grandfather, at college in the 1710s,[159] had survived on £12 a year. Pryse reckoned that his own bursary was 'nearly sufficient to maintain a youth of prudence', although in his second year at King's he ended up £10 in debt. Donald

Sage, at Marischal, did not have the chance as his finances were managed by his master: 'I actually had more money on returning than I had on coming to College.' But others needed something more than prudence or a thrifty minder to survive. Of considerable importance, therefore, were the concessions on public tuition fees linked by the colleges to the value of bursaries. At King's, by the time George Young competed in 1818, 'gainers of £10 to £5 [bursaries] paid half fees' (£1 11s 6d). At Marischal, for much of the period, bursars paid their fees at two rates, £1 11s 6d or £1 2s 2d. By 1813 there were four rates, ranging from full fee to £1 2s 2d; these continued until the end of the period.[160] Concessions on other college charges seem to have been discretionary: at Marischal, in 1787, for example, James Bentley and most of his fellow-bursars paid the lowest rate (£1 18s 10d) for graduation, and at least two others were 'excused' in full or in part.[161] Pryse Gordon does not record paying 'spoon silver', although the levy had been extended from foundation bursars to all bursars in 1753, on the grounds that they were required to eat at the college table. The rate was set at £1 10s Scots (2s 6d) a year and remained at this level until 1860.[162] Also in 1753, but in a more generous spirit, the college offered sick bursars medical treatment, free, from the professor of medicine.[163]

The bursars who were required to live in King's in 1730 were accommodated, rent-free, in the south block. Sixteen of them occupied four garrets; the remaining eight, four closets; all slept two to a bed.[164] In the 1750s, however, 16 bursars remained in the south block, but 12 were housed in the Cromwell Tower. This time they paid rent of 4s, which remained standard until at least 1770.[165] They ate at the second table, paying £2 a quarter. In the 1750s they had 'oat loaf' and milk for breakfast and supper. Dinner was boiled beef and broth two days a week; eggs and vegetable dishes (potatoes, barley, rice and turnips) on three; fresh fish on Friday; and roast beef on Saturday. Nutritious – the college claimed that many bursars ate better there than at home – but not, it seems, enough. In 1763 the bursars complained to the rector about 'irregularitys and scarcity of Provision'. Following his intervention the masters compared menus with St Andrews and concluded that their own bursars were better fed for less money; in fact, they dispensed with the Saturday roast.[166] The bursars remained dissatisfied, however, and not just with their food: in 1765 the college ruled that those who 'desired better rooms, and better diets' should have them, 'if they will put themselves upon the footing of Libertines'.[167] Pryse Gordon seems to have benefited as a result: he dined at the college table for 14s a month, providing other meals and occasional luxuries himself.[168]

Little is known about the cost to bursars of living out. One bursar at King's, subsidised by his family, paid 12s 6d for a room, location unspecified, and £6 5s for his board.[169] William Knight, at Marischal, lived at home: paradoxically, since his response to winning a bursary was that 'a little independence had been obtained'. At all events, he had space for his books in 'a small press under the skylight in

15 Marischal College, classroom, around 1830. Here William Knight and Alexander Bain did mathematics, and Professor Robert Hamilton struggled with rowdy students. AUL, MS M 363.

my room'; more importantly, he had money – £7 17s 8d over four years – to buy more. Books were optional; gowns compulsory. Bursars no longer wore the traditional black gown. It was abandoned at King's – a 'mark of inferiority', the college called it – at some time between 1730 and 1765, and at Marischal well before 1780.[170] Henceforth bursars wore red gowns like those of the libertines but, according to Pryse Gordon, without the velvet collar. Although they were made of 'ordinary red freeze',[171] they were still expensive: when Pryse Gordon, having inherited a gown from his brother, eventually treated himself to a new one, it cost over £1 10s.[172]

Changes of destination

Students who reflected in later life on the quality of the education they had received did so judiciously. 'I quitted college', recalled James Mackintosh, 'with little regular and exact knowledge but with considerable activity of mind and boundless literary ambition.' William Knight was more generous: 'however incomplete any college education must necessarily be . . . how little I should have known without it'. Several regretted their immaturity: 'I think,' said Alexander Thomson, 'I was not at that time sufficiently ripe for improving by such works as those of Reid and Stewart and that I shall profit much more by reading them now, than I could have done then.' They wrote frankly about the masters: realistic about their scholarship; hard on their teaching skills. One, complained James Mackintosh, 'rather declaimed, than communicated (as he ought) elementary instruction'. Another's 'manner of speaking', noted William Knight, 'prevented his being heard distinctly, and his classes were in consequence disorderly and riotous'. Overall, Patrick Copland comes out best; Robert Hamilton – 'total incapacity . . . to maintain his authority' (Donald Sage) – worst.

Masters showed up better on the pastoral side. It was, after all, something on which they prided themselves. 'I verily believe', said Thomas Reid of the residents of King's in 1753, 'there are few boys so narrowly looked after, or so little exposed to temptations to vice, at home as with us at present.'[173] The college was no less assiduous, however, once its rooms were empty. Thomas Gordon not only dispensed tea to his students but visited them in their lodgings: 'if I had observed anything amiss', he assured John Rose's father, 'I would have interposed for the amending of it.' Equal care was shown at Marischal. Writing to the father of a recalcitrant student in 1744, Principal Thomas Blackwell referred proudly to 'the many different Methods I have taken both this Year and the last, to win him to Study';[174] while James Beattie's role *in loco parentis* is documented in his letters.[175] 'Professor Stewart . . . has been exceedingly attentive to me', wrote Alexander Watt; and to James Bentley and his fellow-reunionists, Stewart was 'Our honour'd teacher now our friend much lov'd'.[176]

Fathers, impressed by such attention, entrusted further sons to the colleges; appreciative students in due course sent their own. If Pryse Gordon's long-standing family link with King's was as much to do with the Redhyth bursaries as it was with quality, the multiple family connections within and beyond James Bentley's Marischal class of 1787 certainly denote approval. Six of the 62 members, including two pairs of brothers, followed their fathers there; two of the fathers were, in fact, former classmates. In addition, one member of the class had a brother two years above him; three were following brothers who had graduated earlier in the decade; and 13 were followed by brothers after they themselves left. Finally, 15 members sent their own sons to Marischal, three sending four boys each; at least one had a grandson there.[177]

None of the students commented specifically on the value of his university education in the context of employability. This despite the fact that the reformers of the 1750s had emphasised the utility of the new curriculum, and that, eventually, all the professions except medicine expected entrants to have completed at least part of it.[178] Two years at King's, however, made no difference to Pryse Gordon, who obtained his commission by patronage. James Bentley owed more to his four years at Marischal. His hopes of the ministry frustrated by 'a weak voice and general delicacy of constitution', he secured tutoring posts with 'several influential families in Aberdeenshire', which in turn led to his appointment as professor of oriental languages at King's. William Knight is the foremost example of those whose prospects were re-shaped by their years at college. Fearful of failing the bursary competition for a second time, he had contemplated what the lack of a university education would mean: 'I might have descended in the scale of life or never been put in possession of those advantages which led to a subsequent change of destination.' Successful, he applied himself soberly to his courses and eventually succeeded Patrick Copland, who had done most to inspire him. James McGrigor, in contrast, represents those whose 'change of destination' was largely a matter of chance. He decided in his final year that he did not want to be a 'general merchant' like his father but was instead attracted to medicine by the example of his friends. He finished his professional training as the Napoleonic wars broke out and, susceptible to a smart uniform, became an army surgeon, serving under Wellington and, ultimately, heading the army medical department, where he dispensed patronage to other students from Aberdeen. Of the other students featured in this chapter, Lord George Hay, from King's, later became sixth Marquis of Tweeddale. George Young, James Urqhart and John Munro succeeded to their family estates; the last also fought at Fontenoy. Walter Morison, Abercromby Gordon, William Malcolm and John Macdonald all entered the ministry. Alexander Tawse was a surgeon with the East India Company; George Gordon (Pryse's son), secretary to Sir Walter Scott. Three followed professions in England: Charles Burney as an academic; George Colman in the theatre; while James Mackintosh became an eminent lawyer and philosopher (or, if Hazlitt is to be credited, a prototypical policy wonk).[179] From

Marischal, Donald Sage entered the ministry; James Melvin became rector of Aberdeen Grammar School; James Leith served in the Peninsular War; and Alexander Thomson, as a gentleman of independent means, pursued interests ranging from classical antiquities to industrial schools.

TABLE 3.8 MARISCHAL COLLEGE, CLASS OF 1787, ORIGINS AND DESTINATIONS

Destinations	*Church*	*Med.*	*Law*	*School-teaching*	*Commerce Industry*	*Armed Forces*	*Planting, etc.*	*Other*	*Not known*	*Total*
Origins										
Landowner	2	2		1			1	1	7	
Minister	1	2		1	1	2		1	2	10
Doctor										0
Lawyer			4		1					5
Teacher										0
Other profs										0
Commercial & industrial		3			3		1	2	1	10
Agriculture	1	1	2	2	1				1	8
Crafts/Trades		3			1			1		5
Not known										17
Total	2	11	8	3	8	2	1	5	5	62

Source: AUL, MS M 16, M 222; Anderson, *FAM*, 2. 'Crafts/Trades' covers occupations that appear in subsequent tables as 'Intermediate' and 'Working class'. 'Others' includes higher education and work abroad, excluding planting, etc.

Multiplied, such choices and changes generated considerable social and geographical churn. It is well illustrated by James Bentley's Marischal class of 1787, whose reunions were an occasion for recording the progress of 45 (72.5%) of its 62 members (Table 3.8). The most popular choice was medicine (24.4%), generally as surgeons with the armed forces or the East India Company. Law and business were in joint second place (17.7% each). The church, unlikely to be under-recorded here, came joint lowest: an indication, perhaps, of the limited number of pulpits to be filled. Eight entered the same profession as their fathers, mainly in law and commerce. Sons of the manse and farm chose the widest range of occupations; the latter, almost certainly discontented with their prospects at home. Fourteen (31.1%) spent part, or all, of their working life overseas, the majority in the West Indies; a source of no great surprise to the reunionists. They were more interested in the number, around a third, that had stayed in Aberdeen or Aberdeenshire. They considered it 'a very uncommon circumstance that so many of one class should be settled in one place', and 'happy at this occurrence' assembled in the Lemon Tree on 5 November 1803 for the first of their 'convivial evenings'.[180]

Chapter 4

Grind – grind – grind, 1826–1860

George MacDonald entered King's College in 1840. He had taken what was by then a common route, from elementary school in Huntly to the grammar school in Old Aberdeen, where he was groomed for the college bursary competition.[1] Alexander Bain, who entered Marischal College in 1836, had followed a harder path. Having left school at 11, he spent seven years studying mathematics on his own and at the Aberdeen Mechanics' Mutual Instruction Class, finishing off with three months' free tuition at Aberdeen grammar school to bring his Latin up to competition standard. Recognising his ability, staff at Marischal found him a bursary and he subsequently won another, the Gray mathematical bursary, which gave him a year's postgraduate study.[2] He began this, his fifth year at college, as George began his first.

At King's, where there was no money for new buildings, George did Greek in the sixteenth-century Round Tower; mathematics and natural philosophy in the seventeenth-century Cromwell Tower; Latin and moral philosophy in the eighteenth-century south block; and chemistry in the recently-built west range. He attended college prayers in the original common school and sat examinations there or in the hall above. Before and between lectures he might be found in the sunless piazza along the south side of the quadrangle. At Marischal, in contrast, the old, decaying hulks, embarrassing to both college and town, were demolished soon after Alexander entered. They were replaced in 1844 by a 'modern' granite building, neo-Tudor in style; its hall, library, museum and classrooms fronted by an open forecourt.[3]

The education that George and Alexander received had been scrutinised by the commission of 1826. The colleges pointed with pride to their accessibility through the bursary system: 'bursaries have afforded the means of education to many who could not otherwise have got it at all.' They emphasised the breadth of their curriculum: 'although [students] are by no means complete in any one branch of education, yet [they] are so far well-grounded, as that they can by themselves carry on their studies in every department of literature and science'. And they claimed that intensive study on meagre rations helped to develop the character of the students: '[it] prepares many of them for going through difficulties in life, and at the same time for being industrious and steady men.' But they had also to acknowledge that too much teaching and learning was compressed into the short session; that students entered ill-prepared in Latin, Greek and mathematics, which limited the progress they could make in these subjects; and – especially at King's – that examinations were not sufficiently rigorous, thereby debasing the value of the Master's degree. They also conceded that overwork on a poor diet could seriously damage their students' health: 'nothing affords me more pleasure', admitted one professor, 'than to know that they have got home with their lives.'[4] The commission proposed measures to resolve these problems, but they were not mandatory, and the colleges were slow to adopt them: at Marischal, a chair in Latin deemed urgent by the commission was not filled until 1841.[5] The one suggestion to which they did accede readily, the reform of the examination system, put students under even more pressure, prompting one to a parody of Thomas Hood:

> Grind – grind – grind
> In the dull December light,
> Grind – grind – grind,
> And work with all my might.[6]

The commission's main recommendation, taking into account the overall condition of the colleges, was that they should be united. The proposal was no less contentious then, however, than it had been 40 years earlier. It was raised again by the commission of 1836 and on a further three occasions before it was eventually achieved by the commission of 1857.[7] Inevitably, the issue preoccupied both colleges; not least the students, who expressed their views in the debating chamber, in the fledgling student press, and – at Marischal – during rectorial elections.

Having reclaimed their right to elect a rector of their own choice, Marischal students guarded it jealously, relishing the annual opportunity to assert themselves. The professors, for their part, complained to the 1826 commission that elections were disruptive and irresponsible; bajans and semis, they insisted, were too young to vote.[8] Mistrust on both sides was at its height between 1826 and 1829, as Joseph Hume battled with the Tories' champion, Sir James McGrigor. By the mid–1830s, however, some of the bitterness had gone, and procedure was well established. Elections were held at the end of February or the beginning of March and lasted three weeks. Each class produced a long list of candidates; these were reduced to a short list of two or three at 'aggregate' sessions, dominated by students from divinity and medicine; finally, on election day, the students assembled in the hall and voted in their four nations.[9] Attempts by the college to intervene in the proceedings were strongly resented: in 1838, for example, over 100 students protested against the principal's interference in an aggregate meeting and his veto of a crucial casting vote. Intervention was unavoidable, however, since collective voting often caused problems: in 1829, 1844, 1847 and 1857, for example, when two nations voted for one candidate and two for another, the office was left unfilled.[10]

For most of the period students chose as their rectors men who were eminent or influential – ideally both: men who would, for example, support the college in its struggle against the Militia Act, as McGrigor did in 1826 and the earl of Errol in 1831.[11] When Alexander Bain entered in 1836, the incumbent was John Abercrombie (1794), a Marischal graduate, eminent as a physician and (at the time, anyway) philosopher. He was then enjoying his second year in office and in 1837, the first occasion on which Alexander was entitled to vote, was ready for a third. The students, however, were nervous at the imminent prospect of union and decided they needed a rector with more political clout. They rejected the doctor along with the equally eminent scientist, Sir David Brewster, and chose Lord Lyndhurst, lord chancellor in recent Tory administrations, who was both eminent and influential. In the controversial election of 1838, Lyndhurst was rejected in favour of his Whig counterpart, Lord Brougham and Vaux, also eminent and influential, if no longer the charismatic figure who had triumphed as rector at Glasgow in 1825. In the next three elections church matters predominated, as students were caught up in the Non-Intrusion controversy. In 1839 and 1840 they elected Non-Intrusionists, rejecting in the process both Thomas Campbell, the poet, and Robert Southey, the poet laureate. In 1841, however, the Non-Intrusion candidate was defeated by Sir James McGrigor, recalled after 15 years to the conservative side. In the 1840s and 1850s some students still favoured the eminent as rectors: Macaulay was put forward as a candidate in 1845 and 1846, Carlyle in 1850. As union drew inexorably closer, however, the majority again put its faith in a succession of influential politicians and peers.

Students at King's, having let slip entirely their right to choose the rector, were slow in trying to regain it. Only at the end of the session 1833–34 did 33 of them address a petition to the principal 'stating that they . . . considered themselves as entitled to certain rights and privileges such as the power of electing the Lord Rector etc and respectfully demanding a perusal of the original Foundation Charter'. Three days later 27 of the signatories explained that 'they had been induced to sign under various misrepresentations'. They asked, nevertheless, if representatives might examine the foundation documents; the senate made no objection, thereby deflating the activists and defusing the situation. It was left to graduates to claim and win the right to elect the rector in 1856.[12] College-appointed incumbents did not ignore students' interests: in 1831, as at Marischal, the rector was asked to fight for militia exemption;[13] in 1854 it was to the rector that a student, mistakenly punished by the college, appealed for redress (below, p. 116).

Hard plodding

The 1826 commission asked both colleges to consider extending the academic session in order to spread the load of teaching and learning. King's was unanimously, if regretfully, opposed: 'there is a very serious objection, arising from the poverty of our students.' Marischal was divided, but one professor believed that 'a single week would make a very considerable difference to some students coming from the country.' Unimpressed, the commission recommended a session of six months, accepting that some bright boys would be excluded: 'we are persuaded the cases would be few.'[14] The colleges, mindful of events at King's in the 1750s, resisted: King's kept its 21-week session until 1854, when it added an extra week;[15] Marischal stayed at 22½. In both cases, the session was preceded by a week devoted to the bursary competition and the examination of returning students. Holidays were limited to Christmas Day and New Year's Day, despite the efforts of students at King's to prolong them.[16]

At King's, in 1827, the main course in each year was taught, Monday to Friday, in three periods: 8.15 to 9 am, 11–12 am and 3–4 pm; other courses were fitted around these times. Marischal had similar arrangements, but the teaching week included Saturday morning. As the period progressed, the hours and frequency of meetings changed. Generally, however, bajans worked a maximum, tertians and magistrands a minimum, of 20 hours. Semis, with their overstuffed session, did more: at King's, for example, 25 hours in 1827; 27½ hours in 1855.[17]

Each year of the arts curriculum comprised, in effect, a main course with one or more subsidiary subjects.[18] As a bajan at King's, John Sinclair (1826) did first (elementary) Greek with first Latin; as a semi, first mathematics with chemistry and natural history, second (advanced) Greek and second Latin; and as a tertian, natural philosophy (including mathematics) also with Greek and Latin.[19] Had he returned as a magistrand, he would have done moral philosophy, including logic, rhetoric, English and political economy, again with Greek and Latin. At Marischal, the first year was the same as at King's. The second was devoted to civil and natural history and first mathematics with second Greek and Latin; the third to natural philosophy with second mathematics, third Greek and second Latin (the last two optional); and the fourth to moral philosophy and logic, with Greek, Latin and third mathematics as options. The 1826 commission, convinced that students were overworked – 'more than enough engrossed'[20] – recommended that courses should be sub-divided or re-positioned, but the colleges made no changes. They acceded, nevertheless, to the commission's suggestion that teaching in Latin, Greek and mathematics should be improved and extended.

Teaching methods varied with the courses. In classics, students concentrated on translation: Greek into Latin; Latin into English. At Marischal, James Melvin expected his bajans not only to translate a Horace ode but to 'explain what allusions there were to History, Geography, Antiquities, and Mythology', to scan it, and to comment on the 'beauties of [its] composition.'[21] Mathematics was taught from the blackboard: 'I am kept very bussy,' wrote John Sinclair, doing first mathematics, 'being employed in the morning in solving questions in Arithmetic and in

16 Gowned students of 1859. From W Johnston's record of the last bajans of King's and Marischal, 1899.

Logarithms and in the forenoon in simple and quadratic equations and in the afternoon in demonstrating Simsons Euclid.'[22] Natural history, chemistry, natural philosophy and moral philosophy were taught through lectures or 'extemporaneous speaking from notes'.[23] The first three were illustrated by demonstrations: the professor of natural history at Marischal revealed that when he taught galvanism, '[he gave] every one of the class shocks.'[24] The quality of the lectures depended largely on the age and energy of the lecturer. At Marischal, for example, the middle-aged William Knight continued to be highly-regarded by his students, among them David Masson (1835): 'within the first day or two . . . we felt ourselves in a new kind of professorial presence.'[25] In contrast, the elderly professor of moral philosophy there read lectures that had changed little since he first delivered them as assistant to James Beattie in 1793. He also continued to dictate, to Alexander Bain's annoyance:

> What made matters worse was the want of concurrence in the arrangement of the dictated notes with the read lectures. There was a certain remote parallelism in the run of the two lines; but it was not close enough to be followed by the class. Accordingly, the habit of the students was to take down the notes, and pay no attention to the lectures . . . What aggravated the situation was that the examination questions kept neither to the one line nor to the other.

As many of the staff taught for much of the period, methods changed little in style. At Marischal, however, John Stuart Blackie, the new and innovative professor of Latin, made his students use the language to describe pictures or sculptures: 'we could not only speak,' said John Forbes White (1844), 'but think in Latin.'[26]

Learning became as much a test of character as of ability. As in previous periods, students – especially country boys – entered college with limited Latin, no Greek, little mathematics and less general knowledge. The colleges blamed local schoolmasters, obsessed with the bursary competition.[27] Neil Maclean (1853), however, who reckoned his teacher was 'one of the ablest classical scholars in Scotland',[28] argued that 'if other branches of study were somewhat neglected . . . one could hardly blame [him] when the results were so good.'[29] Striving to make up these deficiencies and to master new subjects, the majority of students became, according to William Walker (1836), formerly of King's, 'a steady-going hard-plodding set of youths, giving their days and nights to patient poring over class-books'.[30] Plodding – slow, steady progress – was good: 'your bright, brilliant scholar soon fades away,' said one of Maclean's characters, 'but your hard plodding, determined student makes his way to the front.'[31] Plodding was reinforced by what William Blaikie (1833) of Marischal called 'the drill-system of Aberdeen', based on daily or weekly tests.[32] In first Greek at King's testing was random: 'no-one', the professor assured the commission, 'can be sure of escaping the next hour to that in which he has been examined.' In first mathematics at Marischal the students' performance was marked and recorded: 'I could', the professor boasted, 'by referring to my books . . . state the proficiency of any student who attended several years ago, at each of the daily examinations . . .' Students also did exercises in and outside the classroom. Outside they were expected to work on their own, especially on problems in mathematics. 'Each [student]' explained the professor at Marischal

> stands up in his place and reads his solution, giving reasons for every step of the process, or he leaves his place and writes his solution with his own hand. I invariably require him to explain every difficulty which occurs; I wish to ascertain whether his exercises are his own production or not, and that is very soon seen.

Such exercises did more than merely reinforce classroom teaching. The professor of moral philosophy at King's, who set his magistrands questions to be answered overnight, claimed that 'the exercise accustoms [them] to express their thoughts in writing.' They needed the practice: they had to write three essays in the course of the session, and few of them were up to it. The professor himself read out their first, anonymous efforts to save them from embarrassment, then he started to train them.[33] According to William Walker:

> [He] laid down sound rules . . . illustrated them from the writings of the best English authors, and enforced them by his criticism . . . [He] was not a severe, but he was a sound critic; noting every departure from simplicity and purity of style . . . especially every ambitious attempt at fine writing.

At Marischal, students began writing essays in their second year. William Mair (1845) had evidently mastered the technique by the time he was a magistrand. He wrote essays on 'The Authority of Common Sense', 'Materialism' and 'The Utility of Logic', showing 'ability, care and attention to the subject'.[34] Finally, tutors were still common around 1827, overseeing the learning of duller students.[35] When John Sinclair lost his in his second year, Professor Tulloch found him another: George Tulloch (1816), a cousin who had completed his course but had yet to graduate. The 1826 commission, encouraged by some professors, approved of tutors, recommending that the colleges themselves should employ tutorial assistants. But when it suggested using bursary funds for this purpose, the colleges quickly lost interest.[36]

Students studied Greek, Latin and mathematics from textbooks, which they were required to buy. On other courses it was different: 'there is no book', the professor of civil and natural history at Marischal told the 1826 commission, 'that comprehends the system.' The professor of natural history at King's solved the problem by publishing his own outline. Professors did recommend works on specific topics but, one explained, 'with caution, because the expense is very great.'[37]

Students who had paid their matriculation fee and could find the returnable deposit were entitled to borrow from their college library. At King's, they had also to submit their requests to the professors for approval. The library there opened for two or three hours on Tuesdays and Fridays. In the session 1826–27, 76 of the 235 students in arts borrowed books. 'They do not take out a great number,' the 1826 commission was told, 'their time being so occupied by the business of the classes, that they have not much leisure for Scientific or Philosophical reading, and for lighter works they usually have recourse to circulating libraries in Aberdeen.'[38] According to John Sinclair, however, the library was 'quite inadequate to meet the demand for books made upon it by the Students.' Consequently, he told his father, 'under the patronage of the Professors', they were setting up a subscription library of their own:

> Instead of containing one copy of the most useful works as is the case in the College Library, our collection will contain five or six copys of the books necessary in the several classes . . . We are to begin with a Library for the moral philosophy Class as the Range of enquiry is wider and the number of Books necessary for reading and reference is greater than in the junior Classes.

This library, established in 1828, was housed in the moral philosophy classroom. It began by acquiring multiple copies of standard works such as 'Stewart's Outline' then proceeded to new works, including those of John Abercrombie, Marischal's rector-to-be. Of the class of 1837, the first for which borrowing records are complete, 13 out of 30 magistrands used the library: John Watt, for example, borrowed 'Reid's Inquiry' three times.[39] At Marischal, the college library opened for a single hour, 1–2 pm, on Saturdays, which may explain why, in 1826–27, fewer than 14 arts students used it. The first arts class library there was for natural philosophy and was set up by Professor William Knight at his own expense.[40]

Students continued to follow extra-curricular courses. John Sinclair, for example, as a semi at King's, took lessons in French, dancing, drawing and music. Elocution was also on offer and, in the 1850s, German.[41] Many students, however, had not the money, still less the time, for such activities: 'every individual', the professor of Greek at King's told the 1826 commission, 'feels unwilling to devote his time to any other object than that which he considers his immediate duty, and upon which his own character depends.'[42] Nevertheless, according to John Hill Burton (1823), even hard-pressed highland magistrands visited a dancing-master before the graduation ball.[43]

Explaining why Aberdeen students worked harder than most, the narrator of Neil Maclean's novel cited 'compulsory examinations, and the opprobrium attaching to those who "stick" [fail]'.[44] He highlighted what was, without doubt, the most distinctive feature of the period at both colleges: the development of an examination system that was rigorous, well-regulated and, accordingly, feared by the students and respected by the public at large. The bursary competition itself was reformed, but this was principally to improve and broaden bursars' skills at entry. At Marischal, translation from Latin into English was made an integral part of the examination in 1846; King's followed suit in 1847; both colleges incorporated Greek in 1849; and Marischal added arithmetic in 1851.[45] The proceedings were no less traumatic than before. Maclean's narrator walked from Aberdeen to King's, 'past small houses alive with occupants peering out at the raw recruits'. John Hill Burton recalled 'groups of anxious whisperers, with books under their arms' gathering silently outside Marischal. For Duncan Anderson (1844), writing his Version in the common school at King's, 'the hours wore on in profound stillness, broken only by the peculiar sound that a hundred and fifty pens, operating all at the same time, make upon a hundreds and fifty sheets of paper.'[46] For John Kennedy (1828), attending in the crowded hall to hear the results proclaimed, 'it was galling . . . to see not a few, whom I considered and whom others considered far inferior to me in their knowledge of Latin, standing before me in the bursary list.'[47]

Annual and final examinations were transformed. At King's, in 1827, there were two examinations each session: the 'Black-stone examination' held in March for all students at the end of their first, second and third years; and the 'entrance examination' in October, for bursars entering their second, third and fourth years. Both, as the 1826 commission was informed, were oral, predictable and, in effect, a formality; both needed to be improved.[48] The commission tacitly agreed and changes were introduced in 1833. Rules proposed for the March examinations stated that they were to be in writing, last not less than three hours, with not more than 40 students in one room, under the supervision of a professor; papers were to be marked anonymously and graded; and results and awards were to be checked by an 'examining committee'.[49] The entrance examination was extended to all students in 1847; it, too, was written by the end of the period.[50] The outmoded final examination for the master's degree was abolished, this time on the commission's insistence.[51] From 1834 onwards candidates had to have passed the four March examinations, answering satisfactorily one-third of the questions in each paper, in order to graduate.[52] At Marischal, the March examination remained oral: in 1837, Alexander Bain recalled, 'students were called up in alphabetic order, and had leading questions put to them, usually in the sequence of the course.' The October examination, also oral, was extended to all students in 1827.[53] The final examination was written; it covered all the courses of the curriculum, was held on six successive days and, when Alexander Bain sat it in 1840, left him 'prostrate and exhausted'.

On the recommendation of the 1826 commission, both colleges introduced schemes to reward students who had done well in their degree examinations. From 1828 onwards Marischal commended students who had 'excelled in all subjects',[54] thereby inspiring Alexander Bain, working 'far above my strength', to gain *optimes* in five subjects, *benes* in two, and share first place in what he called 'the Honours List'. From 1834 onwards King's distinguished between those who had exceeded

17 Alexander Bain, portrayed by Sir George Reid in 1882, during his first term as rector of the university of Aberdeen. Almost 50 years earlier, the young weaver had struggled to win a place at Marischal. Aberdeen University Picture Collection.

the minimum requirements in the majority of their courses, and those who had distinguished themselves throughout. In 1857 it went further and introduced a system of classified honours based on optional, additional examinations in classics, mathematics and science, and philosophy.[55] Prizes, too, were made more effective as both stimulus and reward. In 1827 King's offered 32 class prizes totalling £66. They were still awarded by student votes, however; a practice that the 1826 commission condemned. From 1833 onwards, therefore, they were linked to the results of the March examinations.[56] A disproportionately small number went to second Greek and Latin, although these courses were attended by all three senior classes; as a result, said William Walker, 'comparatively little attention [was] given [by students] to classics.' This problem was partially resolved in 1838 with the foundation of the Simpson prize in Greek, worth £60.[57] At Marischal, class prizes were tied to the March examinations by the time Alexander Bain entered in 1836. Additional prizes (for all students) were also offered by some of the rectors: in 1835, for example, John Abercrombie gave £50.[58] There was a third way of recognising individual progress. At both colleges, class certificates were 'framed so as to indicate what are the attainments, and what has been the conduct of the students', rewarding the diligent and penalising the indolent. They were, enthused the 1826 commission, 'perhaps the most effectual method of influencing the students, and calling forth their intellectual energy.'[59]

Despite these incentives the number of students who stayed on to graduate at both colleges did not increase notably (Tables 4.1, 4.2). At King's, they were deterred, the 1826 commission was told, by the examination, the fee, and the influence of family or 'friends' (patrons); at Marischal, by 'the novelty of the regulations, and the greater strictness of the examination'.[60] By the 1850s, however, the number of bajans at King's who went on to graduate had risen from around 30 per cent to 35 per cent. According to Neil Maclean's narrator, 'it was considered a mark of failure not to take the degree, and all such were placed among the "stuck".'

Maclean, who deeply resented the cost of graduation, gave his narrator some uncharacteristically harsh lines on the ceremony at King's:

> [The graduand] robes his person in a gown generally borrowed from some clerical friend . . . Ranged in a row before the Senatus, they are each covered with a small cap, which scarcely lies on the crown of their heads, but which, having already decorated the craniums of many famous men, is supposed to contain some virtue unknown to the vulgar. A certain amount of Latin being muttered, the farce is concluded by the professor shaking hands with each in turn, and accepting them as brothers.[61]

The ceremony at Marischal differed little in form and impact. According to similarly disenchanted accounts by David Masson and William Mair, the principal officiated and the janitor borrowed black gowns on the students' behalf.

Graduation was celebrated at King's with a class supper, at which the new graduates were joined by respectful bajans, semis and tertians. As described in Maclean's novel, it combined the fun of the valedictory with enough morbid sentimentality for a wake.[62] At Marischal, new graduates dined at the Lemon Tree Tavern,[63] and gown waltzed with town at the graduation ball. John Hill Burton described how shy Highland students, red hair curled, uncomfortable in white stock, kid gloves and dress shoes, would fortify themselves with wine, porter or whisky before approaching a dressmaker's girl, a professor's daughter, or one of 'the high-bred belles of Union street', and inviting her to 'jist tak a daunce wi' me, Mem'.

The leading topic for several years

Arguably as significant an issue as union among students in this period were the convulsions of the church in Scotland. The Non-Intrusion controversy became, said Alexander Bain, 'for several years, the leading topic in the youthful circle with which I was associated.'[64] Institutionally, however, things went on much as before. In 1827 religious instruction was embodied in the Murray lectures at King's and the Murtle lectures at both colleges.[65] This was not enough for the 1836 commissioners, especially John Abercrombie, the former rector of Marischal: 'it appeared a great defect in the educational system of both Universities that no instruction was given to the Students in the Evidences of Christianity . . . a subject which, independently of religious considerations, is so important as a branch of general information.' The commission recommended that a course should be delivered in the third and fourth years and examined as part of the degree in arts. It was anxious, however, not 'to introduce a spirit of religious difference within the walls of the Universities' and waived the examination for dissenters.[66] Both colleges quickly complied: at King's, the course was delivered by the professor of moral philosophy; at Marischal, by the principal, who published a textbook on the subject.[67] Alexander Bain, who 'had never grappled with the authenticity of the Bible', found the course stimulating; the majority of students did not.

At both colleges, there were prayers before teaching began. At King's, they continued to be held in the common school after roll-call.[68] In 1844, however, a professor complained that 'the short prayer . . . was from the previous irregular crowding into the school and preparation for escape of upwards of 200 youths, incompatible with decorum or a pious frame of mind'. In 1854 the practice was discontinued and prayers said in class.[69] Students worshipped in the chapel twice on Sundays, unless they had permission to attend a church of their preference. 'A good many of the Highlanders,' the 1826 commission was told, 'go to the Gaelic Chapel'.[70] Others joined congregations of their own denomination: John and James Kennedy (1831) and George MacDonald attended the Congregational chapel in Blackfriars Street;[71] 'Robert Falconer', after a period of non-attendance, sampled St Machars but settled for the episcopalian church with its organ.[72]

Ram reels

Little is known about college sport, organised or otherwise, in this period. At King's, Neil Maclean's characters went rowing; and a shinty club is said to have existed before 1860. Students who had played cricket at school, however, opted to play for local clubs. At Marischal, a cricket club is said to have been established in 1849.[73] In the same year Peter Bayne (1846) regretted that sport was no longer compulsory at the college, as it had been in the seventeenth century: 'for, by some regular system of healthful exercise, the sunken eyes and sallow cheeks, which we observe at the close of every session, might cease to be such invariable features in the face of a student.'[74]

Dancing was one way of keeping fit, especially the kind performed in the Lobby at King's. Paying an annual subscription of one shilling to cover the cost of candles and a fiddler, students – mainly highlanders – assembled there on Saturday evenings. As women were no longer admitted,[75] they danced single-sex 'ram reels': 'the dignified Magistrand,' rhapsodised William Walker, 'threading the mazes with, it might be, a raw bajan for his partner.' A Christmas ball was held in the common school until 1849, when it took place in the hall. In 1851 there was an attempt to ban it; presumably because it ended with the ram reels and rowdiness that concluded the graduation ball at Marischal.[76]

There were other, less energetic things to do on Saturday nights, mostly in Aberdeen. Donald Fraser (1838) from King's, often went to the theatre there.[77] Others supped there, notably at the Café Royal, where a room was set apart for them. Those who stayed behind in Old Aberdeen regaled themselves at the Red Lion. Students also partied in their lodgings. 'Bursary suppers' were given at the end of February by those who had newly received the first half of their award (below, p. 126). As described by Neil Maclean, a chairman and croupier presided, encouraging the company to offer toasts, tell stories, or make music. The guests talked about 'the inner consciousness of man' and 'the comparative merits of Tennyson and Browning', but most of all about themselves; they excluded anything 'shoppy'. They sang songs like 'The Mermaid', 'The Spring Examination' and 'Ubi Juvenis Fui' but banned the bawdy 'Silver Eel'. They drank punch or toddy, and – a habit unknown to William Walker in the 1830s – smoked pipes and cigars; some – usually the highlanders – took snuff.[78] Suppers of a less convivial kind were hosted by Thomas Davidson (1856) of King's; on Sundays, after church; he served his fellow-baptists coffee, bread and butter.[79]

Students also received hospitality from another quarter. William Walker, anxious to clear professors of charges of aloofness, described early breakfasts at their tables, ending with the 9 am bell. As age at entry rose, however, and students' social skills improved, breakfasts gave way to dinners and suppers. According to one of Neil Maclean's characters, such occasions could be an ordeal for the poor and inexperienced, notwithstanding the warmth of the welcome and the presence of professors' daughters.[80]

College societies met on Friday and Saturday evenings, offering entertainment and – ideally – intellectual stimulation. At King's, there was the literary and debating society. In 1829–30, his second year, John Kennedy attended a debate on the character and writings of Lord Byron; when the house failed to condemn them, he walked out. In the 1830s, recalled William Walker, the authenticity of Ossian was frequently debated, producing a Highland-Lowland split. By the 1840s meetings were run by magistrands but were open to the other classes: George MacDonald depicted a debate in which a row between older and younger students ended in a fight.[81] In 1848 the society reconstituted itself. Under new rules, approved by the college, the magistrand officers were joined by representatives from the other three classes.[82] In its first session, 1848–49, the reformed society attracted audiences of up to 130; afterwards, to repeated concern, numbers fell to between 60 and 30. The debates themselves were robust: good speakers were applauded by ruffing (in John Kennedy's day), or the thumping of sticks on the floor (in Neil Maclean's); bad speakers were shown no mercy. Undeterred, Archibald Forbes (1853), as a bajan, debated phrenology with a magistrand; he lost narrowly but went on to speak in a further three debates; as a semi, however, he was censured for disruptive behaviour.[83]

During the five sessions, 1848–49, 1849–50, 1853–54, 1858–59, 1859–60, the society held over 60 meetings. It prohibited 'strictly Religious [questions], and questions on Church Politics' but tolerated debates on related issues such as a national education system (supported in 1848–49, 1849–50, 1853–54 and 1859–60) and the Maynooth grant (opposed in 1853–54). On constitutional matters the house preferred monarchy to republicanism (1848–49). It opposed the first three clauses of the People's Charter, including universal suffrage, but approved the rest (1848–49); it maintained its opposition to universal suffrage (1849–50) but favoured an extension of the franchise (1853–54). On foreign affairs it opposed the Crimean War (November 1853) and, in February 1860, decided that Napoleon III was not planning to invade England. On social issues the house supported Teetotalism (1853–54) and the abolition of the Game Laws (1858–59); it opposed capital punishment in 1848–49 and 1853–54 but supported it in 1849–50. On culture it was against novel-reading (1849–50, 1858–59) and the theatre (1858–59) but believed in the morality of Burns (1853–54, 1858–59) and the authenticity of Ossian (1858–59). There were frequent debates on historical figures, notably Cromwell (1853–54, 1858–59, 1859–60), and on the influence of certain institutions: in 1859–60, for example, the house voted, 21 to 19, that the press was more beneficial to society than the pulpit. Closer to home, the union of the colleges (1849–50) was opposed by a large majority.

A week after the reconstitution of the Debating Society in 1848, the Hilaric Cachinatory Society began its short life. Its seven members were headed by a

18 King's College around 1860. This lithograph by J Henderson shows students, in tall hats and gowns, entering the college gate and chatting on the street.

tertian, James Joass (1846), under the pseudonym 'Max Meerschaum'. They met 'to encourage mirth and jollity', in contrast to other, un-named societies of 'vain looking coves who cry about Peripatetics and great nonentities'.[84] There was nothing 'vain looking' about the impoverished members of the Celtic Society. Founded in 1853 and open to Gaelic-speaking students in all classes, it held regular debates on familiar topics: in the session 1853–54 the house was against the Maynooth grant but divided equally on the union of the colleges, leaving the chairman to cast his vote in favour of it.[85]

Marischal, too, had societies, although less is known of them. In 1830 the Literary Society met on Saturday in the mathematics classroom. Its members came from all four classes and included private students. By 1832 there were others, including a Theological Society.[86] Late in the 1840s students, graduates and staff met informally to read Latin and, more importantly, Greek. They formed the nucleus of the Homeric, later Hellenic Society, established by Professor Blackie in 1850. Under Greek pseudonyms and in three grades (probationers, ordinary members and 'sworn brethren'), they met weekly for 'the conjoint reading of the most approved Greek authors' and other studies. Of the ten original members, seven were staff or graduates, including John Forbes White and William Geddes; the latter, formerly of King's (1842), now taught at the Aberdeen grammar school. Of the three undergraduates, two were tertians, one a bajan.[87]

College magazines offered an alternative outlet for student opinion, although none lasted longer than a session.[88] The *King's College Miscellany* appeared in 1846–47. Its editors, said to have been two magistrands, intended it to be 'a student's magazine': they mixed poetry, short stories and essays with biographical sketches of college worthies, classical translations and mathematical problems. *The Aberdeen Universities' Magazine*, 1849–50, had a different policy, aiming to promote student journalism and to give expression to students' views: 'Every class in the community is giving forcible utterance to its individual sentiments, and why should *we* be silent?' The editorial team, drawn from both colleges, included James Joass, now a magistrand, from King's, and Peter Bayne from Marischal, whose leading article in the first number advocated the union of the colleges and prompted an outcry.[89] *The Aberdeen University Magazine*, another combined effort, appeared in 1853–54 'as a medium for the interchange of thought, and as incitement to the cultivation of literature.' Its contents ranged from a three-part article on 'Jesuitism' to 'Reminiscences of a "Grinder" ' – yet another parody of Hood:

> I remember, I remember
> The garret where I GROUND . . .

Its role was continued by *The Student; a Literary Magazine*, edited by students and graduates, which ran for ten numbers in 1857–58.

Freaks

'It is generally allowed', wrote John Hill Burton of students at both colleges in the late 1820s, 'that, for the first month or two, they live in a state of peace and tranquillity; but, at the end of this period, the proverbial restlessness of human nature makes its appearance. Feuds are commenced in all quarters.' Not, according to William Walker, at King's in the 1830s: 'work was the main interest . . . occasionally relieved and brightened by good-humoured banter, or amusing incidents'. Fewer offences were recorded there in that decade than in any other, so Walker may be justified in smugly disowning the 'freaks' (pranks) perpetrated by Neil Maclean's characters in the 1850s.

Among traditional offences in and around the colleges themselves, misconduct in the classroom was at its worst under the older and less competent professors. At Marischal, in the 1830s, according to David Masson, magistrands would disappear under the raked seating of the moral philosophy classroom to consume 'bottled porter and mutton pies'; in 1838, over-exuberant graduands damaged the desks there. Fighting was largely the result of drinking or horseplay. At King's, Samuel Davidson (1827) admitted that he was drunk on the night in 1831 when he tried to pick a fight with two other students in the street. At Marischal, John Bothwell (1827), charged with two similar offences in 1829, claimed that they were 'only in joke'; the college, not amused and determined that 'such violent scuffling and giving of blows' should be stopped, punished him nevertheless.[90] Bullying was recorded on only one occasion, at Marischal in 1846; the victim was William Mair, frail and hairless after an illness. The cutting or tearing of gowns was ritualised in both colleges. As a bajan at King's, Neil Maclean's narrator was tossed between two rows of students, 'at each movement hearing a new rent in my precious gown'. At Marischal, according to John Hill Burton, it was an expression of 'party spirit' in early rectorial elections: 'a violent party man . . . may be discovered by the tattered nature of the fragments of [his] gown'. Snowballing, too, had its rites. At King's, bajans and tertians took on semis and magistrands, the battle spreading from the quadrangle into Old Aberdeen and ending, for Maclean's narrator, in the ordeal of a 'snow bath'. Sticks apart, the only weapon recorded was a 'sword-cane', carried to a meeting of the Marischal debating society in 1830 by Charles Stuart (1829) and used 'in a most improper manner' by William Booth (1827).[91]

Misconduct in town resembled that of previous periods, but with a less vicious edge. What John Hill Burton hailed as 'a course of secret mischief and devilry', and William Walker disparaged as 'daring and risky midnight adventures', amounted to little more than antisocial behaviour in the streets. In the 1820s, according to Burton, students of both colleges stank out shops with asafoetida, stole and trashed street-lamps, and switched tradesmen's signs; they carried off old ladies in sedan chairs and dumped them in unsavoury neighbourhoods; and they turned some passages into no-go areas at night. The exasperated townsfolk were themselves not guiltless. Even their children, said Burton, were likely to heave a dead cat at a student in his gown, or yell 'Buttery Willie Collie' as he passed. The origin of this sobriquet, like that of Downie's murder, was the subject of speculation among students of the time but remained – and remains – uncertain.[92] At King's, in the 1850s, according to Neil Maclean, freaks were perpetrated chiefly by 'students from the country, who, being unaccustomed to the ways of the town, and little known to the residents, troubled themselves less whether they were discovered or not.' In fact, it was his more sophisticated characters that stole door-knockers, 'pinned' (overturned and wrecked) carts, and broke windows, loftily placating their victims or, when this did not work, taking them on with fists and sticks.[93]

An incident recorded at King's in 1854, Maclean's first year, shows that he got it right. Following complaints that students had been making trouble at night, not only in the streets of Old Aberdeen but in the grounds of the professors' houses, the college asked the police to patrol these properties. Around midnight on Saturday, 17 March, five students, including Peter Cameron (1851) and his two brothers, disguised themselves and set off 'to see if there were Constables there'. Things went wrong, however, when the constables saw them first and mistook one of them for George Morrison (1850). George, a prominent magistrand, active in the Debating Society, protested his innocence and produced witnesses to confirm it, but in vain; the college ordered him to leave without competing for prizes or taking his degree. Prompted – in some cases, anyway – by guilt, Peter and his fellow-culprits confessed. George's name was cleared, though not before he had appealed to the rector, and he departed with his degree and two prizes.[94]

A new offence – one, at least, that was now much more visible – was cheating. It was prevalent at King's from 1840 onwards, probably because of the greater rigour of the examinations, the importance attached to them, and, accordingly, the students' fear of failure. In some cases cheating was a group activity: in 1848, for example, following the examination in second Latin, 'a paper was handed in signed by a large number . . . of the [tertian] Class in which they confess to having copied or assisted . . . four only of the whole Class were innocent of one or other misdemeanour.' Other offenders preferred to work solo: in 1851 Alexander Murray (1848) was found to have given in 'an almost verbatim copy of a translation of Sallust by Mair' and was detected 'copying from a Translation of the Anabasis of Xenophon'. Among the commonest techniques, according to one of Neil Maclean's characters, were 'finger-nails for dates, and wide arm-sleeves for slips of paper'.[95]

Discipline at King's continued to centre on the weekly assembly of all four classes in the common school. Overcrowding and unruliness, however, were no more conducive to punishment than they had been to prayer, and from 1848 onwards 'public schools' were held only 'as occasion may require'.[96] Serious cases of misconduct, including the Morrison affair, now came directly to the senate; truancy and similar offences were punished in class. The role of the hebdomadar in all this is obscure; the office still existed in 1848 but is not mentioned in the revised college rules of that year. Public and class censors survived, however; the former called the roll on weekdays in the common school and on Sundays in the chapel.[97] There was one major innovation, possibly prompted by the Morrison case, in which several suspects were alibied by their landladies: from 1854 onwards the college kept a register of students' addresses during the session.[98]

At both colleges, serious offences were punished as before by expulsion or fines; bursars were deprived of part or their entire award. At King's, Andrew Murray, the plagiarist, was expelled; the drunk and disorderly Samuel Davidson was fined 10s 6d; and one of the culprits in the Morrison affair lost the final half of his bursary. At Marischal, the over-exuberant graduands were fined one guinea each, plus the cost of repairs; John Bothwell's joke cost him 2s 6d; while the sword-wielding William Booth and Charles Stuart, both first offenders and thus treated with exceptional leniency, paid 2s 6d and 1s, respectively. Delinquents might also be precluded from taking their degree or competing for prizes: not a new punishment but one that had grown in force as the importance of academic honours had increased. George Morrison narrowly escaped it; Peter Cameron did not, although in his case the sentence was suspended. Minor offences, like absence and lateness, were fined in shillings and pence.[99]

The discipline imposed by the colleges was complemented – up to a point, at least – by the students' own code of honour. No doubt something of the sort had existed in previous periods, but it is more apparent in the 1840s and 1850s than at any other time. At King's, the tertians of 1848 accepted that cheating was wrong and that it was widespread, but they preferred to confess as a class rather than name names; Peter Cameron and his friends colluded to give each other alibis but ultimately owned up to save George Morrison. At Marischal, students themselves reported the fracas at the debating society, and when William Mair stood up to his bullies and knocked both of them down, he was admired by all. The code was most clearly articulated by Neil Maclean's characters: crude practical jokes were 'a mark of Bageantdom – the most opprobrious epithet in the college'; incompetent professors might be treated roughly but not to the detriment of class-work; cheating was dishonourable and was to be exposed, although an ingenious system might be secretly admired. In town, it was a 'cowardly trick' to smash the windows of the old and poor – one victim was compensated with a whip-round; but violence against thimble-riggers, who fleeced students and townsfolk alike, was fully justified.[100] Maclean may, of course, have wished to impute a sense of honour to characters whose behaviour otherwise was immature and irresponsible; but his readiness to expose the contradictions in the code and the arguments for and against them, suggests that it was more than a mere narrative construct.

19 Marischal College was built to Archibald's Simpson neo–Tudor design between 1837 and 1844. The students are shown wearing trenchers and gowns.

Jupiter, Homunculus, and Creepie

George MacDonald reckoned that at King's it took three days for new entrants to get to know each other.[101] Bonding took longer; nevertheless, the bajans of 1845 were sufficiently united by the end of the session to submit a petition on behalf of some tertians who had admitted cheating.[102] Magistrands, after four years together, were the most inclined to make written representations: in 1827, for example, they petitioned for the use of the hall at Christmas and in 1850 for changes in the timetable; while in 1844 George MacDonald and his fellow-magistrands in second Greek memorialised the assistant who taught them, testifying to his ability and apologising for the behaviour of the class.[103] At Marischal, many of the bajans already knew each other from the grammar school. As a result, said William Walker, nicknames ('Jupiter', 'Homunculus', 'Creepie') and mock-Latin classroom slang were more prevalent there than at King's.

Inevitably, there were fissures in the class, not least between bursars and non-bursars (now known as 'free students'). John Hill Burton recalled with distaste 'the healthy, smiling Jackanapes, whose parents . . . have sent him to college [to gain] a bursary, that he may shew his talents, his wealth, and his contempt for his poorer competitors, by resigning it.' At King's, however, resentment seems to have eased by the 1850s: Neil Maclean would not have overlooked it. Instead, his characters turned their scorn on private students, who joined the class for a single session, entering and leaving without examination: 'no-one of any spirit would be a "private" in such a University as ours.'[104] At Marischal, however, where private students enrolled in large numbers, they were taken for granted: they attended meetings of the Literary Society in 1830, and those in the class of 1841 were invited to the graduation supper.[105] Social skills – or rather, the lack of them – could also be divisive; again, especially at King's. Staff and graduates more than once likened the college to a mill, where students, by rubbing up against each other, would acquire polish;[106] not surprisingly, some rubbed others up the wrong way. 'I thought I should have much to learn in way of refinement', remembered James Kennedy; 'I was surprised to find that I might consider myself one of the smarter, genteeler class'; George MacDonald complained to his father that 'the lad who lodges along with us is not so much a gentleman as we could wish'; even Neil Maclean's narrator confessed that he found his classmates 'very uncouth', while other characters were not slow to mock the pronunciation and ill-fitting clothes of country boys, highlanders in particular.[107] Whether polish was, in fact, preferable to rude honesty was a serious question. Maclean himself believed that students who had struggled to enter college on a bursary viewed everything except the intellect with contempt, '[which] retards their improvement very much.'

The average annual number of entrants to King's during the period, 71.5, was almost 30 per cent higher than the 53.8 entering Marischal (Tables 4.1–4.2). This owed much to the large number of King's alumni who were parish schoolmasters and directed their pupils to the college; to the number of bursaries available there to support them; and to prejudice in the counties against the utilitarian ethos of Marischal – 'the Broad Street Academy'.[108] It owed something, also, to the rural setting and small size of Old Aberdeen: 'the students here,' said a professor at King's, 'are much more under their professors' eyes'.[109] Nevertheless, some who lodged there, like 'Robert Falconer', found it dull;[110] while pressure on rooms forced a number of King's students, the majority by 1857, to lodge in Aberdeen, whatever their preference.[111] Sometimes sheer pragmatism prompted a student to choose one college over the other: Alexander Bain, sought-after by both, chose Marischal because 'the walks to King's would have entailed an injurious amount of fatigue.'

TABLE 4.1 ENTRANTS AND GRADUATES AT KING'S, 1826–59

Years	*Average annual number entering the first class*	*Average annual number of entrants who graduated*	*Graduates as % of entrants*
1826–29	75.0	30.2	40.3
1830–39	72.3	30.7	42.4
1840–49	75.8	33.8	44.5
1850–59	78.0	35.7	45.7

Source: Anderson, *Roll*, Appendix B. For averages of the period 1852–57: *Evidence* (1857), 120.

TABLE 4.2 ENTRANTS AND GRADUATES AT MARISCHAL, 1826–59

Years	*Average annual number entering the first class*	*Average annual number of entrants who graduated*	*Graduates as % of entrants*
1826–29	56.0	23.0	41.0
1830–39	51.2	19.2	37.5
1840–49	48.2	18.3	37.9
1850–59	59.8	19.9	33.2

Source: Anderson, *Roll*, Appendix B. For averages of the period 1852–57: *Evidence* (1857), ADD.

At both colleges, the relative proportions of bursars and free students changed little from the previous period, or indeed during the period itself. At King's, in the session 1835–36, there were 120 bursars (53.6% of the aggregate number of arts students); in 1855–56, 118 (53.3%). At Marischal, in 1835–36 there were 87 bursars (57.2% of the aggregate – excluding private students); in 1855–56, 92 (52.8%).[112]

Class numbers fluctuated as in previous periods and for the same reasons: 'many [students] change their views,' said James Melvin bluntly, 'and some of them die off.'[113] At King's, poverty changed a lot of views: George MacDonald dropped out of the class of 1840 after his second year almost certainly because his father could not supplement his bursary of £14; having raised additional funds in his year out, he joined the class of 1841 as a tertian. Others could not keep up. James Kennedy reckoned that at the end of his first year, 1831–32, nearly half the class could not read a sentence of Greek: 'I suppose a number of these at the end of the session closed their university career. In every succeeding session the number decreased, till I believe at the end not more than one-half remained.' James was right: of 79 entrants, 22 (27.8%) left after the first year; 11 (19.2%) after the second, and six (13%) after the third, leaving 40 to finish the course. Some students left for purely personal reasons: James himself, in 1832, to join his brothers at Edinburgh. At Marischal, as William Walker and others observed, it was still common for students to leave after their second or third year to enter medicine or law. Numbers were threatened in 1827 and 1831 by the Militia Act,[114] and affected, as always, by migration: among 90 entrants to King's in 1844 were ten from Marischal, who 'came over at the end of the first week' and stayed on for one or two years.[115]

The overall impact of these fluctuations upon aggregate numbers at the colleges is shown in Table 4.3: King's retained its lead, although the high number of private students at Marischal helped to narrow the gap. Nevertheless, it is clear why, when contemplating union, King's students saw no reason to join the smaller community in Aberdeen; why Marischal students feared that they would be swamped by the larger community based in Old Aberdeen; and why staff at both colleges feared that the amalgamated numbers, wherever they were located, would produce classes of unmanageable size. All students now lived at home or in lodgings, the majority in Aberdeen. Living out of college, said Neil Maclean, was 'the great difference . . . between English and Scottish student-life.' Nevertheless, non-residence was not, in his experience, harmful: 'The Scottish student, in the majority of cases, goes to college for the purpose of working . . . He has also generally very limited means at his disposal, and . . . extremely little in the way of dissipation can be done without that.'

TABLE 4.3 AGGREGATE NUMBERS OF ARTS STUDENTS AT KING'S AND MARISCHAL, 1830–51

Session	*1830–31*	*1840–41*	*1850–51*
King's	231	157	268
Marischal	167	121	159

Source: Report (1836), 120–1, 210; *Report* (1857), 119, 138–9. The figures for Marischal exclude private students.

The average age of entrants to King's in 1827 was 14.[116] Donald Fraser, whose father was in Canada, entered much earlier, 'before I had completed my twelfth year'; he was, he admitted, 'too young for University studies, and wasted much of my time in sheer boyish levity and fun.' At Marischal, 12 was said to be the average age at entry.[117] Those who entered earlier, noted one Marischal professor, were 'the students who have made the best figure, perhaps, in the Grammar School, and their parents, perhaps from vanity, wish to push them forward through the whole of their education, not knowing that they cannot make such a figure at College as they do while they are learning the Latin language.'[118] By the 1830s, according to William Walker, the averages had risen to 15 at King's and 13 at Marischal; by the 1850s, to 17 and 16. By this time, at least, the average at King's may have been inflated by its highland students, whose repeated attempts to win a bursary, as described by Neil Maclean, delayed their entry.[119]

The social origins of students at King's were not recorded at matriculation. There is, however, an unofficial list of the bajans of 1859 that includes their fathers' occupations (Table 4.4). Figures for landed families are not available but alongside the other traditional patrons of King's, the professions (30% of the class), there is significant representation (14.2%) from the 'Intermediate' category, including agents, master-craftsmen and tradesmen, the majority from Aberdeenshire and the northern counties. At Marischal, in contrast, fathers' occupations were regularly recorded at matriculation and are tabulated in Appendix IV (Table 1). Those for the classes of 1830, 1840 and 1850 (Table 4.4) reflect the overall trend. The number of students from landed families (15.7%, 15.1%, 7.4%) continued to decline, while those from the 'Commerce and Industry' (23.0%, 15.1%, 18.5%) and 'Working class' (9.6%, 4.1%, 13.6%) categories were volatile. This was probably a reflection of the troubled urban economy or, in the case of the working class, a preference for the Mechanics' Institute, where the instructors included Alexander Bain, passing on what he had learned at Marischal. 'Agriculture' dipped then rose to its previous high level (10.8%, 13.7%, 19.8%), while the 'Professional' (25.3%, 32.8%, 27.1%) and 'Intermediate' (14.5%, 12.3%, 12.3%) categories remained stable.

TABLE 4.4 KING'S AND MARISCHAL, SOCIAL ORIGINS OF STUDENTS, 1830–59

Fathers occupations	*King's (bajans) 1859*	*Marischal, 1830*	*Marischal, 1840*	*Marischal, 1850*
Land	[<20]	13	11	6
Professions	21	21	24	22
Commerce and industry	6	19	11	15
Agriculture	7	9	10	16
Intermediate	10	12	9	10
Working class	6	8	3	11
Unknown	20	1	5	1
Total	70	83	73	81

Source: For King's, Johnston, *Bajans*, which lists two more bajans than Anderson, *Roll*, 211. Students from landed families are not identified and are therefore included in the 20 'Unknowns'. For Marischal, Anderson, *FAM*, 2. The social categories are defined in Appendix IV.

20 Marischal College, 1861, marred by the obelisk erected in memory of Sir James McGrigor, graduate and rector; it was later removed.

The geographical origins of students at King's and Marischal from 1830 onwards are tabulated in Appendix IV (Tables 2–4). At King's, the majority of students continued to come from Aberdeenshire and the counties to the north, but with considerable variation in the latter over comparatively short periods. In William Walker's class of 1836, for example, 20 per cent of the students came from Aberdeenshire, 17 per cent from Banffshire and 11.7 per cent each from Moray and from Ross and Cromarty. In George MacDonald's much smaller class of 1840, the number from Aberdeenshire remained stable at 22 per cent, but the only other high-scoring county was Inverness-shire with 11 per cent. In the session 1854–55 Aberdeenshire, excluding 'Aberdeen and the immediate neighbourhood', provided 29 per cent of the aggregate number of arts students; Banffshire, 15.7 per cent. At Marischal, Aberdeen and Aberdeenshire predominated, although their relative positions also varied. Returns made to the commissions of 1836 and 1857 show that in the session 1834–35, for example, 44.1 per cent of students in arts came from the town and its suburbs; 28.7 per cent from the county; in 1854–55, 30.9 per cent came from the town, and 45.0 per cent from the county.[120]

From croft, farm and what George MacDonald called 'little, grey towns', students walked, rode or coached to and from their colleges. 'Robert Falconer' encountered a troop of them trudging through his town on their way home. He himself was sensible enough to travel down by coach, as did 'Alec Forbes', who 'found himself on the box-seat of the Royal Mail, with his trunk on the roof behind him'.[121] John Kennedy, too, rode on the roof all the way from Inverness: 'Between Keith and Huntly they had a piper upon the coach who played "O'er the hills and far awa'," which indeed affected me very much'.

My father will pay

The only free students known to have left any record of their day-to-day life at college were John Sinclair and John Kennedy, contemporaries at King's in 1828. Sinclair's father allowed him £100 a year, but with little faith in his 'unfortunate and infatuated son' he entrusted him and his money to John Tulloch, professor of mathematics, a fellow-highlander. Neither, the professor discovered, was easy to manage:

> He never has got even a shirt, a neckcloth, a pocket-handkerchief or a pair of stockings but from the Clothier and Linen-draper and these I need not tell you swell the bill enormously and particularly so, when the young gentleman himself is the judge of the necessity of the supply and when I am met by the words 'I could not do without them. My father will pay you at once if you need the money.'

It might have been worse: there were, said the professor, 'men base enough to supply him with money for the purposes of extravagance or folly, but hitherto he has got none from such a source . . . And indeed the moment I learn that he has recourse to such an expedient, that moment my superintendence of his education must cease.' John Kennedy, in contrast, having failed to win a bursary, was supported by 'the kindness of a friend' and duly practised thrift.

Both colleges submitted to the 1826 commission the basic costs of students in arts. At King's, free students paid £3 3s in tuition fees for the four main courses and from £1 11s 6d to 10s for the subsidiaries: a total of £18 8s 6d over four years. John Sinclair himself paid more than the standard rate in his first year, possibly for extra tuition, and less in his second, when he did not take chemistry. Fees for examinations, servants and heating amounted to around £3. Finally, for those who graduated – not Sinclair, who dropped out – there were fees of £2 16s 2d. At Marischal, tuition cost £18 18s; other fees were much the same as at King's. By 1857, the cost of tuition at both colleges had risen to £20 14s.[122]

The colleges also included in their submission the cost of textbooks. At King's, this totalled nearly £5 (including £1 11s 6d for 'Hutton's Course'),[123] although John Sinclair spent double that in his second year alone. At Marischal, textbooks cost £4 10s. The colleges excluded from their calculations the cost of extra-curricular courses: at King's, however, Sinclair's French lessons cost £6 a year.

Sinclair paid 9s a week for the rooms he occupied with his tutor: 'a small parlor, bedroom, and bed closet', plus 'attendance'. He paid 14s a week for his board, £5 a year for fire and candles, and £3 for washing and mending. Although his professor 'expected by the most rigid economy to save two or three pounds on the board and nearly as much on the Lodging by renting a cheaper one during the summer when the demand is less', it is not certain if he succeeded. John Kennedy had a room at Number 26 College Bounds in Old Aberdeen. He paid £3 10s in rent for the session, not £3 as he had hoped, and ate for 2s 6d a week: 'meat (2lbs), 10*d*.; half-stone of meal, 10½*d*.; potatoes, 2½*d*.; barley, 1*d*.; milk, 3½*d*. I do not recollect the rest at present but I keep a memorandum book.' In addition, he paid 1s a week for cooking and 5s a session to have his shoes cleaned. The two sisters with whom he lodged were 'very kind to me, and I may sit at their fire and read my book as long as I please.'

Free students who fell ill were treated by their own doctors; at King's, those who went absent would receive a visit from their professor or the class censor to check their condition.[124] With epidemics the colleges took every precaution: in the session 1832–33, during an outbreak of cholera, King's postponed morning prayers until 8.45 am, 'that time may be given to the Students for breakfasting before leaving their Rooms'; at Marischal, the classrooms were fumigated.[125]

Better to have sixpence than nothing at all

At King's, in 1826, there were 29 endowments capable of providing 128 bursaries in arts. Nine of the endowments supported around 60 competition bursaries: George MacDonald, for example, twelfth in the competition of 1840, was awarded a Fullarton. The remaining endowments were for presentation bursaries, although the college was in several cases patron. At Marischal, 38 endowments supported 99 bursaries, 35 of them competitive: Alexander Bain, having missed the cut in the competition, was later awarded one of these, probably Mitchell's, when it fell vacant. By 1859 a further three endowments at King's had established ten more bursaries, three of them competitive. There were 11 more endowments at Marischal, providing 18 bursaries, four of them competitive.[126]

'A boy with a bursary of twenty-five pounds', declared Andrew Halliday Duff (1844), 'can pay all expenses for the session including fees.'[127] In fact, the value of arts bursaries was generally less – much less at Marischal, where Duff had been a student. There, in 1827, 15 bursaries paid upwards of £10 to £25, while 84 were for £10 or less, including Alexander Bain's. At King's, in 1827, there were 76 in the first category, including George MacDonald's; 55 in the second.[128] The colleges accepted the situation: 'it is better to have sixpence', said Principal Brown at Marischal, 'than nothing at all.' The university commissions demurred, especially as King's was trying to fund even more small bursaries from existing endowments: 'we agree with our predecessors', said the commissioners of 1836, 'in thinking [this] a source of manifest evil to the interests of education, at the expense of a smaller number of liberal endowments, which might be made highly conducive to the promotion of those interests.'[129] The problem remained unresolved, however, and there were numerous students like the 'poor lad from Orkney', a fellow-competitor of George MacDonald, who was awarded a bursary of five pounds 'but wouldn't keep it because it wouldn't keep him.'

Bursars received half of their money towards the end of February; they got the rest when they passed the March examination, failing which, the entrance examination the following October. At both colleges, the value of their bursaries determined the rate at which their tuition fees were charged. George MacDonald, with a bursary of £14, would have paid the full rate; Alexander Bain on £10, would have paid ten-twelfths. There were no reductions, however, on graduation fees, something that irked poorer students: 'it was considered very hard', wrote Neil Maclean, 'to pay for an honour for which they wrought so assiduously'. Like others unable or unwilling to pay, he himself put off graduating for two years.

'Nothing', said James Kennedy, writing of students from King's who lodged in Old Aberdeen in the 1830s, 'could be more miserable than the lodgings occupied by most. I lodged in College Bounds in a little house where there were five or six students, with two in each room and that room so small that I wonder how health was maintained. Others I found still worse lodged.' Things were little better in the 1850s: in the session 1854–55, 36 students were crammed into nine houses in College Bounds, eight of them lodging at Number 25.[130] Nevertheless, evidence in the George Morrison affair of 1854 shows that at least some of the students in these houses – George himself and Peter Cameron, for example – had their own rooms. These offered privacy but little else. Neil Maclean's narrator was shocked when he visited those occupied by bursars from the Highlands:

> down from the bare tiles of some the water was running, and on cold nights this would be frozen and hang in icicles from the roof. A chair, a stool, and a rickety old table composed all the furniture of these rooms, if we except the student's trunk, his few books, and his bed. A small, small fireplace, formed so as to hold the smallest quantity of coals, was fixed into one side.[131]

In Aberdeen itself poorer students, according to John Hill Burton, lodged in garrets in the Gallowgate and the Spital – the latter presumably taken by students from King's. In the 1840s Andrew Halliday Duff reckoned that they could rent a large room in the town, with a box-bed, for 5s a week. Neil Maclean, one of the many students from King's who stayed there in the 1850s, showed that a bursar's fees and living expenses could come to well under £20. After an expensive first session, lodging alone in 'a very respectable part of the town [George Street], and not in a garret', he gladly shared the room with his brother. Between them they paid 4s a week in rent, amounting with food, coal and gas to £8 8s a session. With class fees also at £8 8s, this left him almost £4 for books and other things.

Neil and his brother spent 7s 10d a week on food and ate well: meal and beef; bread and potatoes; syrup and coffee; tea, apples, flour and milk; sugar, barley and sago. The highland students in his novel ate more plainly: 'Though my bursary is small', said one, 'it is quite sufficient for my wants, along with the two bags of meal and potatoes and the barrel of herrings which I brought with me.'[132] Others replenished their stocks monthly with boxes of oatmeal, fowls and eggs delivered by the local carrier: 'Our potatoes and meal are both almost done', George MacDonald informed his father; 'be so good as to send a fresh supply as soon as convenient.' But those for whom this was not an option shared the fate of the student at King's who told his professor 'that he lived, as his phrase was, upon meals-corn. I asked him if he meant that he lived on meal only, prepared in different ways? He said, "Yes." '[133]

Overwork on such a limited diet, claimed William Walker and Neil Maclean, accounted for the notoriously high rate of sickness and death among bursars; James Kennedy believed it was caused 'still more by their wretched quarters.' There are, certainly, regular reports of bursars dying and of bursaries vacated through ill health but not enough detail to say whether the incidence was higher than that

21 George MacDonald, 1868. Also by Sir George Reid, the portrait shows the author at the time when he was producing his college novels.

among free students or working-lads of the same age. In fiction, at least, they were too poor or too proud to call in a doctor; anxious friends had to do it for them.[134] Alexander Bain distrusted doctors, dreaded taking 'physic' and preferred to suffer alone.

Alexander made himself ill competing against graduate students, ministers and teachers for the Blackwell Essay Prize of twenty pounds[135] – unsuccessfully, as it turned out. For bursars who lacked Neil Maclean's skill in managing money, winning prizes, especially class prizes, was a serious business: it was one way of acquiring the books they needed. Many had succeeded in the bursary competition only by borrowing grammars and dictionaries: 'Noo, this is my Riddle and Arnold', Neil MacLean's narrator was told by his schoolmaster; 'every year . . . it has gaen to the Competition, an' every year it has returned bearing on it the name of another bursar.'[136] They either continued the practice, or bought what they needed secondhand (at the very least) in and around the colleges. The bursar living on 'meals-corn' nearly died as a result: he paid under £5 for his bed and board for the entire session, spent the rest on books, and ended up spitting blood. Alexander Bain, in contrast, got indigestion.

Bursars also sought out secondhand (at the very, very least) gowns. Those who could not, and had to find around 15s for a new one, immediately went for the distressed look: 'The respectability and age of the student,' wrote John Hill Burton, 'is marked by the tattered and discoloured condition of his gown.' At King's, in 1831, James Kennedy and his contemporaries wore 'tall hats' with their gowns. In 1840, however, Duncan Anderson's father had him arrayed 'in cap and gown in one of the famous clothing establishments of Bon-Accord'. According to William Mair, 'we of Marischal had . . . a velvet collar; they of King's . . . wore a trencher'; however, pictures of Marischal show the students with trenchers. The correct academic dress of students in arts at both colleges in 1859 was modelled in pictures specially commissioned 40 years later:[137] the King's gown had a cloth collar, the sleeve cut high on the arm; the Marischal gown, a purple velvet collar and long sleeves; both models were bareheaded.

Coming out at eighteen

William Walker told the story of a magistrand of King's, who attended the last meeting of the Literary Society for the session and listened to his class-fellows bidding farewell to the college, its venerable old halls and the learned professors to whom they owed so much. 'He then got up and forthwith struck a very jarring note. He felt no regret at leaving the old halls. He didn't owe much to them. He had learned more solid and practical truth from an eighteen-penny pamphlet, than he had learned from all the professors of King's College with all their lectures and blackboards.' Walker himself was more judicious:

> There was much honest hard work done by good, though somewhat old fashioned professors, and by eager hard-plodding students . . . The 'raw material', as one of the professors would have put it, was pretty efficiently prepared for the 'home market,' but it was not quite fitted to 'wrangle' to much purpose across the border.

Acknowledging that teaching and learning improved in subsequent decades, he assumed that 'students of the Forties and Fifties must have many interesting memories of those stirring times.' As they did. Neil Maclean, for one, wrote fulsome speeches for his characters praising the education they received: 'The foundation is as well laid as the superstructure is raised,' said one, 'and this is proved unmistakably by looking over the lists of the successful candidates for the Civil and Military Services.' 'We work hard before we come up,' said another, 'and when here do the same (I speak here particularly of our own college), so that when any go farther south the work at the English colleges is mere child's play, until they come to the very highest parts of Mathematics.'[138] The snide remark – one of several – about the low work-rate at Marischal might have been justified in the 1830s. As David Masson complained: 'we had among our professors two old men, who ought either never to have been there, or to have been superannuated long before I and my coevals became acquainted with them . . . There is real pain in setting down such things as these, but I hold it to be a duty.' William Blaikie said of the same decade that he was taught nothing in Greek, natural history and moral philosophy: 'what I came to know, I had to pick up from books.' Andrew Halliday Duff had no criticisms of the teaching there in the 1840s but repeated the now-familiar lament: 'A lad who goes to college at fourteen is necessarily but little advanced in learning; and with the same opportunities for the next four years, it is not to be expected that he will come out at eighteen with the same amount of knowledge as an Oxford or Cambridge man of three or four-and-twenty.'

Not much was said about the professors' pastoral role; it was probably taken for granted. Several former students, however, praised the kindness of John Tulloch, professor of mathematics at King's. To John Kennedy he was 'the genial Highlander'; to William Geddes, 'the plucky little Highlander'; while Duncan Anderson remembered him at the bursary competition, limping round the room, 'as anxious and fidgety as if he were one of the competitors himself.' Tulloch came from Caithness, entering King's as a student in 1799 and later teaching in Inverness.[139] Not unnaturally, he took a personal interest in students from the far North. Too much, apparently: 'It used to be thought that Tulloch was partial to [biased towards] the Highland Students,' said William Walker, 'but I never heard any other proof than that he was known to be very kind and considerate to the poorest of them – remitting their fees, and when he could, procuring for them bursaries or other help.' Certainly, Tulloch's concern for the recalcitrant John Sinclair went well beyond paying bills: 'you must allow me to say,' he scolded John's aggrieved father, 'that to be continually addressing him in vituperative language has, and indeed, cannot fail to have a bad effect on his mind.'

TABLE 4.5 KING'S COLLEGE, BAJANS OF 1859, ORIGINS AND DESTINATIONS

Destinations	*Church*	*Med.*	*Law*	*School-teaching*	*Commerce industry*	*Armed forces*	*Planting, etc.*	*Other*	*Not known*	*Total*
Origins										
Landowner										[<20]
Minister		1	2	1			1	1	2	8
Doctor	1	1								2
Lawyer			3						1	4
Teacher	4			2						6
Other profs						1				1
Commercial & industrial	3	1						2		6
Agriculture	3			1	1	1	1			7
Intermediate	3	2						2	3	10
Working class	2			2					2	6
Total	16	5	5	6	1	2	2	5	8	50

Source: Johnston, *Bajans*, which lists two more bajans than Anderson, *Roll*, giving an overall class of 70; the origins of 20 are not recorded. Students from landed families are not identified and are therefore included in the 20. The social categories are illustrated in Appendix IV. 'Other' occupations include: administrative, clerical, and unspecified work abroad.

TABLE 4.6 MARISCHAL COLLEGE, BAJANS OF 1859, ORIGINS AND DESTINATIONS

Destinations	*Church*	*Med.*	*Law*	*School-teaching*	*Commerce industry*	*Armed forces*	*Planting, etc.*	*Other*	*Not known*	*Total*
Origins										
Landowner										0
Minister	1	1			2		1		1	6
Doctor		2						1		3
Lawyer						1				1
Teacher	1	2		1						4
Other profs								1		1
Commercial & industrial		5	1		1			1	1	9
Agriculture	1	3	1	6			2	1		14
Intermediate	2	3	1		3	1			6	16
Working class		1		3					1	5
Total	5	17	3	10	6	2	3	4	9	59

Source: Johnston, *Bajans*; Anderson, *FAM*, 2.

John's father wanted him to enter a profession. The widowed mother of 'Alec Forbes' hedged her bets: 'he would be no worse a farmer for having an *A.M.* after his name; while the curriculum was common to all professions.'[140] Other parents saw a college education simply as a stopgap: '[they] send up their children to us from not knowing what to do with them', a professor at King's told the 1826 commission.[141] Whatever their motives, however, most parents seem to have appreciated the education their boys received and showed it in the usual way: at Marischal, for example, in the class of 1836, 44 of the 74 students were either preceded or succeeded by their brothers, some by as many as four.

At King's in the 1830s, said William Walker, 'the pulpit . . . was the aim of the great majority of graduates, and many of them made the parish school a stepping-stone to the parish church'. The church remained in pole position throughout the period: when magistrands of the class of 1854 were asked what careers they intended to follow, almost half put the church first, well ahead of teaching and medicine.[142] By this time the Disruption had extended the number of vacant pulpits: among the 16 members of the class of 1859 who entered the church, six entered the Established Church, four the Free Church and two the United Presbyterian. As in 1787, however, ministers' and farmers' sons diversified most in their choice of careers; while students from the working class stuck to the church and teaching (Table 4.5). Among Marischal students, the church came well behind medicine, teaching and business; those from the 'Intermediate' category diversified as much as those from church and farm; while those from the working class again clustered in teaching (Table 4.6). The solid, if not spectacular, number of students from both colleges who entered teaching is at first sight a testimony to the efforts of the Dick Bequest to raise the profile of parochial teaching in the North East; in fact, only eight of the 16 taught in local parish schools.

Students in every category went overseas: mostly as missionaries, teachers, army doctors and planters. Of the King's class of 1859, at least four went to India, and one each to Australia, Canada, Ceylon, Guyana, China, and the USA. Of the Marischal class of 1840, at least three went to India, three to Ceylon, and one each to China and the USA; while James Grant explored Africa. Of the class of 1845, at least four went to Australia, and one each to India and Ceylon. Lastly, of the class of 1859, six went to India, five to Africa, four to Australia, two to Ceylon, and one to Burma. Given the size and scale of this diaspora, it was not unfitting for Neil Maclean to set the epilogue to his novel in 'some outlandish place'.

Conclusion

Some 15,000 students attended King's College and Marischal College between 1600 and 1860. Very few described the experience; relatively few left a footprint in the records, other than as bursars, matriculants and graduates. The present study has drawn on the words and careers of 127 in all, augmented by several hundred counted heads. This is hardly the stuff that solid conclusions are made of. The documentary evidence, too, has its weaknesses, due mainly to the nature of the academic business of the colleges and the way in which it was recorded. Substantive business (pedagogic, curricular and regulatory) was for the most part carefully minuted. But it was largely prescriptive, with little to show how and when it was implemented and to what effect. Sessional business (the routine of teaching, examining, graduating and maintaining discipline) was cyclical and repetitive. It was recorded briefly and inconsistently, taking for granted an awareness of facts and procedures, and offering little by way of context or explanation. For these reasons, it is difficult to date precisely the ways in which patterns of student work and conduct changed. The periods into which the study has been divided are almost certainly fuzzier round the edges than the joined-up dates of the chapter-headings imply.

The first period, 1600 to 1639, saw King's and Marischal operating the system of education imposed upon them by the Reformers; it ended as they were caught up in war. Each college contained around 50 boys and young men. At King's, they came from Aberdeenshire and the counties to the north; at Marischal, from Aberdeen and its hinterland. Some paid their way; others lived on charity and were not allowed to forget it. Within the walls, they were expected to follow an almost monastic regime, acquiring the knowledge and skills, practising the piety and modesty, that would equip them to serve as ministers of the church and teachers in its schools; or as lairds, lawyers and burgesses, protecting and furthering its interests. Beyond the walls, they were required to behave in a way that maintained the credit of the colleges, impressing and reassuring the communities that hosted, supported and invested in them. They lived behind locked gates, crammed into dilapidated buildings, under strict regulation and close supervision, with only organised games of football to relieve the pressure. Inevitably, there was trouble: in some cases little more than mischief; in others, the product of a culture in which offence was readily taken and violence easily provoked. Beyond a single reference to fighting between the colleges, however, the extent of serious misconduct is unknown.

The second period, 1640 to 1717, encompassed the wars of religion and revolution, military occupation, more religion and revolution and, finally, the 'Fifteen'. There was regime-change in both colleges and bitter recrimination between them over recruitment. It is scarcely surprising, then, that as numbers rose, to around 150 at King's and over 100 at Marischal, so did the incidence of violence. Students were infected by the turbulence of the times; some had known nothing but war or the threat of war; more and more lived out, beyond the surveillance of hebdomadar, censor and janitor. Religion, politics and college rivalry gave them a chance – virtually a licence – to fight amongst themselves or on the streets. Riots, tumults and disorders were the result, reaching levels of violence unacceptable not just to the college and the town but to the government.

The third period, 1718 to 1825, centred on the reform of the college curricula in the 1750s. At Marischal, this went smoothly and successfully; less so at King's, where there was a counter-productive effort to revive the fully residential college. In the 1770s numbers began to rise again, eventually topping 200 at each college. The number of bursars also rose; the size of their bursaries did not. King's recruited from its traditional sources, the professions and the land; Marischal from a widening social base. Some students entered the colleges to kill time; the majority to follow the modernised curriculum, in whole or in part, and acquire the polite learning needed to enter a profession, run a business, or manage an estate. Taught over a five-month session, with walk-through examinations, the courses ultimately challenged only the very thick or very idle, and both colleges became targets for reform. Holed up in Old and New Town garrets, the concept of 24/7 control buried along with full residence, students now managed their own time and activities: ram reels replaced organised sport; literary and debating societies came and went; church attendance was, up to a point, a matter of personal choice. Violence persisted, mainly against townsfolk and not unprovoked: neither the 'Forty-five' nor the French Revolution, however, brought Aberdeen students onto the streets. At Marischal, however, encouraged by the reformers, students reclaimed their role in the election of the rector: as a result they acquired a voice, a measure of self-esteem, and a legitimate occasion for misrule.

The final period, 1826 to 1860, was dominated by proposals for union, which soon passed 'if' and proceeded to 'how' and 'when'. By the 1850s King's had over 250 students a year; Marischal's total of around 200 was inflated by its traditionally strong private contingent. Bursar numbers rose and with them bursar pride. Both colleges recruited steadily from the amorphous 'Intermediate' category of clerical workers and master-tradesmen; spasmodically from the working class. Some students, mainly at King's, were straight out of George MacDonald: self-taught on remote hillsides, destined to win baseline bursaries, grind on an empty stomach, and 'wag their pow in a pulpit'. The majority, however, came from modest to affluent families, progressing from grammar school to college and into the church, medicine, law or commerce at home and in the colonies, with the same degree of diligence but rather less angst. The curriculum they followed remained largely unchanged, despite the efforts of the commission of 1826; but the examinations they sat were comprehensively reformed and restructured, thereby restoring the credibility of the Master's degree. This made no immediate impact on the numbers graduating, but it did force students who feared the embarrassment of failure to plod away in their rooms for at least five nights in the week. Those with sufficient energy then thumped their sticks at debates at King's on Friday evenings or indulged in laddish behaviour – moderated by an honour code – in town on Saturday nights.

On the eve of union, the features that had traditionally distinguished students in arts at King's from those at Marischal remained in place, if less pronounced: their numbers, their origins, their destinations and – in the matter of sleeve-length and collar, at least – their gowns. There were, however, strong similarities between the two communities: the broad-based education they received, the curricula they followed, the ways in which they learned, and the methods by which they were taught and examined. There were similarities, too, of lifestyle: the unlovely rooms they occupied in Old and New Aberdeen; their choice of entertainment; the topics that aroused them in debate or at rectorial elections. At the end of their college careers, however, students departing from King's experienced something that students of Marischal did not: a sense of loss. On his final night, Neil Maclean's newly-graduated narrator went with the rest of his class for a last look at 'the old pile'; gathering in the quadrangle, they sang a song of farewell, then quietly drifted away. If Marischal students sang sad songs in its neo-Tudor courtyard, behind a huddle of houses and shops, no-one treasured the memory enough to record it.

Appendix I

Statutes of Principal Gilbert Gray, Marischal College, 1605
AUL MS M 2, ff. 170r.–174v.
Edited and translated by Morton A E Gauld and Colin McLaren

Editorial Notes

The use of capitals in the text has been restricted to personal and place names. The original punctuation has been reproduced; additional punctuation has been added sparingly. Letters, words and phrases that are interlineated, overwritten or inserted from the margin have been italicised. Those that are crossed out have been underlined. Obscured or illegible words, and suggested readings, have been placed in square brackets. Scribal peculiarities, for example, 'accademia' have not been signalled or corrected. Sections of the text, or parts of sections, that are crossed out or marked 'delete'; and additional text that has been written in the margin without a clear mark of insertion, are indicated with an asterisk. For ease of reference, paragraphs have been numbered consecutively.

TEXT

[1] Statuta accademiae Abredonensis [proposita] a magistro Gilberto Graio gymnasiarcha anno 1605 qui octavus est annus prefecture eius.

[2] Quia sine ordine ne mundus consistere potest sine sine legibus nulla societas coli aut respublica regi feliciter valet decet imprimis in nostra republica literaria sanctis et salutaribus legibus studiosam iuventutem dirigi harum igitur capita quaedam et fundamenta sequentibus proponimus.

[3] 35* Nulli in gymnasium nostrum aut studiosorum numerum incipiantur nisi prius accademiae et disciplinae nostrae observ[acionis] suae juramento praestito. Cuius formula haec sit.

*Numbered out of sequence.

[4] Formula juramenti studiosorum qui membra accademiae huius et eius privelegiis frui cupiunt.
Ego A N juro et sancte promitto vobis gymnasiarchae ac praeceptoribus accademiae huius vestrisque in hoc officio successoribus debitam obedientiam et reverentiam. Et quod (per dei graciam) volo servare leges et statuta ac per membra gymnasii statuenda pro *pro religione* pace et disciplina accademiae huius cuius imposterum dignitati simul et incolumitati quantum in me est semper studebo. Sic me deus adiuvet.

[5] 1 Volumus studiosios nostros ante omnia summa concordia pacis inter se vivere, neminem alteri injuriam verbo vel facto inferre.

[6] 2 Nunquam cuiquam nec domi nec foris contumeliose in quemque loqui licet sed qui pro verbis dat verbera solus verberator [luito] penas, et mutuam pugnam mutua pena [maneat] *nam veritas convicii non excusat injurantem.*

[7] 3 Pasquillos latino vel scotico sermone in socios cives aut [*socios alios*] quoscunque qui composuerit [et . . .] ab omnibus preceptoribus publice luerit accademia eiiciatur ab aliis factos et a se inventos qui sparserit transcripserit et non statim combusserit [luito] publice.

[8] 4 Vetamus ne studiosorum quisquam arma quaevis aut inferrendam aut propulsandam injuriam apta ut loricam thoracem ferream cassidem chirotaecas ferreas gladium pugionem machinas sclopos aut id genus alia habeat aut quovis modo iis utantur sive intra gymnasium sive extra sed scalpellis dumtaxat utantur qui secus fecerint pro primo armorum confiscacione mulcentur [secundo] in publicis scholis puniantur tertio deprehensi accademiae [ejiciantur].

TRANSLATION

[1] Statutes of the Academy of Aberdeen [set forth] by Master Gilbert Gray Gymnasiarch in the year 1605, which is his eighth in office.

[2] Because the world cannot exist without order, no society flourish and no state be governed successfully without laws, it is proper in the first place that youths studying in our commonwealth of letters should be governed by sacred and beneficial laws; we therefore put forward certain heads and bases of such laws, as follows.

[3] 35* None are to be admitted to our gymnasium or numbered among the students unless the oath of the academy as to their observance of our regulations has first been taken. This is the form of the oath.

*Numbered out of sequence.

[4] Form of the oath taken by students who desire to be members of this academy and to enjoy its privileges.
I, A N, swear and solemnly promise due obedience and reverence to you the gymnasiarch and teachers of this academy and to your successors in this office. And that (through the grace of God) I wish to keep the laws and statutes and other rulings which may yet be made by the members of the gymnasium for *the godliness* the peace and order of this academy. And that to its honour, as also its safe preservation, I will ever devote myself in time to come to the utmost of my ability.

[5] 1 We wish that our students before all things should live together in the utmost harmony and peace; that no-one should harm another by word or deed.

[6] 2 A student is never allowed to speak abusively to another, either at home or abroad but he who returns words with blows, is alone to pay the penalty, and a shared punishment should [await] a shared fight. *For the truth of an insult does not excuse the one who inflicts the injury.*

[7] 3 He who composes lampoons in the Latin or Scots language against his fellow-students, citizens or any others of his acquaintances [and] has undergone punishment by all the teachers in public, is to be expelled from the academy. He who has found verses made by others and has not immediately burned them but has spread and copied them, is to be punished in public.

[8] We forbid any of our students to have any weapons capable of inflicting injury when wielded against or thrown at someone, such as a cuirass, an iron breastplate, a helmet, iron gauntlets, a sword, a dagger, instruments of war, firearms or other things of that kind, or to use them in any way either inside or outside the gymnasium, but let them use small knives only. Those who do otherwise are to be penalised by the confiscation of their weapons on the first occasion, punished in the public school on a [second] and if caught for a third time [they are to be expelled] from the academy.

[9] *de togis urgendum semper.* Togis nigris studiosi nostri ut et galeris aut pilaeis nigris [ita] *et togis* omnes utantur, togas non laxas aut vagas habeant, sed induant easdem decore in accessu et vestitu publice et privatim urbanitati nitori munditiei studeant qui secus fecerint, [nisi] admonitioni preceptorum paruerint puniantur.*

*'togis non . . . puniantur', crossed out.

[10] Comam studiosorum nullus alat, prolixiores capilli capitis foemin[eus] ornat[us] virum omnem dedicent [dedecent] nisi luxuriosus aut effiminatus haberi velit miles item studiosorum ergo scandalum sunt et opprobrium.

[11] 5 Qui preceptoribus gymnasii omnibus et singulis non assurexerit, et cum reverentia caput aperuerit qui obloquitus fuerit aut irreverenter verbo aut gestu acceperit instanter publice luito, similiterque qui pastoribus civitatis, magistratui parentibus et senioribus debitum honorem non exhibuerit; hic quam studiosis qui morum observantia bene audire solent, maculam inurit, eam poena sua eluat [*bibliothecario*] idemque expectent qui civium alicui artificumve aut ipsis filiis servis aut familiae iniuriam aliquam dicto aut facto inferre aut mollestiam creare presumpse[rint] ut discant nostri omnes non solum cum seipsis sed et cum ceteris in pace et charitate vivere.

[12] [Nemo] aus praeceptoribus [vel] publice vel privatim familiariter sese ausit [injun]gere, nedum aequare [. . . a] enim huiusmodi familiaritas contemptum parit.

[13] 6 Ante januam gymnasii nemo consistito, aut antequam conveniatur aut postquam dimissi fuerint studiosi, imprimis etiam diebus dominicis a concione ne coram foribus nostris studiosi conspiciantur aut colloquia agitentur cum in preterentium animis scandalum hoc creet, gymnasio scilicet non studiosos intus literis exerceri quos ociosos pro foribus stare publice aut errones plateas obambulare vident qui *igitur* in hoc deliquerit vapulato.

[14] 7 Nemo matulos per fenestras exonerato.

[15] 8 Aditus publicos ne urina aut sordibus *ne* conspurcanto itaque in janua ostiis scholarum aut locis publicis et conspectui omnium expositis nemo urinam reddito. *Secus faciens publice luito.*

[16] 9 Horti aut accademiae muros nemo transilito qui secus faxit publice ab omnibus preceptoribus vapulato.

[17] 10 Omnes intra septa accademiae cubanto qui nocte aliqua *manserit* emanserit publice vapulato saepius sic peccans accademia omni exulato.

[18] 11 Nulli extraneo intra gymnasium cum studiosis versari aut cubiculo inibi frui fas esto.

[9] *Concerning gowns, to be impressed on the students at all times.* Let all our students wear gowns, as also hats or caps, of black. They are to have have gowns that are not ample or loose but must put them on in a seemly fashion on their admittance. And in their dress, in public and in private, let them strive for refinement, neatness and cleanliness. Those who do otherwise, [unless] they have submitted to the admonishment of their teachers, are to be punished.*

*'They . . . punished', crossed out.

[10] Let none of the students grow his hair. Hair that is too thick and feminine attire are unbecoming in a man, unless he wishes to be taken for a flamboyant or foppish knight; in the same way, therefore, they bring shame and disgrace on students.

[11] He who does not rise to each and all of the teachers of the gymnasium and bare his head to them with reverence, who slanders them or acknowledges them irreverently in word or gesture, let him atone for it immediately; and likewise, he who does not show the respect due to ministers of the city, the magistrates, his parents and elders. Let him by his punishment cleanse the stain with which he has marked students, who are usually well esteemed in the observance of good manners, [. . .] And let them expect the same, who presume to harm or harass by word or deed any of the citizens or tradesman or their sons, servants or household, in order that all our students may learn to live in peace and love not only with themselves but with others.

[12] Let [no-one] dare to [impose himself on his] teachers in a familiar way [either] in public or in private, still less act as if he were their equal, [for] familiarity of this kind produces contempt.

[13] Let no-one stand in front of the door of the gymnasium, either before assembly or after the students have been dismissed. In particular, furthermore, on Sundays after the sermon students are not to be seen before our doors or to hold conversations, since this will cause outrage in the minds of passers-by; namely, that at the gymnasium they see not students inside intent upon their books but idlers standing in front of the door in public or vagrants roaming public places. He who transgresses in this, therefore, is to be beaten.

[14] 7 Let no-one empty chamber-pots through the windows.

[15] 8 They must not defile the public approaches with urine or filth. And so let no-one urinate in the main doorway or the entrances to the schools or in places that are public and exposed to everyone's view. Let anyone doing otherwise pay the penalty in public.

[16] 9 Let no-one climb over the walls of the garden or the academy. He who does otherwise, let him be beaten in public by all the teachers.

[17] 10 All students are to pass the night within the bounds of the academy. He who stays out on any night is to be beaten in public. He who offends in this way frequently, let him be expelled from the entire academy.

[18] 11 It shall be impermissible for anyone from outside to stay with the students inside the gymnasium or have the use of a bedroom there.

[19] 12 Sacras conciones omnes studiosi singuli pleno agmine *et ordine* adeunto diebus operariis tertio, dominico vero secundo signo dato, eodem die dum ab omnibus conveniatur novi testamenti greci publica interpretatio esto. Qui sacrum hoc excer[ci]ium clamore garritu discursu aut quavis irreverentia violaverit cras vapulato.

[20] 13 In templum summa cum modestia et gravitate omnes uno agmine eunto et una ingrediuntor. Finita concione pomeridiana die dominico studiosi in accademiam *omnes* redeunto et in schola publica vel privata prout preceptoribus videbitur commodum concionum eo die habitarum rationem reddere parati sunto.

[21] 14 In templum euntes aut quotiescunque sive cum funere sive alias in publicum prodeuntes sine colloquii murmure, strepituque decore *et ordine* omnes incedant, ut studiosorum accademiae gravitas morumque civilitas potius quam levitas ulla populo spectanda preponatur inter eundum coetum nemo *nulli* deserant in templum ingressi sedes *solitas in solio* solummodo vacuas et humiliores capescant ut nec magistratuum civium seniorumve loca invadant. Nudo capite et aperto, dei verbum, audiant *aut alias similiter* nec semel collocati discurrere alio aut ullatenus exire presumant qui in horum aliquo a preceptore aut censorum aliquo deficere notabitur cras publice penas dato.

[22] 15 Supellectilem cubiculi sui salvtam quisque prestato si quis ostio fenestris mensae tecto fulcris lecto aut id genus aliis [vim] dederit aut horum aliquid alio transportarit aut quavis ratione violarit, duplum damni solvito priusquam promotione ulla gymnasii frui liceat *predem et vadimonium idcirco initio prestato.*

[23] 16 Locarium.* Locarium in introitu pro cubiculo solvito, marcam quottanis.

*In margin.

[24] 17 Qui templi aut gymnasii tectum, pinnacula ostia fenestras vitreas violare aut ostiorum seras revellere parietes lapide iacto ferire, cultelo aut re aliqua comminuere tentaverit penas luito et damnum insuper prestato.

[25] 18 Omnes a cena ad signum campanae magnae quod hora 9 datur in suis cubiculis adsunto ibidem dicta hora ut et mane quottidie hora 5 ab hebdomodario invisantur et ad diligentiam in studiis excitentur, et in dubiis si que monentur juventur instruantur, absentes a cubiculis suis dictis horis [aut . . . res] sed sociis molesti aut ipsi ociosi et ignavi cras puniantur.

[19] 12 Each and every student shall go to hear sacred sermons; in full procession *in class order* at the third bell on work days but at the second bell on Sunday. On Sunday, while all are assembled, there is to be a public exegesis of the Greek New Testament. He who profanes this sacred exercise with noise, chatter, running about or any form of irreverence, is to be beaten the following day.

[20] 13 Let our students go to church with the utmost modesty and dignity in one procession and enter it together. When the afternoon sermon on Sunday is finished, let *all* students return to the academy and let them be prepared to give an account, in the public school or their classrooms as seems fitting to their teachers, of the sermons they have heard that day.

[21] 14 When going to the church or whenever they go out in public either in a funeral procession or on other occasions, all students are to proceed without the murmur of conversation and without noise, with dignity *and in class order*; so that dignity and civility in the behaviour of the students of the academy may be displayed rather than any levity perceived by the people. None *no members* of the company are to leave it as they process. When they have entered the church they are to take *their usual seats at the lowest level,* only those seats that are empty and in a humble position, so that they do not encroach on the places of the magistrates, the citizens or the elders. Let them hear the word of God with their heads bare and uncovered *and similarly on other occasions.* When they have once been settled in their place, let them not presume to rush off elsewhere or on any account to leave. He who is observed by a teacher or any of the censors to be at fault in any of these things is to be punished in public on the following day.

[22] 15 Let each student be responsible for maintaining the furniture of his bedchamber in good condition. If anyone treats violently the door, windows, table-top, bedposts, bed or anything else of that sort, or removes any of these things anywhere else, or for any reason damages them, he is to pay double the cost of the damage before he is allowed to enjoy any advancement in the gymnasium. *For that reason he shall give a bond and pledge at the beginning.*

[23] 16 Rent of bedchambers.* Let the student at his entrance pay the sum of one mark annually for his bedchamber.

*In margin.

[24] 17 He who tries to damage the roof, pinnacles, doors and glazed windows of the church or the gymnasium or force the locks from the doors, strike the walls with a stone he has thrown, damage them with a knife or anything else is to be punished and pay the cost of the damage in addition.

[25] 18 Let all be present in their bedchambers after supper at the signal from the great bell, which is given at nine o'clock, and at the aforesaid hour as also at 5 am daily they are to be visited there by the hebdomadar and encouraged to be diligent in their studies, and advised, helped and instructed in matters where they have doubts, if any. Those who are absent from their rooms at the aforesaid times [or who . . .] but are troublesome to their room-mates or are idle and lazy are to be punished the following day.

[26] Hepdomadario in visitatione ullatenus molestus aut inobediendus cras ab omnibus preceptoribus publice luito.*

*In margin.

[27] 19 Hora sexta matutina ut et vespertina ad scholam publicam pulsetur, ibidem cum hepdomadario preceptores reliquos omambulare [obambulare] volumus, ut cuique ex studiosa juventute libeat, liceat quoque difficiliora quaeque expiscari, hinc nomina citari, absentes inspiciente hebdomodario in catalogum a censore referri, tandemque preces celebrari convenit, qui sacrum excertitium discursu a loco in locum jurgiis clamore strepitu pedum luminum extinctione aut quavis irreverentia violare aut interrumpere ausit instanter publice ab omnibus preceptoribus luito.

[28] 20 Precibus finitis mane summa cum modestia in scholas singuli suas secedant ubi per quartam [*iii*] horae partem lectione partis bibliorum et observatione locorum preceptores singuli suos excerceant* tum in cursu suo doceant dictentque quae opus sunt intermittentes diebus sacrarum concionum tertio signo dato.

*'ubi . . . exerceant', marked 'delete'.

[29] Eandem lectionem, hora 10 *undecima* cursus ipsi preceptores semel repetant et examinent denuo ab hora *sesqui* quarta pomeridiana in sesquiquintam *sextam*, ignarum lectionis in sua schola puniat instanter sine venia saepius vero in ignorantia deprehensum nec quicquam admonitionibus proficientem in publicum producat ut a gymnasiarcha palam coarguatur et vapulet.*

*Marked 'delete'.

[30] Ut vero faelicius procedant repetiones [repetitiones] studiorum et collaciones clascem singuli preceptores suam pro discipulorum numero in factiones et tribus dividant duobus aut tribus uno praefecto qui socios ingenio et industria precedat eosque in lectionum repetione, dubiorum solutione juvet et omnino in studiorum ratione et cursu promoveat.*

*Marked 'delete' and crossed out.

[31] 21 Fiat in singulis ordinibus aut preceptoris constitutione aut sortium judicio catalogus nominum ordine eorum qui lumina per vices sociis suppeditare in scholis debeant item eorum qui diebus saturni publice declamare debeant aut theses tueri qui catalogus extet in loco publico affixus, tam in schola publica quam privata.

[26] He who is in any way troublesome or disobedient towards the hebdomadar in the course of his rounds, shall undergo punishment from all the teachers the following day in public.*

*In margin.

[27] 19 At six o'clock in both the morning and evening let the students be summoned by the bell to the public school. We wish that the remaining teachers, together with the hebdomadar should walk there with them, in order that each young student who wishes may be at liberty to enquire about any things which they find particularly difficult. After this, it is time for the roll to be called, for those who are absent, under the eye of the hebdomadar, to be entered in the register by the censor, and finally for prayers to be said. He who dares to profane or interrupt the sacred exercise by running hither and thither, by quarrelling, shouting, making a noise with his feet or putting out the lights or any sort of irreverent behaviour, shall undergo punishment from all the teachers immediately in public.

[28] 20 When morning prayers are finished, let the students disperse individually with the utmost propriety to their own schools, where for a quarter *a third part* of an hour let each teacher exercise his students with a reading of part of the bible and a discussion of topics arising from it.* Then they are to teach their course and dictate what is necessary, stopping on the days of sacred sermons at the third bell.

*'where . . . from it', marked 'delete'.

[29] At 10 *11* o'clock the teachers of the course are to repeat the same lesson once and examine their students again from 4 *30* to 5.30 *6 pm*. The teacher shall punish immediately, without leniency, any student in his school who does not know the lesson. He shall produce in public, however, any student who is found to be ignorant on a number of occasions and who has not learned anything from his admonishments, in order that his fault may be publicly exposed by the gymnasiarch and that he may be beaten.*

*Marked 'delete'.

[30] In order, however, that repetitions and collations of studies may proceed more fruitfully, every teacher is to divide his class according to the number of pupils into groups and sets, with one student, who surpasses his class-fellows in intelligence and industry, set over two or three of them, and this student shall help them in the repetition of the lessons and in resolving problems and generally bring them on in the matter and course of their studies.*

*Marked 'delete' and crossed out.

[31] 21 There is to be in every class an alphabetical list of names, either decided by the teacher or established by lot, of those who should supply lights in turn for their class-fellows in the schools; likewise of those who should give declamations in public or defend theses on Saturdays. This list shall be prominently displayed in a public place in both the public and private school.

[32] 22 Cui munus candelas suppeditandi incumbit si ea hora venia impetrata absit *curet lumina relinqui ordini suo et per aliquem sociorum eius loco exhiberi si vero huius officii sibi incumbentis immemor abierit tum ordine sequens et cetera ut hic est [scriptum]* ordine sequens sine dilacione eius vices suppleat et privatim et publice quod si in scholam publicam postquam signo vocati sint absque lumine ingrediantur [pub]lice luant, cui vero ea septimana declamandi onus incumbit ei nulla ratione venia absentiae a preceptorum ullo detur aut [si] perigrinandi fas fiat in quatuor *sex* ad minimum ante diebus sequentem se ordine moneat publice ut vices suas in declamando obeat qui si sic admonitus officio desit luat si vero qua ratione thesium tentorem [tentatorem] *propugnatorem* avocari hora disputacionis contingat quilibet [sociorum sive dux] iussu preceptoris respondentis partes [. . .]

[33] 23 Die saturni mane precibus finitis in ordinibus singulis ab ordinariis habeantur publicae declamationes de honesta *honesta* necessaria aut utili aliqua materia quas memoria recitent actone [actione] oratoria exornent, libroque ad id comparato inscriptas preceptori offerant ut eius chirographo et signo publico notentur ne iteracione fucum faciant. *Preceptores qui recitationi intersunt si quid in puritate dictionis sit delictum a declamatore de eo eum coarguant et rectius instruant eius item eius in actione oratoria et elocutione defectum diligenter ei notent et de eodem admoneant ut vice sequenti in his omnibus rectius et ex arte se gerat. Ubi placide errores defectusque suos sic ab audientibus didicerit emendationis proxima declamatio argumentum faciat et testimonium sit.*

[34] Nemo interim in preceptorem socium civem aut perigrinum invectiva oratione uti presumat in vitia non personas bachari permittimus qui secus fecerit publice luito easdemque penas dato qui declamandi munus cum ad se ordine venerit absentia detrectarit aut quavis ratione non legittime *non* implerit.

[35] Has declamationes ordinarias auspicari quottannis volumus secundo *tertio* die saturni mensis novembris et concludi secundo die saturni mensis julii.

[36] 23* A quibus declamationibus summos ad cursus repetionem felicius instituendam post primum diem saturni mensis aprilis liberamus ad quem etiam diem usque primos seu tyrones ab eodem officio immunes esse permittimus qui tamen post eum diem summorum in declamando vices suppleant imposterum.

*sic.

[37] Disputationes singulis sabbathi[s] publicae instituuntor*

*In margin.

[32] 22 If he whose duty it is to provide candles has permission to be absent at that time, *he must ensure that the lights are left for his class and displayed by one of his class-fellows in his place. If, however, he goes off, forgetting the responsibility imposed upon him, then the next in order, etc as it is written here* the next in order is to take his turn without delay, both in private and in public. But if they should enter the public school without a light after they are summoned by the bell, they are to be punished for it [in public]. To the student, however, on whom is imposed the task of declaiming that week leave of absence is on no account to be given by any of the teachers or, [if] permission to travel should be given, let that student warn the next to him in order, in public, at least four *six* days beforehand, that he should appear in his place to declaim; if the student who is advised in this way should fail in his duty, he is to be punished. If, however, it should happen for some reason that the student who is to attack *defend* theses is called away at the time of a disputation, anyone from among his class-fellows [or their leader] by order of the teacher, [may take] the part of respondent.

[33] 23 On Saturday after morning prayers are finished, public declamations are to be held in each class by class members on some worthy, needful or useful subjects. The students are to recite these from memory, embellish them with oratorical gestures and give them to their teacher written in a book obtained for that purpose, in order that the declamations may be annotated with his signature and public mark, lest students should act fraudulently by repeating them. *If anything should be lacking in the purity of the diction of the student who gives the declamation, the teachers who are present at the recitation shall explain it to him and instruct him in the correct way. Likewise, if there is anything wrong with his oratorical gestures and delivery, they are to take care to draw his attention to it and admonish him about it, in order that on the next occasion he should conduct himself in all these things in a more correct fashion and as the art requires. When the student has quietly learned his errors and failings in this way from those who are listening to him, his next declamation shall be proof of his improvement and bear witness to it.*

[34] Let no-one, meanwhile, presume to use abusive language against a teacher, a class-fellow, a citizen or stranger. We permit students to inveigh against vices not people. He who does otherwise shall be punished in public and the same penalties shall be imposed on one who, when the task of declaiming comes to him in turn, refuses it by absenting himself or for some other reason does not discharge it according to the rule.

[35] We wish these class declamations to begin each year on the second *third* Saturday of the month of November, and to end on the second Saturday of the month of July.

[36] 23* We release the highest class from these declamations after the first Saturday of the month of April so that it can work more fruitfully on the revision of its course. Also we permit students of the first class, or beginners, to be exempt from that duty until the same day; after that day, however, they are to take the place of the highest class in declaiming thereafter.

*sic.

[37] Let public disputations be organised every Saturday.*

*In margin.

[38] Quo melius etiam lingua latina apud nos efflorescat statuimus ut preter ordinarias dierum saturni declamatiunculas quatuor celebres et elaboratae declamationes utriusque quottannis fiant pastoribus magistratu adeoque omnibus viris doctis publico programmate ad eas audiendas invitatis incipiant duo e summa clasce hoc prestare ad festum divi Martini pro et contra in eadem materia perorare unusque eiusdem clascis theses in schola public*a* de auditis contra quosvis opponentes asserere et tutari conabitur secundum publicum specimen exercitii suum, tertiae clascis studiosi tribus post mensibus edant, scilicet secundo februarii secundarii vero suum specimen edant ultima septimana mensis aprilis et primi mense julio in fine qui finitis declamationibus suis vice disputationis sint singuli ad interpretandum quamvis sorte oblatam partem novi testamenti aut Isocratis libro ad periculum faciendum prefectus [profectus] eorum [ab] episcopo aut urbis prefecto porrecto explorent vero preceptores diligenter priusquam in publicum suos producent eorum in pronunciando adeoque declamando actionem oratoriam eamque in quibus opus est juvent et promovent [pre] promoveant et instruant [. . .] ut etiam predicta facilius et felicius a studiosis agantur, ut singulae clasces quaque septimana ter partem aliquam probati autoris a suis preceptoribus sibi praelectam habeant volumus et ordinamus audiant primi ex Salustio et epistolis Ciceronis familiaribus aut ex Plinii epistolis secundarii Florum audiant et ex ipso Livio commentarium petant hinc in fine anni Chronicon Carionis aut Sleidanum de monarchis tertii officia Ciceronis tractent hinc Senecam perlustrent summi Plinii naturalem historiam et Senecam semper ob oculos habeant habeantque singuli studiosi chartacios suos libellos in quibus fruses [fruges] linguae latine que toto anno vel docendo vel legendo occurrunt similia item gnomas et oraciones suas accipiant.*

*Marked ‘delete’ and crossed out.

[39] Post lectiones doctas studiosi in *cubiculis* clascibus suis et scholis privatis se contineant, maxime a 10 in duo*un*decimam et a secunda pomeridiana in *sesqui*quartam.*

*Marked ‘delete’.

[40] Estate etiam volumus et ordinamus ut omnes studiosi a cena hora 8 in schola publica conveniant ut de auditis quotidie placide tunc inter se disputent vel seorsim saltem in suis scholis a preceptoribus exerceantur, quos eadem etiam hora interresse par est absens a cetu publico aut suorum dicta hora luat.*

*Marked ‘delete’ and crossed out.

[41] 24 Dies nostris ad ludendum ordinarii in septimana hi tres sint dies lunae, mercurii, veneris, ludatur, singulis dictis diebus si faverit coelum a meridie a secunda in quartam in arenis, *iisdem publice* ab hepdomadario emittantur qui studiosis in arenas comitetur colludat eosdemque reducat prodeuntium nomina in campis citantur redeuntium ad posticam gymnasii *non certabunt pecuniam aut potu ullatenus.*

[38] In order that the Latin language should flourish even better amongst us, we order that in addition to the minor class declamations on Saturdays, there are to be four solemn, formal declamations by each class annually, which the ministers, magistrates and indeed all educated men should be invited by public proclamation to hear. Two students from the highest class shall begin this undertaking at the feast of St Martin, speaking for and against on the same topic, and one student from the same class will attempt to assert and defend theses based on what he has heard in the public school against any opponents. Students of the third class shall perform their second public demonstration of the exercise three months afterwards, namely on the second of February. The students of the second class, however, shall perform their demonstration in the last week of the month of April and the students of the first class at the end of the month of July. These students, when their declamations have finished, in place of a disputation, shall each interpret some part of the New Testament, chosen by lot, or from a book of Isocrates offered by the bishop or the provost of the town to test their progress. The teachers, before they put their students forward, shall carefully examine their oratorical delivery in diction and equally in declamation and give help, encouragement and instruction where it is needed. In order that the aforesaid exercises should be performed with greater ease and success by the students, we wish and ordain that every class should have lectures on some part of an approved author from its teacher three times a week. Let the students of the first class hear readings from Sallust and the letters of Cicero Ad Familiares or from the letters of Pliny. The students of the second class shall hear Florus and from Livy himself they are to look for a commentary, and after this the Chronicon of Carion or Sleidan's De Monarchis. Students of the third class shall deal with Cicero's De Officiis and hereafter go through Seneca. Students in the highest class are to have the Natural History of Pliny and Seneca forever before their eyes, and each student is to have a notebook of paper in which he is to collect the fruits of the Latin language that present themselves throughout the year either in what he is taught or in his reading, likewise similes, maxims and his own prayers.*

*Marked 'delete' and crossed out.

[39] After the taught lessons the students are to remain together in their *bedchambers* classes and private schools especially from 10 to twelve *eleven* and from two pm to *half-past* four.

[40] In addition, we wish and ordain that in summer all students should assemble in the public school after supper at 8 o'clock in order that they may then discuss quietly among themselves what they have heard each day or should at least be given individual work in their schools by their teachers, who should also be present at that time; he who is absent from the public assembly or his class at the aforesaid time is to be punished.*

*Marked 'delete' and crossed out.

[41] 24 The usual games days for our students in the week are to be these three, Monday, Wednesday, Friday. There are to be games on each of the aforesaid days, when the weather is favourable, in the afternoon from two until four on the Links. The students are to be sent out *on these days in public* by the hebdomadar, who is to accompany them to the Links, join in their games and lead them back. Let the names of those who go out be called over on the playing-fields; let the names of those returning be taken at the back gate of the gymnasium. *They will not under any circumstances play for money or drink.*

[42] 25 Nostri colludant omnes una euntes et redeuntes sponsui omni cum veteranis interdicimus nostris, solitum etiam studiosis nostris campum occupent solummodo nec ultra tentent aut aggrediantur.

[43] [. . .]modo adhuc [vidi] ludendi genus legibus vetitum vale [. . .] induci [. . .] apud nos tolerandum sit *nam bona consuetudo excutere debet quod malo introduxit.**

*In margin, crossed out.

[44] Adsint in campis pilae pedales duae a primis ut moris est suspeditande usque ad medium mensis maii *dumtaxat* nec ultra harum una serviat natu maioribus qui promiscue ex omnibus ordinibus ad primam sponsionem et certamen eligantur altera minoribus et junioribus qui inter primos cui suarum erit partus in pila suspeditanda defuerit a reditu publice luat.* *Nullus pilam praeter alienare summos alienare presumat usque [ruinam].*

*'Adsint . . . luat', crossed out.

[45] Qui campanam iniussus pulsarit funem involverit aut in altu miserit petulantie penas publice luito.*

*In margin.

[46] 26 Qui inter summos primos ad lusum impetrandum protruserit aut ullatenus molestiam iis exhibuerit aut inter ludendum verberibus acceperit publice vapulato, similiterque qui ultra quam unam dictarum pilarum eamque quae maxime detrita et inidonea fuerit idque sub finem solum quatuordecim dierum alienare quibusvis praesumpserit aut tentarit poenas publice ab omnibus preceptoribus dato.*

*'similiterque . . . dato', marked 'delete' and crossed out.

[47] Tantum singulis diebus octo distribuere liceat eamque grammatico.*

*In margin.

[48] A communibus et statutis campis nemo aliorsus ingrediatur.*

*In margin.

[49] 27 Nunquam nostris de vicinae accademiae preceptoribus aut discipulis male loqui aut eosdem ulla ratione calumniari permittimus sed volumus ut honorifice iis passim loquantur et sensiant nec enim ii sumus qui ex aliorum infamia nobis famam queramus, nec ullam nobis cum iis nisi de virtute et honore contentionem intercedere patimur hanc tamen non temere a discipulis excitari aut suscipi permittimus sed in presentione dominorum et preceptorum qui disputacionem moderantur ne a verbis ad verbera ut moris *eorum* fuit procedatur.

[42] 25 Our students shall have games together, all of them going out and returning in a single body. We forbid our students to enter into any match with experienced players. In addition, they shall occupy only their usual playing-field and not attempt to go beyond it.

[43] [I have recently seen a kind of game hitherto forbidden by our laws . . . let it be tolerated among us] *for good practice must drive out what it has introduced by mischance.**

*In margin, crossed out.

[44] There are to be on the playing-fields two footballs, supplied by the students in the first class as is the custom, until the middle of the month of May *only* and not beyond. Of these, one shall be for the use of those who are of higher birth, who are to be drawn from all the classes irrespectively for the first game; the other for those who are of lesser birth and for the younger boys. The student in the first class who is entrusted with obtaining their footballs and fails to supply the ball is to be punished in public after their return.* *Let no student other than a member of the highest class presume to dispose of a ball until . . . it is in a dilapidated condition.*

*'There are . . . return', crossed out.

[45] He who rings the bell without being ordered to, coils up the rope or puts it high up out of mischief, is to be penalised in public.*

*In margin.

[46] 26 He among the fourth class who pushes aside students of first class in order to get a game or causes them trouble or uses violence while playing is to be beaten in public, and likewise he who presumes or tries to dispose of one of the said balls to anyone, other than one in very bad condition and unsuitable for use and that only at the end of a fortnight, shall be given penalties by all the teachers in public.

[47] On <u>eight</u> single days only, the grammarian is to distribute [dispose of] it.*

*In margin.

[48] Let no-one trespass from the common and specified playing-fields to any other place.*

*In margin.

[49] 27 We do not ever permit our students to speak ill of the teachers or pupils of the neighbouring academy or to accuse them falsely for any reason, but we wish that they should speak and think of them honourably everywhere, for we are not men to seek our news from the gossip of others; nor do we suffer any dispute to occur between us and them unless it concerns virtue and honour. We do not, however, permit a dispute of this sort to be aroused or undertaken rashly by our pupils except in the presence of masters and teachers, who are to moderate the argument lest it should proceed from words to blows as has been the custom amongst them.

[50] 28 In gymnasio aut cubiculis ludere aleis foliis lusoriis capitale esto, similiter studiosis nostris in tabernis conspici aut in cellis bibentes deprehendi aut hieme noctu plateas oberrantes conspici, post unam admonicionem ejectio e gymnasio pena esto.

[51] *Ne ex turpiter loquendi licentia turpiter faciendi impudentia sequatur* domi vetamus studiosos nostros cum ancillis culinariis aut scurris misceri anilibus fabulis aut profanis colloquiis aut cantilenis recitandis indulgere sed statim ac a mensa cum gratiarum actione et morum civilitate se subduxerint in cubicula sua recta intra gymnasium sese recipere eos volumus et ibidem studiis operam dare donec horae ordinariae eos vocent.

[52] In mensa non nisi rogati et de rebus quas probe sciant loquantur senioribus et dignioribus cedant et in omnibus civilitatis et urbanitatis atque officii curam diligentem agant cum turpe *sit* studioso et literas profitenti in hisce ab idiotis et plebeis aut superari aut notari et vere dictum ut habeant qui proficit in literis et deficit in moribus plus deficit quam proficit quare probent re et opere ipso omnes se diligenter didicisse quos decet in mensa eandem curam gestus incessus et verborum habeant cum in plateiis conspiciuntur.

[53] 29 Pro disciplinae nostrae observatione commodiore constituatur singulis septimanis publicus censor et tabularum custos is omnium nomina citet quater quotidie mane hora 6 ante preces vesperi eadem hora, horis item 10 et secunda, absentes fideliter notet et die saturni aut lunae gymnasiarc[h]ae deferat vernacule loquentes etiam jurantes et rixas inter studiosos excitantes errones etiam et discurrentes per aream aut cubicula gymnasii *et templum*.

[54] Delatus in septimana semel absens [*aut*] luat palma simpliciter *aut assem solvat* bis vero delatus utroque *2o asses* ter venia non impetrata corpore luat publice, veniae vero impetratae argumentum sit chyrographum preceptoris aut viva vox dumtaxat.

[55] Jurantes semel luant palma *aut asse multentur* bis asse *assibus 2* multentur ter corpore luant vulgariter loquentium eadem sit ratio.

[56] 30 Sint et in singulis clascibus censores qui de iisdem deferant die censurae et privata crimina que quotidie occurrunt in clasce apud suum preceptorem privatim in dies deferant et absente quavis hora preceptore exeundi sociis potestatem faciat*, garrulos ociosos aut sociis molestos notet.

*'et absente . . . faciat', marked 'delete'.

[50] 28 It shall be a most serious offence to play at dice or cards in the gymnasium or in bedchambers, likewise for our students to be seen in taverns or to be caught drinking in back rooms or to be seen wandering the streets at night in winter. After one warning, the penalty shall be expulsion from the gymnasium.

[51] *Lest from licence to speak in an unseemly manner, licence to behave in a shameless fashion should follow* We forbid our students when at home to associate with kitchenmaids or clowns, or to indulge in telling old wives' tales, talking together profanely or singing popular songs. Instead, we wish that as soon as they have left the table with thanksgiving and in a civilised manner, they should retire to their appropriate bedchambers within the gymnasium and there devote themselves to their studies until it is time for their classes.

[52] At table students are not to speak unless they have been asked a question and then only of things they know well; they are to yield to their elders and superiors; and in all things let them pay careful attention to civility, refinement and morality, since *it is* shameful for a student and one professing learning either to be outdone in such behaviour or observed in the breach of it by fools and common people and that they should consider it a true saying, 'he who is proficient in learning and deficient in manners lacks more than he gains'. They must therefore show by actual practice that they whom it so behoves have carefully learned to show at table the same attention to gesture, deportment and conversation that they display where they are on view in public places.

[53] 29 For greater convenience in the observance of our regulations a public censor and keeper of the register shall be appointed each week. Let him call the names of all the students four times each day, at 6 am, at the same time in the evening before prayers, likewise at 10 o'clock and 2 o'clock. Let him note faithfully those who are absent and report [them] on Saturday or Monday to the gymnasiarch, together with those who speak in the vernacular, those who swear and cause quarrels among the students, those who wander off and also those who run about in the courtyard <u>or</u> the bedchambers of the gymnasium *and the church.*

[54] He who is reported absent once in the week <u>shall be punished simply with [a stroke on] his palm</u> *or pay one penny.* He who is reported twice shall pay *2 pennies* for each occasion. He who is reported three times, where permission was not obtained, let him be punished corporally in public; proof that permission has been obtained should be in writing, signed by the teacher, or simply by word of mouth.

[55] Let those who swear once be punished on ther palm *or be fined one penny.* Let those who do so twice, be fined <u>a penny</u> *2 pennies.* Let those reported three times be punished corporally. Let the same scale apply to those speaking in the vernacular.

[56] 30 There shall be also in every class censors to report on the classes on censoring day. And they shall report private offences which occur daily in class to their teacher in private each day. And, in the absence of the teacher at any time, the censor shall grant permission to his class-fellows to go out of the college.* The censor shall note those who chatter, who are idle or annoy their class-fellows.

*'And, in . . . college', marked 'delete'.

[57] 31 Sit et quottannis publicum omnium ordinum examen de profectu in literis studiosorum, huic totum mensem octobris qui a reditu primus est tribuimus, omnibus tandem *sigillatim* examinatis exeat preceptorum de singulis censura qui industriam suam et profectum in hoc examine praeceptoribus non probaverit in eadem adhuc clasce maneto aut si qua ratione pretervolarit detrudatur a quarta in tertiam a tertia in secundam a secunda in primam clascem denuo.

[58] 32 Qui a calendis octobris accademiae defuerit pro singulis absenciae suae diebus ultra hoc tempus praescriptum duos sollidos aerario gymnasii pendat antequam recipiatur nec in clascem admittatur nisi examinatus cuius examen pro dilacione eo severius sit [bell . . . sit] pecunia in reparatione scholarum impendatur quas quottanis magis magisque exornari par est.*

*In margin.

[59] Primi seu tyrones nulli admittantur nisi quos digna prehabita in resolucione probatorum tum oratorum tum poetarum e latino in vulgarem sermonem et composione [composicione] e vulgari in latinum examinatione ad id idoneos preceptorum omnium concensus [probarit].

[60] Primi examinatoribus sex solidos et octo denarios sigillatim pendant, secundi marcam, tertii viginti solidos summi trigenta *aut potius omnis clascis quisque marcam summi in fine anni 30 40 solidos.**

*'Primi . . . trigenta', marked 'delete' and crossed out.

[61] Librorum singulis clascibus docendorum ratio et numerus sic se habent. Audiant primi institutiones lingue graece Cleonardi selectas aliquot oraciones Isocratis et Demosthenis *Zenophontis Cyropaideiam aut eiusdem autoris [partem aliam] ex Aeschina [. . . ro] [historieque] ex Herodoto Thucid [. . .] [Hesiodi] prout a senatu a[lmae] a[cademiae] academico ordinabitur* dialogos Luciani tabulam Zebetis ex Homero libros duos vel alterum ex Pindaro *Euripide* et novum testamentum grece eo anno totum horis matutinis et diebus dominicis percurrant sub finem anni dialecticam Rami et die dominico sacram lectionem ex Catechesi Ursini aut simili.

[62] Secunda clascis post praxin inventionis et indicii et retoricam Talei et tractatum de forensi *audiant*, praxin autem petendam e latinis ex oracione aliqua Ciceronis e grecis ex Demosthene [aut contio quem senatus academiae] prescribet post inquam hanc praxin que fiet tribus primis mensibus reliquo anni audiant organum logicum Aristotelis integrum si fieri poterit si quid sit omittendum sint libri posteriora analitica et die dominico habeant sibi explicata acta apostolorum.*

*'Secunda . . . mensibus, die . . . apostolorum,' marked 'delete' and crossed out.

[57] 31 Let there also be each year a public examination of all classes concerning the students' proficiency in learning; for this we have allotted the whole of the month of October, the first after their return. When all the students have finally been examined *individually*, the opinion of the teachers on each student shall be made known. He who has not demonstrated to the teachers his industry and proficiency in this examination, let him remain in the same class as hitherto, or if for any reason he should have slipped through, let him be put down from the fourth to the third class, from the third to the second, from the second to the first again.

[58] 32 He who is not present in the academy after the first of October shall pay for each day that he is absent after this specified time two shillings to the treasury of the gymnasium before he is received there; and let him not be admitted into his class unless he has undergone an examination, which is to be harder according to the length of the delay. The money shall be laid out on the repair of the schools; it is fitting that they should be embellished more and more each year.*

*In margin.

[59] No students of the first class or aspirants shall be admitted except those who have been approved as suitable for admission by the unanimous agreement of the teachers after a proper examination, held beforehand, in the translation first of approved orators then of poets from Latin into the vernacular, and in composition from the vernacular into Latin.

[60] Students of the first class shall each pay six shillings and eight pence to the examiners; students of the second class, a mark; students of the third class, twenty shillings; the highest class, thirty shillings *or rather, each student in each class shall pay a mark, the highest class paying 30 40 shillings at the end of the year.**

*'Students of the first class . . . thirty shillings', marked 'delete' and crossed out.

[61] The apportionment and number of the books to be taught to each of the classes shall take this form. Students of the first class shall have lectures on the Institutions of the Greek Language of Cleonardus, a number of selected orations of Isocrates and Demosthenes, *the Cyropaedia of Xenophon or another part of the same author* [. . .] *from Aeschines and histories from Herodotus, Thucidides* [. . .] [*Hesiod*] *as will be ordained by the Academic Senate of the* [*bountiful academy*], the dialogues of Lucian, the Tabula of Zebetis, two books of Homer or one from Pindar, Euripides. And they shall go through the whole of the New Testament in Greek that year in the morning hours and on Sundays. Towards the end of the year they shall read the Dialectic of Ramus and on Sunday a sacred reading from the Catechism of Ursinus or a similar work.

[62] The second class, after practice in invention and rhetorical proof *shall have lectures on* the Rhetoric of Talaeus and the tract on eloquence. Practice, moreover, is to be sought, in Latin authors, from any oration of Cicero; in Greek, from Demosthenes [or a speech which the Senate of the academy] may prescribe. After, as I say, this practice, which is to take place in the first three months, they are to have lectures in the rest of the year on the Organon Logicum of Aristotle in full, if that is possible; if anything is to be left out, let it be the Posterior Analytics. On Sunday they shall have the Acts of the Apostles expounded to them.*

*'The second . . . months, On Sunday . . . to them', marked 'delete' and crossed out.

[63] Tertia classcis audiat e greco Aristoteli textu selectiores libros *maxime 5 et 6.1.2 et [principium] 3* ethicarum et politicarum Aristoteli officia Ciceronis philosophice tractata geometriam Rami arithmeticam et sub finem anni libros akromatikeis die vero dominico epistolam ad Romanos.

[64] Vel tertii audiant geographiam hebream grammaticam.*

*In margin.

[65] Quarta classcis reliquum phisices ex Aristoteli textum breve insuper anatomiae compendium geographiae similiter et chronologiae astronomiae etiam principia et hebream grammaticam cum aliqua praxi die vero dominico epistolam ad hebreos.

[66] Nota. Audiant insuper omnes die lune hora una lectionem theologicam in schola publica a gymnasiarcha cuius rationem reddere singuli sint parati statuto ab eo tempore.*

*In margin, marked 'delete' and crossed out.

[67] Hi *4ti* sub finem anni examinentur de quadriennii cursu *tam mathematico quam philosophico* theses stato die tueantur de eodem, hinc ad pileum vocentur digni, indigni nulla nec prece nec precio eodem donentur qui examinatorum suffragiis erudicione et morum probitate ceteros precedat in promocione quoque eosdem preeat, nulla generis aut prosapiae racione habita virtuti enim hic honos a nobis paratur non nobilitati, die laureationis admissi ordine suo inducantur prout in publica citacione edicti censurae vocantur et sollenni juramento adstringante [adstringente]. Cuius formula est

[68] Ego N A me confiteor coram deo omnipotente et celebri hoc coetu me orthodoxam catholicam et christianam religionem quae ex puro dei verbo in ecclesia scoticana proponitur ex animo profiteri et promitto me eandem per dei gratiam assistente dei spiritu constanter semper professurum, contra detestari me omnes hereseis vel olim in ecclesiam invectas vel recens [s . . .] *pontificis* Romani tyrrannide natas accademiae [deinde huic] cui hanc ingenii culturam debeo nutricia quantopere potero liberaliter relaturum si fidem fallam deum quem antea testem tunc judicem et vindicem non recuso.

[69] Juramentum.*

*In margin.

[70] Ad examen 4 ann[o] ne admittantur nisi omnibus publicis et privatis muneribus prius satisfecerint preceptorum omnium janitorisque chyrographum pro hoc ostendant, secus ad lapidem ne admittantur, admissi deinde ante omnia iuramento adstringantur hoc se mod-

[63] The third class shall have lectures on the Greek text of Aristotle, the more important books *especially 5 and 6.1.2 and the beginning of book 3* of the Ethics and the Politics of Aristotle, Cicero's De Officiis treated in a philosophical context, the Geometry and Arithmetic of Ramus, and towards the end of the year the Acroamatics. On Sunday, however, the Epistle to the Romans.

[64] Or let students of the third class hear geography, Hebrew grammar.*

*In margin.

[65] The fourth class shall have lectures on the rest of the short text of the Physics from Aristotle and in addition the compendium of anatomy and likewise of geography and the principles of chronology and astronomy and Hebrew grammar with some practice. On Sunday, however, the Epistle to the Hebrews.

[66] Note. In addition, on Monday at one o'clock all the students shall have one lecture in theology by the gymnasiarch in the public school. Let them each individually be prepared to give an account of it at a time fixed by him.*

*In margin, marked 'delete' and crossed out.

[67] These students of the fourth class shall be examined shortly before the end of the year on their four-year course, *both in mathematics and philosophy*. On a pre-determined day they are to defend theses pertaining to the course. Afterwards, those worthy of it shall be called to receive their cap; those who are unworthy shall be given nothing, neither in response to prayers or payment. He who, in the opinion of the examiners, surpasses the other candidates in [learning] and good conduct, shall precede them also when they are promoted irrespective of race or family, for this honour is bestowed by us for virtue not for rank. On the day of laureation, the students who have been admitted shall be inducted in their order as they are named in the public proclamation of the report of examiners' judgement and bound with a solemn oath. The wording of this oath is:

[68] I N A confess before almighty God and this distinguished assembly that I sincerely profess the orthodox catholic and Christian religion which, in accordance with the pure word of God, is set forth in the Scottish church, and I promise that I will always profess it through the same grace of God, with the constant assistance of the spirit of God; conversely, that I abhor all heresies, either those introduced into the church in former times or those recently [. . .] sprung from the despotic rule of the Roman pontiff. And next that I will liberally give back to [this] academy to which I owe the cultivation of my mind, as much support as I can. If I should break my faith, I do not refuse that God, formerly my witness, should then be my judge and punish me.

[69] The oath.*

*In margin.

[70] No students shall be admitted to the examination in the fourth year unless they have first paid the public and private dues of all the teachers and the janitor. They shall show a written receipt for this, otherwise they shall not be admitted to the stone. Next, those

estiam in respondendo polliceri et contentos fore eo loco quem iis preceptores assignabunt nec violaturos eos [se] censurae ordinem die laureacionis.*

*In margin.

[71] A laurea donatis convivia nulla agitentur sed gratitudinis suae [ele]emosinen *quatuor . . . ad minimum libellarum* vel in libris relinquant bibliothece gymnasii vel in pecunia pro sua sorte et arbitrio aerario nostro ad tecta resarcienda.*

*Either the whole entry or '*quatuor . . . libellarum*' is marked 'delete'.

[72] Iidem ad exteras regiones profecturi si nostro testimonio ornari desiderent pro sigillo gymnasii viginti solidos *4 libras* solvant ab his omnibus dictis oneribus pauperes immunes sunto.

[73] 34 Solvant singuli studiosi *minoris gradus ab introitu in academiam in primo statim ingressu* preceptori suo quottannis *10 20 marcas ad minimum* didactron quinque libellas idque ad festum pascalis *purificationem Mariae ad festum Martini aut saltem calendas januarii nec ultra prorogetur qui ante hoc tempus discedere conatus fuerit stipendium nihilominus integrum persolvat et primo statim ingressu pridem sistat qui ultra festum purificationis Mariae solutionem distulerit bis monitus a gymnasiarcha publice monitus nomine citetur* potentiores et nobiles *generosi etiam maioris gradus* pro dignitate augeant quum illis liberalitatis modum praescribere nefas sit.

[74] Item pro locario cubiculis *singuli* locario marcam [. . .] *vilioribus pro commodioribus 20 30 ad minimum solidos* ad festum pascatos *idque sub primum introitum* pendant collectori publico quae pecunia in prestandis aedibus gymnasii tectis sartisque impendatur nisi quantum exinde pro janitoris mercede ordinatum est. Collectae vero residuae bona et aequa ratio gymnasiarchae reddatur a collectore quottannis mense antequam dissolvatur accademia.

who have been admitted shall be bound, before all things, by an oath that they promise to be seemly in responding and that they will be content with the place that the teachers assign to them and that they will not violate the order of the examiners' judgement on the day of laureation.*

*In margin.

[71] No feasts shall be held by those who have been laureated but let them leave a token of their gratitude *of . . . at least four pounds* either in books for the library of the gymnasium or in money, according to their condition and judgement, to our treasury for repairing the roofs.*

*Either the whole entry or '*of . . . four poundo*' is marked 'delete'.

[72] Laureated students about to set out for foreign parts, if they should desire to be furnished with our testimonial, shall pay twenty shillings *4 pounds* for the seal of the gymnasium; poor students shall be exempt from all these charges.

[73] 34 Let every student *of minor rank* pay after his entry into the academy *immediately upon his first entry* to his teachers each year *10 20 marks at least* a tuition fee of five pounds and let him pay it at Easter *the Purification of Mary at the feast of Martin or at least the calends of January and let there be no farther extension. He who attempts to leave before this time shall pay the whole sum notwithstanding and shall deliver it beforehand immediately upon his first entry. He who delays payment beyond the feast of the Purification of Mary, having been twice admonished by the gymnasiarch, shall be named in public.* The more highly-born students and the nobility *also gentlemen of higher rank* shall pay more in accordance with their status, since it is wrong to lay down to them the limit of their liberality.

[74] Likewise in rent for their bedchambers *every student* shall pay in rent a mark at Easter [. . .] *for the cheaper kind, for the larger at least 20 30 shillings and they shall pay it around the time of their first entry* to the public collector. Let the money be spent on providing that the buildings of the gymnasium, be kept roofed and in good repair, except as much of it as is decreed for the wages of the janitor. Of the residue of the money collected, however, let a good and fair portion be delivered to the gymnasiarch by the collector each year in the month before the academy disperses.

Notes

[19, 28] 'at the third . . . second bell'. The 'second bell' of the church marked the beginning of the service; the third, beginning of the minister's sermon: Cowan, *Reformation*, 141.

[38] 'from Livy himself'. Presumably after hearing the master lecture on Livy, students would seek out a recommended commentary.

[70] 'to the stone'. For the origin of this expression: Cant, *St Andrews*, 20n.; Durkan and Kirk, *Glasgow*, 92–3.

Appendix II

Laws of the new academy of Aberdeen, undated.
AUL, MS M 391
Edited and translated by Morton A E Gauld and Colin McLaren

For Editorial Note: Appendix I.

TEXT

[1] Leges Novae Academiae Aberdonensis

[2] Cum nulla hominum societas sit que ad equitatem invitari vel in officio contineri potest, si non monitores et censores qui aliis ingenio, authoritate, et morum gravitate praelucent, eam subinde officii moneant et rationem quoque exigant [tum] vel inprimis juventus quam ataxia et aetatis fervor eo impellit ut vel minimum prospiciat pr[o]futura, vel obfutura, his opus habet maxime. Nam quod [quae] alii vel aetate vel rerum adversarum experientia edocti didicerunt, unde se ad aequabilitatem componunt et modestiu[a]m, haec nec per aetatem intelligere, vel per eorum usum animadvertere potest sed effreni licentia in obvia quaeque ruit, eaque amplectitur modo placitura.

[3] Quare prudenter judicarunt judicarunt quibus juventutis instituendae cura commissa fuit, qui eam non tantum institutione ad pietatem et modestiam efformandam, sed et legibus et disciplina in officio continendam et coercendam esse putarunt; ut praemiorum [*spe*] et poenarum metu tanquam stimulis ad ea praestanda excitaretur, ad quae alias institutione et sanis consiliis impelli non potest. Nobis quoque in eandem curam et cogitationem incumbentibus visum est coetum hunc scholasticum legibus et disciplina coercere, ut dum mature sanis consiliis et sanctis actibus assuescit, usus bene vivendi verti possit in naturam. Ea quibus discipulos nostros astringi volumus, partim spectant ordinarios eorum labores, ut progressus in studiis, partim vitam privatam intra academiae septa, partim publicam.

[4] Progressus in studiis gradus suos habeto incrementa et terminum, nam per quatuor ordines intra quadriennium juventus in studiis philosophicis decurrens, proaemio laborum tandem adepto in libertatem se vendicato.

[5] Ordinibus his statae horae praelectionum tum publicarum tum privatarum sunto.

[6] Nullus, qui fidem orthodoxam amplexus non sit et eandem ad ultimum vitae spiritum professurum se se in juramento, chirographo et sacrae caenae perceptione testatum fecerit in academiam recipiator, qui renunciarit ejicitor.

[7] Horae publicarum lectionum et congressuum hae sunto.

[8] Hora sexta matutina post precum celebrationem (quas praecentor totius coetus nomine . . .) gymnasiarcha praelectionem capitis novi testamenti et ca*te*cheticam subjungito.

[9] Precibus vespertinis gymnasiarcha itidem praelectionem capitis novi testamenti praemittito.

[10] Dies mercurii lectioni historicae et chronologicae dicatus esto.

TRANSLATION

[1] Laws of the new academy of Aberdeen.

[2] Since there is no society of men which can be asked to conduct itself justly or held to its duty, if counsellors and judges, outshining others in ability, authority and dignity of conduct, do not admonish it continually in its obligations and also hold it to account, then youth in particular, which indiscipline and the ardour of its age urge on to the point that it does not in the least look to the good or bad to come, especially has need of them. For the things that others have learned, informed by age or the experience of adversity, from which they dispose themselves towards fairness and moderation, youth can neither understand through age or heed through the experience of them but, with freedom of the unbridled, rushes at everything that presents itself and favours only what will give pleasure.

[3] For this reason, those to whom the care of educating youth has been entrusted have judged wisely in supposing that youth can be shaped not only by educating it in piety and moderation but also by holding it to its duty and controlling it by laws and discipline, so that it can be aroused by hope of rewards and fear of punishment, acting as a spur, to excel in those things to which it could not otherwise be impelled by teaching or sound advice. It seems [fitting] to us also, who are dedicated to the same care and concern, to control this academic body by laws and discipline, so that while it matures in sound thinking and pious deeds, the habit of living a moral life may be capable of being converted into a natural disposition. The things by which we wish to bind our pupils concern in part their daily work, such as their progress in their studies, in part their private life within the bounds of the academy, and in part their life outside.

[4] Let progress in studies have its own stages, each building on the one before, and a finishing-point, for let youth, going in its philosophical studies through four classes in a four-year period, having finally obtained the reward for its labours, claim its liberty.

[5] In these classes, there shall be fixed hours of teaching, both public and private.

[6] No student is to be received into the academy who has not embraced the orthodox faith and has testified on oath, in writing and by receiving the holy supper, that he will profess it to the last breath of his life. He who renounces it, is to be expelled.

[7] The hours of public lessons and assemblies shall be as follows.

[8] At 6 am, after the offering of prayers (which the precentor . . . in the name of the entire assembly) the gymnasiarch shall add a reading of a chapter of the New Testament and catechism.

[9] The gymnasiarch shall precede evening prayers with a reading of a chapter of the New Testament in the same way.

[10] Wednesday is to be dedicated to a reading of history and chronology.

[11] Dies sabbati publicis exercitiis declamationum et disputationum totus impenditor.

[12] Reliqui dies, praeter dominicum privatis praelectionibus consecrator [consecrantor].

[13] Prima classis praecepta graecae grammaticae ex Clenardo eorundem praxin ex Isocrate, Demosthene, Platone et aliis addiscito, cum graecis latina ex Cicerone, Salustio et aliis coniungito; in utriusque linguae Genesi subinde exercetor. Sub calendas februarias publicum specimen latinae geneseos declamando exhibeto. Eodem mense et martio rhetoricam ex Talaeo addiscito. A calendis aprilis in calendas augusti in dialecticis quae ex Ramo addiscet exercetor. Cum his perpetuo, et praelectio graeca conjungatur.

[14] Secunda Classis sub reditum examini se subjicito. Geographiam deinde et Aristotelis libellum de mundo addiscito, et in graecis et latinis ad calendas usque Februarias exercetor. Inde in calendas Augusti in Aristotelis organo logico versantor.

[15] Tertiani ingressi examini se denuo subjiciant, ut ubi probarint diligentiam in graecis, latinis, rhetorica et dialectica [p]primo honoris gradu quem baccalau[reatum] vocant ornentur; ornati hoc honore si quid in logicis adhuc superest addiscant; et ad ethicam progrediantur quam ex Aristotele et Ciceronis officiis haurient. Eodem anno acroamaticos Aristotelis libros praeceptor proponito.

[16] Quartani ingressi ante calendas februarii physicam Aristotelis absolvant cum quo Plinii et questionum Fregii praelectionem conjungent. A calendis februarii ad calendas maii arithmeticon et geometriam addisc[a]nt, inde ad calendas augusti doctrinam sphaericam, seu astronomiae rudimenta, et grammaticen hebraeam; in quibus studiis si diligentiam probarint doctoris philosophiae, et artium insigniis ornantor.

[17] Unusquisque socium cum quo praelecta a preceptore repetat sibi adjungito; nullus ex auditorio ante repetitam lectionem digreditor; alterutro in praelectionis exactione ignaro uterque ple[c]tatur.

[18] Preceptori debitam reverentiam ut parenti exhibeto; didactri loco libellas tres sub calendas februarii quotannis pendito.

[19] Intra gymnasium omnes pernoctanto, in [a]bnoctantem severe animadvertito, sub nonam vespertinam signo dato omnes intra gymnasium adsunto, clausis gymnasii januis, praeceptorum unus cubicula invisito, absentem notato. Hora matutina signo dato janitor cubicula adito, et juventutem ad labores excitato.

[11] The whole of Saturday is to be spent in the exercises of declamation and disputation.

[12] The remaining days, Sunday excepted, shall be devoted to private lessons.

[13] The first class shall learn the rules of Greek grammar from Clenardus and the practice of them from Isocrates, Demosthenes, Plato and others, and it shall combine Latin from Cicero, Sallust and others with the Greek authors, and after that it shall have practice in original composition in each of the two languages. Towards the calends of February it shall give a public demonstration of its Latin by declaiming [its compositions]. In the same month and in March it shall learn rhetoric from Taleus. From the calends of April to the calends of August it shall have practice in dialectics, which it should learn from Ramus. The teaching of Greek is constantly to be combined with these.

[14] The second class shall submit itself for examination about the time of its return. Thereafter it shall learn geography and the short book of Aristotle concerning the world, and it shall have practice in Greek and Latin [authors] right up to the calends of February. From then on to the calends of August they shall study the Organon Logicum of Aristotle.

[15] When students of the third class have entered, they are to submit themselves again to examination, in order that when they have demonstrated their industry in Greek authors, Latin authors, rhetoric and dialectic, they may be adorned with the first grade of honour which they call the baccalaureate. Furnished with this honour, they are to learn what, if anything, remains of logic and to proceed to ethics which they should take from Aristotle and Cicero's On Duties. In the same year the teacher shall set before them the Acroamatic books of Aristotle.

[16] When students of the fourth class have entered, they are to complete the physics of Aristotle, with which they will combine the reading of Pliny and the questions of Fregius. From the calends of February to those of May they are to learn arithmetic and geometry; thereafter up to the calends of August the doctrine of the spheres or rudiments of astronomy and Hebrew grammar. If they have demonstrated their diligence in these studies, they shall be adorned with the insignia of a doctor of philosophy and of arts.

[17] Let each and every student join a class-fellow, with whom he should repeat the lessons taught by their teacher. Let no student leave the classroom before the lesson has been repeated. Both are to be punished if either is ignorant when asked to repeat the lesson.

[18] Let the student show due respect to his teacher as if to a parent; let him pay, as a tuition fee, three pounds around the calends of February each year.

[19] Let all spend the night inside the gymnasium; severe steps are to be taken against a student who spends the night outside it. Towards nine pm, when the signal has been given, all are to be present inside the gymnasium; when the doors of the gymnasium have been shut, one of the teachers is to visit the bedchambers; let him note anyone who is absent. At the morning hour, when the signal has been given, the janitor shall go to the bedchambers and rouse the youths to their work.

[20] Intra cubicula et gymnasium mundicies adsit, absint sordes, per fenestras matulas ne ejicito, sed janitorem appellato, publicum locum sordium recipiendarum adito secus mulctator.

[21] Extra gymnasium nisi impetrata venia ne egreditor; omnes intra gymnasium hora decima a jentaculo, et secunda pomeridiana a prandio adsunto; quem, in plateis oberrantem praeceptor, vel censor, vel civis observarit discursationis paenam luito.

[22] Quem censor vernacule loquentem notarit, asse in singulas vices mulctator.

[23] Juventutem in campos horis animi relaxationi constitutis deducito, urbem ne ingreditor; idem in academiam reducito.

[24] Qui condiscipulo vel civi injur injuriam fecerit, pro delicti gravitate paenam luito.

[25] Qui gladio, pugione, bombarda instructus fuerit, armis ipsis mulctator, et ne in juventutem exemplum serpat, paenas praesente academiae decano et urbis consule luito.

[26] Aleae, tesseris vel ejusmodi ludis obnoxium pari paena mulctat[o], non resipiscentem ex academia ejicito.

[27] Is in honoribus academicis primas teneat qui diligentiam in studiis, in tota vita modestiam, et sanctitatem supra condiscipulos probarit.

[28] Ad honores doctoris philosophiae ante anni quarti decursum ne admittitor, nec nisi didactro prius persoluto honore eo ornator.

[29] Pro cubiculis locarii loco, singuli quotannis marcam pendunto quam in cubiculorum ipsorum reparationem praeceptor convertito.

[20] The bedchambers and the gymnasium shall be kept clean, and no filth shall be present. No-one shall empty chamber-pots through the windows but shall call the janitor and the janitor shall go to the public place for the reception of ordure.

[21] No-one shall go out of the gymnasium unless he has first obtained permission. All shall be present inside the gymnasium at ten o'clock after breakfast and at two o'clock after dinner. He whom a teacher or a censor or a citizen sees wandering in public places shall pay the penalty for wandering about.

[22] He whom the censor observes speaking in the vernacular, shall be fined a penny on each occasion.

[23] The censor shall lead the youths into the playing-fields at the times fixed for relaxation of the mind; he shall not go into the town; he shall also bring them back.

[24] He who harms a fellow-pupil or a citizen, let him pay a penalty according to the seriousness of his offence.

[25] He who is armed with a sword, a dagger, a firearm, shall be deprived of the weapons themselves, and lest the example spread to the youths, he shall be penalised in the presence of the dean of the academy and the [provost] of the town.

[26] The teacher shall punish anyone guilty of playing games of chance, with dice or at games of that kind with a fitting penalty. He shall expel from the academy anyone who does not reform

[27] He who demonstrates diligence in his studies, moderation in all aspects of his life and piety exceeding that of his fellow-students, shall hold the first rank in academic honours,

[28] No-one is to be admitted to the honours of doctor of philosophy before completing the fourth year of the course and no-one is to be adorned with that honour unless his tuition fee has been paid beforehand.

[29] Every student shall pay a mark each year as rent for his bedchamber; the teacher shall direct this sum towards the repair of those same rooms.

Notes

[8] A space has been left after 'precentor'.

[13–16] Printed in P J Anderson, ed., *Records of the Arts Class, 1868–72* (Aberdeen, 1882), 232–3.

Appendix III

John Row, Regimen mensae (1657)[1]
AUL MS K 3, pp. 15–17; Innes, *Fasti*, 250–3.
Translated by Morton A E Gauld and Colin McLaren

'Everything in an orderly fashion'.

A set of rules for the table, Christian, salubrious, temperate and honourable. A poem of one hundred lines of epistrophic rhythms of various sorts,[2] elaborated in the Hebraic fashion.

No-one shall eat his food until a blessing has been said.
While you eat, you shall. . . .
. . . not take precedence over a senior.
. . . keep the place assigned to you.
. . . sit at the table assigned to you.
. . . eat with clean, bare hands.
. . . not cover your head and face after uncovering them.
. . . have cheerful countenances.
. . . eat in a proper fashion in company.
. . . take the salt on your knife.
. . . not overturn the saltcellar.
. . . offer cutlery by the handle, not the blade.
. . . take your food in three fingers.
. . . cut it with your knife before rending it with your teeth.
. . . not ask for what should be eschewed[3]
. . . not lick your fingers when they are dirty.
. . . not soil your upper garments.
. . . have a linen napkin in your hand.
. . . clean your knife and fingers with the napkin.
. . . not cut the table linen with your knife.
. . . occupy yourself with your plate not the world.
. . . not sit on anything cold.
. . . not eat uncooked food.
. . . refrain from chattering, we beg you.
. . . show obedience to those in charge of you.
. . . not drink, when swallowing hot foot.
. . . alternate dry and cold food.
. . . set bones down on your plate or
. . . throw them on the floor.
. . . do everything in moderation.
. . . not complain if you are beaten if you throw bones at your companions, nor yet if you hurt them.
. . . not swallow food without chewing it; if you do, you will certainly harm yourselves and you will resemble Molossian hounds.
. . . not pick up something that has been set down, lest you look like the Harpies.
. . . avoid quarrels and mutterings.
. . . not disturb your table companions.
. . . not look sharply at your companions.
. . . sit with your head erect.
. . . keep your eyes on your hands.
. . . sit at the table with your feet still.
. . . not take two successive draughts from your cup.
. . . wipe your lips after swallowing.
. . . drink a moderate amount, but often.
. . . regard your drink with pleasure.
. . . take your cups in three fingers and
. . . say nothing over your cups.

. . . draw your table-companions' attention to the cup-bearer.
. . . not fill your cup to the brim.
. . . not pour drink [lavishly].
. . . offer nothing to anyone who does not ask for anything.
. . . not place your cup down on the table if you are not to give the impression that you are ill-mannered.
. . . empty your mouth before you take a drink.
. . . avoid having grubby finger-nails.
. . . not rub a sore spot.
. . . turn your back when spitting or urinating.
. . . not suck back your spittle.
. . . turn your back when you belch.
. . . take care not to scratch.
. . . not talk idly during the meal
. . . grant other people a share [in the conversation].
. . . not gnaw but scrape a bone.
. . . not disgorge what you are eating
. . . not lick back things that have come from your mouth.
. . . take out small bones with your hand.
. . . take the reading in with your ears.
. . . store the explanations in your mind.
. . . not pick out delicacies with your fingers.
. . . not take large mouthfuls.
. . . avoid gluttony.
. . . guard against drunkeness.
. . . eat to live, remember.
. . . not live to eat.
. . . stop short of overeating when you eat.
. . . stop short of inebriation when you drink.
. . . pay attention to your gestures.
. . . not reject what is offered.
. . . take things with a knife or fork.
. . . show yourself to be dexterous not gauche.
. . . thank anyone who offers you something.
. . . say *prosit* to anyone who drinks your health.
. . . not soil your hands or clothes.
. . . not have a drip at your nose.
. . . clean your nostrils with a handkerchief.
. . . take what is near you.
. . . give way in turn to your companions.
. . . eat whatever you cut up.
. . . behave courteously to all.
. . . beware of all excess.
. . . finish your meal with something dry.
. . . wash your hands after the meal.
. . . bend the knee when sitting down to table.
. . . do likewise when leaving it.
. . . honour the giver of good things.
. . . not be slow to accept them for thus you add to your sins.
. . . listen reverently to the holy word.
. . . not disregard the blessing of the table.
. . . return thanks to God through Christ.
. . . listen keenly to the explanation of His word, and observe the sound things therein and reconcile what appears contradictory and refute heterodox opinions and
. . . adduce parallel texts
. . . join together in singing hymns after the meal.

May the student deservedly suffer sharp pains
And be banned from the table, who these rules disdains.

Old Aberdeen, 1 December in the year of our Saviour, 1657.

Notes

1 For a comparable text: J Sulpicius, *De moribus et civilitate puerorum carmen* (various edns, including Edinburgh, 1654)

2 Possibly referring to the absence of set metre in favour of a random rhythmic patter.

3 The text reads *odendum*: possibly for *odiendum*.

Appendix IV

Social and geographical origins of students at King's College and Marischal College
Compiled by Rachel Hart

Social Origins

This analysis of students' social origins is based on the occupations of their fathers as recorded in the college matriculation albums. It uses methods adopted for similar studies of students at the universities of Aberdeen, 1860–1939 (Anderson, *Community*, 138–41), and Glasgow, 1740–1839 (Mathew, 'Origins', 78–84). The registers of King's are not detailed enough to be suitable. The registers of Marischal give comparatively few occupations in the eighteenth century; although information from other sources can been used to supplement them, it is neither consistent nor comprehensive. The analysis therefore starts in 1810, taking entries for every five years up to 1859. It uses the published Marischal registers (*FAM*, 2).

The classification of occupations is based on that used in Anderson, *Community* and by the same author in *Education and Opportunity in Victorian Scotland* (Oxford, 1983). As there, the process raises problems. For example, the term 'merchant' has been included in 'Commercial & industrial', embracing the upper business strata, although it is unclear what scale of business the man might be in; it might, in some cases, be more appropriately listed in the 'Intermediate' category. The same caution is needed with 'engineer'. Similarly, 'farmer' could refer to a landowner, or proprietor, or a small landholder, but the term has been included throughout in the 'Agricultural' category. Latinised terms are used on occasion up to 1850: *artifex*, *operarius* and *opifex* have been taken to refer to manual workers (Mathew, 'Origins', 75). In the 'Intermediate' category, 'builder' includes 'builder/contractor'; 'ship's captain' includes 'master mariner'; 'chemist' includes 'druggist' Other illustrations of the categories are in notes to the table.

TABLE 1 MARISCHAL COLLEGE, SOCIAL ORIGINS OF ARTS STUDENTS[1] EXPRESSED AS A PERCENTAGE OF THE NUMBER IN THE CLASS, 1810–59

Occupation	*1810*	*1815*	*1820*	*1825*	*1830*	*1835*	*1840*	*1845*	*1850*	*1855*	*1859*
Landowner	35.0	8.9	12.1	15.1	15.7	9.1	15.1	11.7	7.4	2.4	0
Minister	5.2	7.9	10.9	4.7	6.0	13.0	11.0	9.4	8.7	7.3	10.2
Doctor	2.6	1.0	2.4	3.5	4.8	6.5	9.6	0	4.9	4.9	5.0
Lawyer	2.6	0	1.2	4.7	2.4	3.9	6.9	4.7	6.2	4.9	1.7
Teacher	2.6	2.9	9.6	7.0	4.8	2.6	2.7	2.4	4.9	6.1	6.8
Other profs[2]	2.6	2.0	4.8	3.5	7.2	6.5	2.7	1.2	2.5	3.7	1.7
Commercial & industrial[3]	13.0	14.9	19.3	24.4	23.0	25.9	15.1	15.3	18.5	17.1	15.3
Agriculture[4]	3.9	21.8	14.5	15.1	10.8	10.4	13.7	30.6	19.8	24.4	23.7
Intermediate[5]	13.0	4.9	9.6	8.1	14.5	10.4	12.3	12.9	12.3	8.5	27.1
Working-class[6]	11.7	14.9	9.6	6.9	9.6	9.1	4.1	4.7	13.6	19.5	8.5
Not known	7.8	20.8	6.0	7.0	1.2	2.6	6.9	4.7	1.2	1.2	0
No. in class	77	101	83	86	83	77	73	85	81	82	58

Notes

1 Since it is not always possible to identify and exclude private students in some of these classes, they have been included throughout.

2 Other professions: civil servant, military officer, supervisor of Excise, architect.

3 Commercial & industrial: merchant, manufacturer, engineer, manager, banker, railway contractor, ship-owner.

4 Agriculture: farmer, crofter, factor, planter.

5 Intermediate (occupations mentioned twice or more): builder, ship's captain, chemist, tailor/clothier, weaver, foreman/overseer, Excise/Inland Revenue/Customs employee, auctioneer, innkeeper, brewer, keeper of reading room, dyer, baker, secretary/clerk, minor official, fishery official, cabinet-maker, flesher, cooper, plumber/brass-founder, post-horse master.

6 Working class: labourer, joiner/carpenter, bookbinder, mason, shoemaker, forester, gardener, gamekeeper, ploughman, candlemaker, sailor, soldier, hairdresser, housepainter, glazier, miller, stabler, jailor, shepherd, dyker, smith, wright, mechanic.

Geographical Origins

The analysis is based on Anderson, *Roll* and *FAM*, 2, taking entries every ten years: at King's, from 1720, and at Marischal, from 1770, to 1859. The amount of information varies between the colleges. At King's, generally speaking, only the county of origin is recorded until 1830; thereafter, a place name is provided. These are in Latin until 1830 when a mixture of Latin and English is used, giving more information with greater precision. At Marischal, intermittent entries are replaced by fuller details from 1770 onwards. Place name and county are frequently given, initially in Latin, increasingly in English, until 1850 when, halfway through the entries, English becomes standard. The difference in the quality of information recorded by the colleges was revealed when the 1836 commission ordered them to return 'the number of students in arts [whose] parents had their settled residence in New Aberdeen, and the number whose parents resided in other parts, specifying the counties in which the latter respectively reside.' King's had 'no record to enable [it] to make a return'; Marischal produced figures for the period 1827–36, arranged by class, explaining 'that it is the parents' *or Guardians*' residence that is given' (*Report* (1836), 122, 210).

The classification of locations employs a modified version of that used in Anderson, *Community*. The categories are: 'Aberdeen city'; 'Aberdeenshire and the North East' (Aberdeenshire and the counties of Banff, Moray, Nairn and Kincardine); 'The Highlands and the North' (the counties of Caithness, Inverness, Sutherland, Ross and Cromarty; Orkney and Shetland); 'The rest of Scotland' (the counties of Argyll, Bute and any not listed above); 'England, Wales and Ireland' and 'Overseas', which replace 'Outside Scotland' in *Community*; and 'Not known', used where no place of origin is given or the Latin form is unclear (e.g., 'Abriensis', *Roll*, 119). Place names were identified in F H Groome, ed., *Ordnance Gazetteer of Scotland: a survey of Scottish topography*, 3 vols (Edinburgh, 1885).

The main problem in interpreting the record is in the use of the terms 'Aberdeen', 'Aberdonensis', 'Aberdonen'. At King's, until 1830, and Marischal, until 1810, it is unclear whether these refer to the city or the county. Accordingly, before these dates students from the city are included in the category of 'Aberdeenshire and the North East'. After the specified dates it is usually possible to confirm from a father's occupation, the increased use of English, or additional information, whether the city or county is meant. Where 'Aberdeen' appears after a place name, it clearly refers to the county not the city (e.g., 'Lumfanan, Aberdeen', *FAM*, 2, 371). 'Old Machar'. 'St Nicholas' and 'Old Aberdeen' have been assigned to 'Aberdeen city'; but some places that are now within its boundary (e.g., Woodside, Peterculter, Dyce and Gilcomston) fell outwith 'Aberdeen' in the period and have therefore been allocated to 'Aberdeenshire and the North East'.

TABLE 2 KING'S COLLEGE, GEOGRAPHICAL ORIGINS OF ARTS STUDENTS EXPRESSED AS A PERCENTAGE OF THE NUMBER IN THE CLASS, 1720–90

	1720	*1730*	*1740*	*1750*	*1760*	*1770*	*1780*	*1790*
Aberdeen	0	0	0	0	0	0	0	0
Aberdeenshire & North East	74.5	68.6	72.0	82.6	49.1	64.5	49.0	63.9
Highlands & North	19.6	28.6	8.0	4.4	40.4	29.0	42.9	22.2
Rest of Scotland	2.0	0	12.0	13.0	10.5	6.5	6.1	8.3
England, Wales, Ireland	0	0	0	0	0	0	0	0
Overseas	0	0	0	0	0	0	0	0
Not known	3.9	2.8	8.0	0	0	2.0	5.6	0
No. in class	51	35	25	23	57	31	49	36

TABLE 3 KING'S COLLEGE, GEOGRAPHICAL ORIGINS OF ARTS STUDENTS EXPRESSED AS A PERCENTAGE OF THE NUMBER IN THE CLASS, 1800–59

	1800	*1810*	*1820*	*1830*	*1840*	*1850*	*1859*	–
Aberdeen	0	0	0	4.4	7.5	6.8	20.6	–
Aberdeenshire & North East	53.3	42.2	42.6	51.0	54.8	66.7	60.3	–
Highlands & North	39.5	46.7	47.9	30.4	30.2	16.7	5.9	–
Rest of Scotland	0	8.9	8.5	9.8	7.5	8.8	10.3	–
England, Wales, Ireland	0	0	0	1.1	0	1.0	0	–
Overseas	7.0	0	1.0	3.3	0	0	2.9	–
Not known	0	2.2	0	0	0	0	0	–
No. in class	43	45	94	92	53	102	68	–

TABLE 4 MARISCHAL COLLEGE, GEOGRAPHICAL ORIGINS OF ARTS STUDENTS EXPRESSED AS A PERCENTAGE OF THE NUMBER IN THE CLASS, 1770–1859

	1770	*1780*	*1790*	*1800*	*1810*	*1820*	*1830*	*1840*	*1850*	*1859*
Aberdeen	13.1	38.3	28.1	14.3	36.4	31.3	43.4	47.9	32.1	30.5
Aberdeenshire & North East	29	40.5	52.6	49.0	40.2	38.6	38.6	32.9	48.2	45.7
Highlands & North	2.6	2.1	5.3	16.4	5.2	3.6	1.2	4.1	2.5	6.8
Rest of Scotland	5.3	10.6	3.5	6.1	1.3	7.2	4.8	2.7	4.9	6.8
England, Wales, Ireland	0	0	0	2.0	3.9	1.2	3.6	1.4	4.9	1.7
Overseas	2.6	2.1	7.0	6.1	2.6	10.9	7.2	2.7	6.2	6.8
Not known	47.4	6.4	3.5	6.1	10.4	7.2	1.2	8.3	1.2	1.7
No. in class	38	47	57	49	77	83	83	73	81	59

Totals of students with a known county of origin compiled over two long periods, 1750–99 and 1800–49 (R N Smart, 'Some observations on the provinces of the Scottish universities, 1560–1850' in *The Scottish Tradition*, ed. G W S Barrow (Edinburgh, 1974), 102–3), show that in the first period, at King's, 57.9% of those recorded came from Aberdeenshire and the North East; 26.9% from the Highlands and the North; and 11.4% from the rest of Scotland; at Marischal, the percentages were, respectively, 79.7, 6.5 and 7.0. In the second period, at King's, 56.7% came from Aberdeenshire and the North East; 33.0% from the Highlands and the North; and 8.1% from the rest of Scotland; at Marischal the percentages were 80.7, 4.4 and 5.6. These support the class-based profiles: the one major discrepancy with class figures, at Marischal in the first period, is attributable to under-recording for the class of 1770.

Abbreviations

Anderson, *FAM*	P J Anderson, ed., *Fasti Academiae Mariscallanae, 1593–1860*, NSC, 3 vols (Aberdeen, 1889–98).
Anderson, *Officers*	P J Anderson, ed., *Officers and Graduates of the University and King's College of Aberdeen*, NSC (Aberdeen, 1893).
Anderson, *Roll*	P J Anderson, ed., *Roll of Alumni, University and King's College, 1596–1860*, AUS 1 (Aberdeen, 1900).
Anderson, *Studies*	P J Anderson, ed., *Studies in the History and Development of the University of Aberdeen*, AUS 19 (Aberdeen, 1906).
AUL	Aberdeen University Library.
AUR	*Aberdeen University Review.*
AUS	Aberdeen University Studies.
Evidence (1826)	*Royal Commission on the Universities of Scotland, Minutes of Evidence, IV, Aberdeen . . .* (1837); in AUL, QL f. Aa P2 1826 3^4.
Innes, *Fasti*	C Innes, ed., *Fasti Aberdonenses. Selections from the Records of the University and King's College of Aberdeen*, SC (Aberdeen, 1854).
NAS	National Archives of Scotland.
NLS	National Library of Scotland.
NS	*Northern Scotland.*
NSC	New Spalding Club.
QS	Quincentennial Studies in the history of the University of Aberdeen.
RPCS	*Register of the Privy Council of Scotland*, 38 vols (Edinburgh, 1877–1970).
SC	Spalding Club.
SHS	Scottish History Society.

Notes

Introduction, pp. 1–3

1 For a brief history of the university, containing illustrations of the principal figures and buildings: J J Carter and C A McLaren, *Crown and Gown 1495–1995: An Illustrated History of the University of Aberdeen* (Aberdeen, 1994). For the history of Aberdeen and its hinterland: P Dennison, D Ditchburn and M Lynch, *Aberdeen Before 1800: A New History* (East Linton, 2002); H Fraser and C H Lee, *Aberdeen 1800–2000: A New History* (East Linton, 2000).

2 The correct term is 'college–universities': J J Carter and D Withrington, eds, *Scottish Universities: Distinctiveness and Diversity* (Edinburgh, 1992), 1; (hereafter Carter and Withrington, *Scottish Universities*). 'College' is less clumsy.

3 For the history of the students at the modern university: R D Anderson, *The Student Community at Aberdeen, 1860–1939*, QS (Aberdeen, 1988) (hereafter Anderson, *Community*).

4 For a translation of the New Foundation and a note on surviving texts: D Stevenson, *King's College, Aberdeen, 1560–1641: From Protestant Reformation to Covenanting Revolution*, QS (Aberdeen, 1990), Appendix II, 149–66 (hereafter Stevenson, *King's College*). For the text and a translation of the Foundation Charter: Anderson, *FAM*, 1, 39–77.

5 AUL, MS M 2, ff. 170r–174v, 'Statuta accademiae Aberdonensis [proposita] a magistro Gilberto Graio gymnasiarcha anno 1605 . . .' (hereafter *Statuta*); MS M 391, 'Leges Novae Academiae Aberdonensis', undated (hereafter *Leges*). For a discussion of the texts and problems in dating the *Leges*: Carter and Withrington, *Scottish Universities*, 136. It now seems likely, from the absence of any reference to bursaries in the *Leges*, that it should be dated before 1616. For the text and a translation of the two documents: below, Appendices I and II.

6 Registers of the matriculation and graduation of students in arts at King's, 1600–87, are transcribed in Innes, *Fasti*, 449–531. For annotated rolls, 1600–1860, based on registers and other sources: Anderson, *Officers*, 177–311, and *Roll*. For annotated rolls of Marischal, 1605–1860: Anderson, *Fasti*, 2, 186–586. The use of these and other biographical sources is discussed by D B Johnston in 'Registers, receipts and personal reminiscences: sources for investigating the student membership of King's College and Marischal College, *c.* 1600–1860,' *AUR*, 51 (1985–86), 456–75. Unless otherwise stated, academic information about students at King's and Marischal is taken from Anderson, *Roll* and *FAM*, 2.

7 Innes, *Fasti*, 273–80, 280–3, 283–5, 392–404.

8 In Aberdeen City Archives. For extracts relating to Marischal: AUL, MS M 109–16, W Knight, 'Collections regarding Marischal College', undated (hereafter Knight, 'Collections'), and Anderson, *FAM*, 1.

9 'lachrymoso caepe': AUL, BK MS E1, W Lauder, 'Panegyricus Paraeneticus Encomiasticus et Postulatorius Pro eximendo Candidatis in Lycaeo Regio Aberdonis

Servitutis scholasticae Jugo . . .', 1632, p. 5 (hereafter Lauder, 'Panegyricus'). For a transcription: ibid., MS K 139.

10 The date in brackets after a student's name is the first year of the class which he attended: thus 'William Lauder (1628)' entered the class of 1628, graduating in 1632.

11 For the laws of Principal Guild, 1641: Innes, *Fasti*, 33, 225–31. For those of the 1640s: ibid., 35–7, 232–9. For those of Principal Row, 1653–61: ibid., 37–40, 240–50, 254–5. For those of the 1680s: AUL, MS K 130, 'Leges et statuta Collegii Regii Aberdonensis', [1686]. For the dating and ascription of the codes: Carter and Withrington, *Scottish Universities*, 135–6. For Row's rules for the table: Innes, *Fasti*, 250–3. For a translation of the last: below, Appendix III.

12 AUL, MS K 36–9; K 54–5; K 256/42/1. For extracts: Innes, *Fasti*, 392–444, 599–610.

13 AUL, MS M 91/9–14.

14 Ibid., MS M 57–8.

15 For visitations at Aberdeen: Innes, *Fasti*, 310–91.

16 AUL, MS K 46, ff. 2v–4r; K 48, ff. 66v–67r; 118r–119r; K 50, pp. 60–2.

17 Ibid., Lib R, L, ff. Aa AU, Bro 12^2, *Statuta Academiae Mariscallanae Universitatis Abredonensis* (1741); Lib R, L, ff. Aa Au, Bro 15, *Leges et Instituta Academiae Mariscallanae Abredonensis* (Aberdeen, 1799); Lib R, L, ff. Aa Au, Bro, 16^1, *Leges et Instituta Academiae Mariscallanae Abredonensis* (Aberdeen, 1816). The 1816 edition is printed in *Evidence* (1826), 242–3.

18 AUL, MS M 41–3.

19 Ibid., MS 30. For a detailed study of the papers in this context: D B Johnston, 'James Beattie and his students at Marischal College, Aberdeen', *NS*, 11 (1991), 11–28 (hereafter Johnston, 'Beattie').

20 AUL, MS M 404/1–20; I M Beavan and J Pirie, ' "Neatness and order": the diaries and papers of William Knight . . .', *NS*, 21 (2001), 129–39.

21 AUL, MS M 222–3; W K Leask, 'The Oldest Class Record', *Alma Mater*, 28 (1911), 201–3.

22 [T Gordon], 'University and King's College of Aberdeen' and [J Stuart], 'Historical account and present state of the Marischal College and University of Aberdeen' in Sir J Sinclair, ed., *Statistical Account of Scotland*, 21 vols (Edinburgh, 1799), 21, Appendix, 51–104, 105–40 (hereafter *OSA*).

23 *Evidence* (1826); *Report [of Scottish Universities Commission] relative to the University and King's College of Aberdeen* (1831) (hereafter *Report* KC) (1826); *Report [of Scottish Universities Commission] relative to Marischal College, Aberdeen* (1831), hereafter *Report* MC (1826); both *Reports* in AUL, QL f. Aa P2 1826. For full bibliographical details of these publications and the following two: Anderson, *Studies*, 447–8, 450, 455.

24 *Second report of the Commissioners appointed . . . 1836 and re-appointed . . . 1837 for visiting the Universities of King's College and Marischal College, Aberdeen* (1839); in AUL, QL f. Aa P2, 1826 (hereafter *Report* (1836)).

25 *Report of H M Commissioners appointed to inquire into the state of the Universities of Aberdeen with a view to their union. Together with the evidence and appendices* (1858) (hereafter *Report* (1857)).

26 *Evidence* (1826), 89.

27 A Bain, *Autobiography* (London, 1904), v (hereafter Bain, *Autobiography*).

28 Both published in London (hereafter MacDonald, *Falconer*, *Forbes*).

29 [N N Maclean], 'University life in the north of Scotland', *Chambers's Journal* (1872), 276–80 (hereafter Maclean, 'University life').

30 N N Maclean, *Life at a Northern University*, ed. W K Leask (Quatercentenary edn, Aberdeen, 1906) (hereafter Maclean, *Life*).
31 W Johnston, *Some Account of the Last Bajans of King's and Marischal Colleges . . .* (Aberdeen, 1899) (hereafter Johnston, *Bajans*).

Chapter 1, pp. 4–32

1 G Burnett, *The Family of Burnett of Leys with collateral branches*, ed. J Allardyce, NSC (Aberdeen, 1901), 41 (hereafter Burnett, *Family*).
2 A M Munro, *Memorials of the Aldermen, Provosts and Lord Provosts of Aberdeen, 1272–1895* (Aberdeen, 1897), 142 (hereafter Munro, *Memorials*).
3 Anderson, *FAM*, 1, 111.
4 For bursaries, their historical and cultural background and their operation at Marischal: S Vance, 'Mortifications (bursaries and endowments) for education in Aberdeen 1593–1660 and their implementation in the seventeenth century' (Ph D, University of Aberdeen, 2000), notably 276–317 (hereafter Vance, 'Mortifications').
5 A Garden, *A theatre of Scottish worthies: and the lyf, doings, and deathe of William Elphinstone, bishop of Aberdeen*, Hunterian Club (Glasgow, 1878), 62.
6 Anderson, *FAM*, 1, 357.
7 This paragraph is largely based on Stevenson, *King's College*, chapters 1–4. There is no equivalent, recent study for Marischal.
8 W Orem, *A Description of the Chanonry, Cathedral, and King's College of Old Aberdeen, in the Years 1724 and 1725* (Aberdeen, 1832 edn), 250 (hereafter Orem, *Description*).
9 Anderson, *FAM*, 1, 85.
10 Thomas would have voted in the Angus nation, Alexander in Mar, had the occasion arisen, but no election is recorded until 1634.
11 D Chalmers, *De Scotorum Fortitudine, Doctrina et Pietate* (Paris, 1631), reprinted in J Robertson, *Collections for a History of the Shires of Aberdeen and Banff*, SC (Aberdeen, 1843), 213 (hereafter Chalmers, *De Scotorum Fortitudine*). Although the general reliability of this account has been questioned (Stevenson, *King's College*, 140), most of its references to college routines can be corroborated from other sources, and it has therefore been used – but with a health warning.
12 The steward's accounts for the academic year 1628–29, for example, show a gradual rise in provisioning over the first six weeks: AUL, MS K 2, ff. 228v–234r.
13 Innes, *Fasti*, 284.
14 Anderson, *FAM*, 1, 186. For convenience, 'master' has been used in place of 'regent' and 'professor' until 1800, when both colleges had professors.
15 Ibid., 1, 185.
16 Timetable constructed from the New Foundation and Chalmers, *De Scotorum Fortitudine*, 212–13 (King's); the Foundation Charter, the *Statuta*, the *Leges* and AUL MS M 2, f. 175r, Duties of the janitor, [1605] (Marischal).
17 'literis multum sudetis': Lauder, *Panegyricus*, p. 8.
18 AUL, MS K 225/2, 'Nomina eorum qui aliquam graecae linguae praxin memoriae commiserunt' [1604]. For 'Nonnus': Nonnus of Panopolis, *Paraphrasis Evangelii S Joannis* (Venice, 1501 and other edns). For 'praxis of Antesignanus': [Pierre Davantes], 'Praxis seu usus praeceptorum grammaticis . . .' in N Clenardus, *Institutiones ac Meditationes in graecam linguam cum scholis et praxi P. Antesignani* (Paris, 1566).

19 J Durkan and J Kirk, *The University of Glasgow, 1451–1577* (Glasgow, 1977), 291 (hereafter Durkan and Kirk, *Glasgow*).
20 Anderson, *FAM*, 2, 33.
21 Ibid., 1, 132.
22 AUL, MS 116, ff. 3–5. The volume is inscribed with the names, Thomas Forbes, John Forbes and Thomas Johnston; in the absence of records of admission for those years, it is impossible to confirm that they were students at Marischal. Nevertheless, the volume has a former shelf-mark that accords with those of other, authentic, Marischal lecture-notes.
23 Ibid., MS 150, 151; M 181; R K French, ed., *Anatomical Education in a Scottish University, 1620* (Aberdeen, 1975).
24 'Ibi disputando inter se ad duodecimam, tempus terunt; Professoribus interim in medio simul deambulantibus': Chalmers, *De Scotorum Fortitudine*, 213.
25 Unless otherwise stated, money is expressed in Scots in this chapter.
26 Anderson, *FAM*, 1, 135; 2, 199, 203.
27 J Lundie, *Oratio Eucharistica & economiastica* . . . (Aberdeen, 1631), 21–2.
28 Comparable information is not available for King's.
29 Comparable information is not available for King's.
30 Anderson, *FAM*, 1, 230.
31 AUL, MS K 283, Draft letter from David Rait to an unnamed correspondent, 1605.
32 Ibid., MS K 36, f. 20v.
33 For comparison: J Bevan, 'Seventeenth-Century Students and their Books' in *Four Centuries. Edinburgh University Life, 1583–1983*, ed. G Donaldson (Edinburgh, 1983), 16–27.
34 Anderson, *Fasti*, 1, 175.
35 The principal bequest of books to Marischal, by Thomas Reid in 1624, anticipates their use by 'the Scholars and Clergy': ibid., 197. It is not clear, however, what is meant by 'scholars'.
36 Anderson, *FAM*, 1, 134.
37 Durkan and Kirk, *Glasgow*, 325.
38 AUL, MS K 10, K 225/2 'Censura Studiosorum'; Innes, *Fasti*, lxxi–lxxiv.
39 'ingenio primus, morum probitate postremus'; 'quia fuci desides et prophani sunt': Innes, *Fasti*, lxxi.
40 'varias concertationes, tum privatas, tum publicas': Chalmers, *De Scotorum Fortitudine*, 213.
41 Based on theses listed in Anderson, *Studies*, 390–401.
42 An undated amendment to the *Statuta* states that the examination should be 'in mathematics and philosophy.' The only occasion on which mathematics is recorded as a topic is at King's in 1631: ibid., 396.
43 AUL, BK Aid, [*Theses*] (Edinburgh, 1616).
44 'omnem fidem exsuperet, nec facile ab ijs qui oculis non conspexerunt credi possit': Chalmers, *De Scotorum Fortitudine*, 213; J Fraser, *Chronicles of the Frasers. The Wardlaw Manuscript*, ed. W Mackay, SHS (Edinburgh, 1905), 260 (hereafter Fraser, *Chronicles*).
45 Anderson, *Officers*, 349–50; Innes, *Fasti*, 501.
46 Anderson, *FAM*, 1, 155.
47 AUL, MS K 281/3/3. See also Table 1.2.

48 The flavour of Lauder's prose comes through in his opening words to the third class: 'Even if . . . the third of the Graces particularly invites us to extol your willing obedience to us and to celebrate your constant friendship, and the first of the Muses despatches us to the regions of the third Muse in order to praise your intellect . . .'. 'Etiamsi . . . ad voluntaria vestra in nos obsequia extollenda et indeclinatam amicitiam celebrandam tertia [charitum] nos magnopere invitet, et musarum prima in tertiae musae arva ad vestram laudandam solertiam releget . . .': *Panegyricus*, p. 8. Also: 'ut studium graecum cum nocturna diurnaque manu versetis impellunt', p. 7; 'ardua principia, logicae fel vobis exhibent sed mel dabit exitus', p. 8; 'bene equidem incipientibus debetur facti dimidium . . . iis solum qui ad finem perseverant', p. 8.
49 Anderson, *FAM*, 1, 155.
50 The passages in the published texts of the Foundations which describe the profession of faith before the principal and the rector are almost identical, but have significantly different punctuation; this has led to a marked difference in the published translations: Anderson, *FAM*, 1, 56, 74; Anderson, *Officers*, 346; Stevenson, *King's College*, 164. Moreover, the description of the profession before the dean of faculty has for long been recognised as ambiguous: Anderson, *FAM*, 1, 70. The text of the New Foundation of Glasgow does not contain an equivalent passage: Durkan and Kirk, *Glasgow*, 447. The question of profession at entry and/or matriculation is not clarified by other sources: surviving texts of matriculation oaths in this period, all from Marischal, do not contain a profession; under the *Leges*, however, students were to profess at entry by oath and in writing.
51 Innes, *Fasti*, 411.
52 According to the *Statuta*, this was given on Mondays at 1 pm.
53 Chalmers, *De Scotorum Fortitudine*, 213.
54 As at Glasgow: Durkan and Kirk, *Glasgow*, 319.
55 It was used for other purposes involving the students, however; graffiti in the stalls date from 1610, 1623 and 1625: C A McLaren, 'The Chapel, the College and the University, 1560–1945' in *King's College Chapel, Aberdeen, 1500–2000*, ed. J Geddes (Aberdeen, 2000), 163 (hereafter Geddes, *Chapel*).
56 Although Greyfriars was known as 'the college church', as in Anderson, *FAM*, 1, 251, it was not used for college services until 1769: Knight, 'Collections', pp. 969–78, 981.
57 A M Munro, ed., *Records of Old Aberdeen, 1157–1891*, NSC, 2 vols (Aberdeen, 1899–1909), 1, 41 (hereafter Munro, *Old Aberdeen*); I B Cowan, *The Scottish Reformation. Church and Society in sixteenth century Scotland* (London, 1982), 140 (hereafter Cowan, *Reformation*).
58 Times of attendance are not known, however; they may have varied seasonally: Cowan, *Reformation*, 139.
59 Innes, *Fasti*, 398.
60 Anderson, *FAM*, 1, 120.
61 Around 1675, when the wearing of gowns was discussed, there were references back to the king's letter: AUL, MS M 91/10, 'Return from Marshall College to . . . Overtures [from] King's College', undated.
62 Fraser, *Chronicles*, 258: 'ballown', a game played by striking an inflated ball with the arm; 'cachpole', hand-tennis; 'byars', possibly billiards; 'bowmarks and rovers', archery at fixed and random distances. Rigged competitions: a suggestion from Professor D Stevenson, who points out that high-born competitors shooting for a similar trophy at St Andrews invariably won.

63 King's students who lived in the Old Town were to return at 1 pm; those who went for dinner to the New were given until 2 pm.
64 Anderson, *FAM*, 1, 126.
65 The fastened gown and the belt were originally symbols of tutelage: Durkan and Kirk, *Glasgow*, 197.
66 Chalmers, *De Scotorum Fortitudine*, 212. Both Foundations encouraged conversation in Greek; with what success is uncertain.
67 *RPCS, 1607–10*, xxxvi.
68 Anderson, *FAM*, 2, 186.
69 Ibid., 2, 192.
70 Ibid., 2, 186–7; see also *Statuta*, [4].
71 An insertion in the *Statuta* requires the hebdomadar to join in the games; it has been firmly deleted.
72 Chalmers, *De Scotorum Fortitudine*, 213.
73 See, for example, K Thomas, *Rule and Misrule in the Schools of Early Modern England* (Reading, 1976), 12.
74 AUL MS M 2, f. 175r, Duties of the janitor, [1605].
75 The conviction of the King's porter that year for a breach of the peace, and the appearance of his successor on a charge of fornication in 1627 raise doubts about their integrity: Munro, *Old Aberdeen*, 1, 34; St Machar's Cathedral, MS CH2/1020/1, p. 107.
76 See also Anderson, *FAM*, 2, 192.
77 Beatings were said to take place 'in public' or 'in public by all the masters'. The last two phrases were also used to describe other, unspecified punishments, which are assumed here to have been corporal.
78 AUL, MS K 36, f. 20v.
79 Munro, *Old Aberdeen*, 1, 38, 52.
80 Aberdeen City Archives, Burgh Registers, 49, p. 381.
81 Vance, 'Bursaries', 291.
82 'Condiscipulatus quadrennialis insolubile vinculum': Lauder, *Panegyricus*, p. 19.
83 Anderson, *FAM*, 1, 154–5; 2, 190–3.
84 The classes of 1604 and 1608 were notable exceptions to the pattern. The first attracted 38 entrants, 20 of whom (52.6%) graduated; the second attracted 33 with only 15 (45.4%) graduating. Both were taught by the same master, John Chalmer, and the unusually high number of entrants clearly owes something to his reputation. He left halfway through the course of the class of 1608, however, which may explain why fewer students than usual graduated.
85 Two members of the class had migrated to King's. The ninth member in its final year was a latecomer. There is no graduation list for the class but that was the stated objective of its members.
86 A Jaffray, *Diary of Alexander Jaffray . . .*, ed. J Barclay (London, 1833), 15.
87 Andrew Strachan (1600), who was placed in the first grade of his class when he was assessed in his final year but nevertheless failed to graduate, is thought to be the Andrew Strachan buried in the college chapel in 1604: G D Henderson, 'A Benefactor of King's College: Professor Andrew Strachan', *AUR*, 22 (1934–35), 23.
88 Anderson, *FAM*, 2, 186.
89 Fraser, *Chronicles*, 257, 260.

90 J D Mackie, *The University of Glasgow, 1451–1951* (Glasgow, 1954), 103; D B Horn, *A Short History of the University of Edinburgh, 1556–1889* (Edinburgh, 1967), 30 (hereafter Horn, *Edinburgh*).

91 His portrait in Marischal College is inscribed 'Anno 1624, Aetatis 33'; the painting is ascribed to 1636, however, by M Apted and S Hannabuss, *Painters in Scotland, 1301–1700: A Biographical Dictionary*, Scottish Record Society (Edinburgh, 1978).

92 Alexander Brodie joined in the second year of the class of 1631. If John Middleton, later Earl Middleton, was indeed in the class of 1628, he would have been nine when he entered: Orem, *Description*, 279.

93 Anderson, *FAM*, 1, 134.

94 Anderson, *Officers*, 4.

95 Anderson, *FAM*, 1, 124, 150, 227.

96 Other families identified in the period are: in Aberdeenshire, Fraser of Philorth (1619), Forbes of Monymusk (1626), Johnston of Caskieben (1632), Baird of Auchmeddan (1634) and Gordon of Straloch (1636); from further north, Abercrombie of Birkenbog in Banffshire (1628).

97 AUL, MS K 283.

98 Under the *Statuta* and *Leges*, the rates fluctuated. In the *Statuta* a standard rate of £5, later raised to £6 13s 4d, then to £13 6s 8d, was introduced for all except the nobility and 'gentlemen of higher rank', who were allowed to pay what they chose. Under the *Leges*, however, the fee is given as £3.

99 Knight, 'Collections', pp. 797–8; Vance, Mortifications', 301–2. A record of the decision of 1619 itself has not been found.

100 AUL, MS K 281/3/3; 278/1/1, Miscellaneous accounts, 1623–24, 1626–27. For comments on the former: Stevenson, *King's College*, 167–8.

101 Stevenson, *King's College*, 166, n. 12; L J Macfarlane, *William Elphinstone and the Kingdom of Scotland, 1431–1514. The Struggle for Order* (Aberdeen, 1985 edn), 361–2; AUL, MS K 281/3/3; 278/1/1.

102 AUL, MS K 278/1/1; K 281/3/3; K 283; MS 2379/1/10, 'Inventarie of plenishing within the Kingis Colledge of Aberdein, 1634'. For a transcription of the last: C A McLaren, 'An Inventory of King's College, 1634,' *NS*, 15 (1995), 123–7.

103 'singulorum cubicula quotidie scopis verrat lectos probe sternat supellectilem salvam praestet': AUL, MS M 2, f. 175r.

104 Ibid., MS K 2, 'Album rationum, 1579–1653', ff. 228v–270v. For brief excerpts for 1579, 1628 and 1650: Innes, *Fasti*, 578–99; see also C A McLaren, 'Visiting the Charter Chest: the Early Records of the University and King's College, Aberdeen' in *Freedom and Authority: Historical and Historiographical essays presented to Grant G Simpson*, eds T Brotherstone and D Ditchburn (East Linton, 2000), 196–8. No comparable information is available from Marischal.

105 For the observance of Lent and 'fish-days': Durkan and Kirk, *Glasgow*, 362. At King's, although Lent in 1629 began officially on 18 February, fresh beef and veal were eaten on the 19th, salt beef as late as the 22nd. On 22–3 February mustard, figs, raisins, plumdames (damsons), and peis (pease) were bought in, but it is not known when they were consumed and by whom.

106 Innes, *Fasti*, 534. Reid is said to have been a graduate of King's; he refers to the college as 'a mother': ibid., 401.

107 Anderson, *FAM*, 1, 77.

108 Based on Vance, 'Mortifications', 189, 304.

109 Innes, *Fasti*, 276; AUL, MS K 281/3/3, 'Spoone selver Michaelmas 1623'.
110 AUL, MS K 36, f. 7v.
111 No comparable information is available for the private bursars at Marischal.
112 AUL, MS 2379/1/10.
113 Anderson, *FAM*, 1, 126.
114 AUL, MS K 2, f. 320v.
115 W D Geddes and W K Leask, eds, *Musa Latina Aberdonensis*, 3 vols, NSC, (Aberdeen, 1892–1910), 3, 257–9.
116 'ingenii acumen, pietatem, amorem, benevolentiam, humilitatem, et vitam sinceram': Lauder, 'Panegyricus', p. 7.
117 Innes, *Fasti*, 284.
118 Ibid., 410, 414–15.
119 Anderson, *FAM*, 1, 171.
120 Ibid., 230.
121 Unless otherwise stated this paragraph is based on Anderson, *Roll* and *FAM*, 2. Inevitably, a disproportionate number of identifications in these volumes come from sources relating to the professions. Although the manuscript annotations in the *Roll* are helpful in other cases, they are for the most part unsourced and have been used only when they can be corroborated.
122 Anderson, *Studies*, 400.
123 Burnett, *Family*, 72.
124 Innes, *Fasti*, 160–3.

Chapter 2, pp. 33–65

1 During this period, 'bajan', 'semi', tertian' and 'magistrand' were used for a student in his first, second, third and fourth years. They remained in use throughout the period covered by this book and accordingly are used hereafter. 'Graduand' is used to designate a magistrand who has passed his final examination and is about to graduate. In 1677 it was stated that third-year students, 'at the years end are Batchelours of Arts', but the term does not seem to have been in common use: T Middleton, *An Appendix to the History of the Church of Scotland* (London, 1677), 42 (hereafter Middleton, *Appendix*).
2 D Stevenson, 'Who was John Spalding?', *AUR*, 51 (1985–86), 102–15; J Spalding, *Memorialls of the Trubles in Scotland and England*, ed. J Stuart, SC, 2 vols (Aberdeen, 1850–51), 2, 113–14. (hereafter Spalding, *Memorialls*).
3 'pastoris et praeconis aberdonensis filio': AUL, MS 3077, 'Commentarius in logicam', 1641–42, p. 1.
4 Spalding, *Memorialls*, 1, 321.
5 C A McLaren 'New work and old: building at the colleges in the seventeenth century', *AUR*, 53 (1990), 208–17 (hereafter McLaren, 'Building'). For the privies: Spalding, *Memorialls*, 2, 188.
6 There is no modern institutional history of either King's or Marischal for much of this period. For 1640–41: Stevenson, *King's College*, chapter 5. For 1690–1717: R L Emerson, *Professors, Patronage and Politics: The Aberdeen Universities in the Eighteenth Century*, QS (Aberdeen, 1992), 1–45 (hereafter Emerson, *Professors*); P B Wood, *The Aberdeen Enlightenment: The Arts Curriculum in the Eighteenth Century*, QS (Aberdeen, 1993), 1–14 (hereafter Wood, *Enlightenment*).

7 For the academic and intellectual history of the colleges in this period: C Shepherd, 'A National System of University Education in Seventeenth-Century Scotland?' in Carter and Withrington, *Scottish Universities*, 26–33; 'The Arts Curriculum at Aberdeen at the Beginning of the Eighteenth Century' in *Aberdeen and the Enlightenment*, eds J J Carter and J H Pittock, (Aberdeen, 1987), 146–54 (hereafter Shepherd, *Arts Curriculum*), and other works by this author.

8 'Primarius studiorum finis esse debet religio Dei . . . divinorumque operum et beneficiorum cognitio': Innes, *Fasti*, 33, 226.

9 AUL, MS K 227. The 'Litany' refers, cryptically, to the principal, the professors of mathematics, Hebrew, law and medicine, three regents, and three masters; and, by name, to 'Drummond' and 'Gray', who have not been identified. Verses entitled, 'Drummond further described . . .' are appended. The 'Description of the . . . Masters' begins with the professor of mathematics but is incomplete. The allegations in all three texts are mainly of drunkenness and dishonesty.

10 John certainly came into that category if, as seems likely, he was one of those students who chafed at the principal's mid-week sermons in 1642, 'wissing rather to be at thair lessonis': Spalding, *Memorialls*, 2, 185.

11 'qui solent impallescere chartis': W Douglas, *Academiarum Vindiciae* . . . (Aberdeen, 1659), 13 (hereafter Douglas, *Vindiciae*). For the context of this oration: H Kearney, *Scholars and Gentlemen. Universities and Society in Pre-Industrial Britain, 1500–1700* (London, 1970), 110–22 (hereafter Kearney, *Scholars*); G D Henderson, 'Professor William Douglas', *AUR*, 32 (1947–48), 87–8 (hereafter Henderson, 'Douglas').

12 AUL, MS M 91/7, Articles agreed at Edinburgh, 1672.

13 NLS, Mackenzies of Delvine Collection, MS 1277, letters of George Fraser to John Mackenzie, advocate, Edinburgh, ff. 121–62, 26 October 1690–98 July 1695; ff. 181–91, 29 October 1703–July 1704. Kenneth Gordon was related to the laird of Clava, Inverness-shire, and a nephew of John Mackenzie. George Mackenzie was John's son. Unless otherwise stated, further information about Kenneth and George as students is taken from this source.

14 Innes, *Fasti*, 340.

15 The case was 'tryit': Spalding, *Memorialls*, 2, 188. The crime seems to have been committed in the college and therefore within its jurisdiction. There is no reference to it in the council archives. Andrew is said to have escaped punishment through the influence of his father.

16 C A McLaren, 'The College and the Community, 1660–1860' in *Old Aberdeen: Bishops, Burghers and Buildings*, ed. J S Smith (Aberdeen, 1991), 62 (hereafter Smith, *Old Aberdeen*). Marischal students accused of similar crimes might have been expected to appear in the Aberdeen Justice Court but this does not seem to have been the case: G Desbrisay, '"Menacing their persons and exacting on their purses": The Aberdeen Justice Court, 1657–1700' in *From Lairds to Loons. Country and Burgh Life in Aberdeen, 1600–1800*, ed. D Stevenson (Aberdeen, 1986), 70–90.

17 For the riots of 1658 and 1668–69: C A McLaren, 'Affrichtment and riot: student violence in Aberdeen, 1659–1669', *NS*, 10 (1990), 1–17 (hereafter McLaren, 'Affrichtment').

18 Anderson, *FAM*, 2, 244–6.

19 AUL, MS K 37, f. 30v.

20 Innes, *Fasti*, 310, 333, 345, 424; AUL, MS K 256/31/1, Agreement, 1648; M 91/7.

21 NLS, MS 1277, f. 121, 26 October 1690.

22 E D Dunbar, *Social Life in Former Days, Chiefly in the Province of Moray* (Edinburgh, 1865), 3–4 (hereafter Dunbar, *Moray*). The master in question, William Black, was notorious for his cynical and sceptical views: NAS, Records of the Privy Council, PC1/24, ff. 64–7. I am grateful to Dr T Clarke for this reference.

23 Innes, *Fasti*, 238, 254, 344; Middleton, *Appendix*, 42.

24 C Innes, ed., *The Family of Rose of Kilravock*, SC, (Edinburgh, 1848), 351–4, 367–9 (hereafter Innes, *Rose*). Unless otherwise stated, further information about Hugh as a student is taken from this source.

25 Innes, *Fasti*, 326, 327, 382; AUL, MS M 91/7, 9, 12.

26 Bajans had to arrive by 1 February; the rest by 15 November; bajans, semis and tertians could not leave before 1 June; magistrands, before 30 April: Innes, *Fasti*, 344–6.

27 NLS, MS 1277, f. 158, 13 February 1695.

28 They imposed finishing dates of 1 May for magistrands, 30 June for the rest: Innes, *Fasti*, 369.

29 A and H Tayler, comps, *The Book of the Duffs*, 2 vols, (Edinburgh, 1914), 1, 32–3; 2, 369–70. Unless otherwise stated, further information about William and Robert as students is taken from this source.

30 Spalding, *Memorialls*, 2, 218, 301, 484; AUL, MS M 57, 1667.

31 Innes, *Fasti*, 436. At King's, 'colledge bonfyres' celebrated, amongst other things, the king's birthday and his 'victorie over the dutch' in 1685: AUL, MS K54/5, 1664–5. At Marischal, 'publict occasions' in the academic year 1684–85 comprised 'the present King's Nativity, Argile and Gray's defeat and a generall thanksgiving': ibid., MS M 58, 1684–85.

32 Innes, *Fasti*, 230; Anderson, *FAM*, 2, 34; AUL, MS K 36, f. 34v. At Marischal, the change seems to have caused logistical problems, so that, as a semi, Andrew Cant was taught by the principal himself, 'hoc anno [1641–42] studioso sub domino dune': AUL, MS 3077, p. 1.

33 The idea had been mooted at Aberdeen as early as 1676: AUL, MS M 91/10. The chair did not become operative at Marischal until 1714–15: M A Stewart, 'The Origins of the Scottish Greek Chairs' in *'Owls to Athens': Essays on Classical Subjects Presented to Sir Kenneth Dover*, ed. E M Craik (Oxford, 1990), 392–3 (hereafter Stewart, 'Greek Chairs').

34 Innes, *Fasti*, 432; Anderson, *Officers*, 73, 75–6; Wood, *Enlightenment*, 2. George Mackenzie, as a semi, had Hebrew lessons twice a week in February 1704.

35 Anderson, *FAM*, 1, 264, 269–71. Gilbert Burnet attended the humanist's class in Greyfriars church before entering the college in 1653, although he was already 'master of that tongue': H C Foxcroft, *A Supplement to Burnet's History of my own Time* (Oxford, 1902), 454.

36 'Oriente solis animus ad studia qualiacunque capescenda promptissimus': AUL, SBL 1651 B3, D Liddel, *Artis conservandi sanitatem libri duo*, ed. P Dun (1651); Innes, *Fasti*, 228, 234, 235, 236, 243. Students, nevertheless, often overslept: AUK, MS M 91/9.

37 Innes, *Fasti*, 311, 437. Comparable information is not available for Marischal.

38 NLS, MS 1277, f. 184, 14 January 1704.

39 Based on curricula of 1641, 1648, 1653–58, 1677 (King's); 1648, 1695 (Marischal): Innes, *Fasti*, 230–1, 247; AUL, MS K 256/23/6/2A, 'Register of the actis [of] the Comissioneris of all the four universities', 1647–48, ff. 3v, 4r; Middleton, *Appendix*, 42; P J Anderson, *Records of the Arts Class, 1868–72* (Aberdeen, 1892 edn), Appendix, 'The Arts Curriculum', 233–4 (hereafter Anderson, *Arts Class*); Shepherd, *Arts*

Curriculum, 146–7. It should be noted that the curricula of 1648 and 1677 make no mention of Hebrew; and that after 1676, as part of the effort to raise standards in Greek, a weekly lesson in the subject was introduced in each year at both colleges: Innes, *Fasti*, 346.

40 British Library, Add. MS 63057 A, f. 10v. Unless otherwise stated, further information about Gilbert as a student is taken from this source. I am grateful to Dr D J Milne for this reference.

41 'subdolam novitatem et heterodoxiam Cartesianam': Anderson, *Studies*, 409.

42 Kearney, *Scholars*, 155. For Alexander Campbell: C Innes, ed., *The Book of the Thanes of Cawdor . . . 1236–1742*, SC (Edinburgh, 1859), 341. Unless otherwise stated, further information about Alexander as a student is taken from this source.

43 'judicii suspensionem . . . tanquam utilem et licitam esse, absque aliqua impietatis labe, censemus; ast necessariam . . . non judicamus': AUL, SBL 1695 F 1, G Fraser, *Theses philosophicae* . . . (Aberdeen, 1695), 3.

44 Ibid., MS K 256/23/6/2A, f. 3v.

45 Innes, *Fasti*, 237, 246. Those who could not keep pace with the master were allowed to copy a classmate's notes afterwards, although they had to continue to listen to the lecture: ibid., 246. How Walter Birnie (1664), a blind student at King's, coped with dictation or, indeed, his studies generally, is not recorded.

46 AUL, MS M 183, John Stewart, 'Phisica generalis', [1691–92].

47 Innes, *Fasti*, 382; Shepherd, *Arts Curriculum*, 147.

48 NLS, MS 1277, f. 184, 14 January 1704.

49 Innes, *Fasti*, 236, 240, 243–4, 426.

50 Ibid., 228, 236, 243; AUL MS K 37, f. 18v; NLS, MS 1277, f. 184, 14 January 1704.

51 AUL, MS M 91/12. There are no references in this period to the open disputations formerly given at Marischal.

52 AUL, SBL 1675, A Shirreff and others, *Quakerism Canvassed . . . A most true . . . accompt of a Dispute betwixt some Students of Divinity at Aberdene, and the Quakers . . .* (Edinburgh, 1675), 2. See also: G DesBrisay, 'Quakers and the university: the Aberdeen debate of 1675', *History of Universities*, 13 (1994), 87–98.

53 NAS, Seafield Papers, GD 248/556/7, letter, [19] January 1677.

54 AUL, MS M 91/9; Innes, *Fasti*, 366.

55 Stewart, 'Greek Chairs', 393.

56 Innes, *Fasti*, 226, 229, 230, 233, 241, 425.

57 'Omnes et singuli non solum caveant vernacule et studeant Latinum loqui; sed et Latine et alii aliis aemulatione laudabili latinius imo et latinissime; in quem finem praecepta de copia ornatu observatione delectu situ et reciprocatione diligenter observentur; Et ut barbarismus et soloecismus cacotonus et traulismus quatuor Latinitatis pestes his eliminentur aedibus, a singulis tabula barbarismorum et soloecismorum teneatur et de singulis quatuor observanda': ibid., 241.

58 Ibid., 311, 328, 342; 346; AUL, MS M 91/9.

59 G Chalmers, *Life of Thomas Ruddiman* (London, 1794), 5–6, 12–15. Unless otherwise stated, further information about Thomas as a student is taken from this source.

60 Stewart, 'Greek Chairs', 393.

61 Spalding, *Memorialls*, 2, 216; NLS, MS 1277, f. 121, 26 October 1690.

62 'Buchanan's Psalms': possibly G Buchanan, *Psalmorum Davidis paraphrasis poetica . . .* ed. N Chytraeus (London, 1648).

63 Innes, *Fasti*, 347.
64 Anderson, *FAM*, 1, 365–6. Unless otherwise stated, money is expressed in Scots in this chapter.
65 After 1687 but before 1701: AUL, MS K 257/21/3, Memorial . . . Anent the Bibliotheck money', [1716]; p. 2; Anderson, *Officers*, 87.
66 I M Beavan, 'Marischal College, Aberdeen, and its earliest library catalogue: a re-assessment', *The Bibliotheck*, 22 (1997), 4–19; and other works by this author.
67 AUL, MS M 91/10, 12.
68 NLS, MS 1277, ff. 92, 97, 11 December 1683, 8 March 1684.
69 Innes, *Fasti*, 248, 254.
70 Ibid., 345, 424; AUL, MS M 91/9.
71 NLS, MS 1277, f. 158, 13 February 1695.
72 Innes, *Fasti*, 374.
73 Ibid., 345, 370, 425, 430. The commissioners also ruled that classes were to be publicly examined at the end of the year before they were dismissed, but there is no evidence of this at Aberdeen.
74 Strictly speaking, with his brother William; not to be confused with his cousin of the same name.
75 AUL, MS M 91/7, 9; Innes, *Fasti*, 425.
76 AUL, MS K 37, f. 30v.; K 281/7/3, letter, Andrew Massie to Patrick Sandilands, 10 July 1662.
77 Orem, *Description*, 330; Douglas, *Vindiciae*, 25; Henderson, 'Douglas', 88.
78 AUL, MS M 91/7; Innes, *Fasti*, 426, 436.
79 Orem, *Description*, 307–8.
80 Innes, *Fasti*, 341; Middleton, *Appendix*, 42.
81 AUL, MS M 57, 1663, 1664, 1665.
82 Middleton, *Appendix*, 42. Thereafter, at King's, it was held on dates ranging from 30 April to 15 June: Anderson, *Studies*, 415–21.
83 Spalding, *Memorialls*, 2, 381. At King's, public graduation was in abeyance in 1715 and in 1716, but in 1717 it was reinstated and opened to 'such as were in the Magistrant class the Last year that are desirous of the degree who have behaved Loyallie under the Government'; only Alexander Fullarton took up the invitation: AUL, MS K 41, f. 15v.
84 Comparable information is not available for Marischal, but the practice seems to have been as common: four students out of 16 paying graduation fees in 1678 had graduated privately; nine out of a total of 34 in 1681, 1683 and 1686; four out of 19 in 1691, 1694 and 1695: based on information in Anderson, *Officers* and *FAM*, 2.
85 Innes, *Fasti*, 321, 340, 369.
86 AUL, MS K 41, f. 23r.
87 Ibid., MS M 57, 1673; Innes, *Fasti*, 230, 248; F Douglas, *A General Description of the East Coast of Scotland* . . . (Paisley, 1782), 113 (hereafter Douglas, *General Description*).
88 AUL, MS K 37, f. 18v; M 58, 1688–89; NLS, MS 1277, f. 185, 7 February 1704.
89 AUL MS M 91/2, 'Act Anent the Colledge of New Aberdeen, 1640'.
90 Spalding, *Memorialls*, 2, 113–14; Munro, *Old Aberdeen*, 2, 39, 40.
91 AUL, MS M 91/2; Innes, *Fasti*, 231, 311.
92 'pro vetere eaque laudatissima consuetudine': Innes, *Fasti*, 232.
93 Ibid., 237. The water was more likely to be for finger bowls than for drinking.

94 'omnia fundamenta religionis Christianae quae 50 capitibus continentur, quam synopsin singuli scribunto': ibid., 244, 248. The Latin text was the *Hymnus Trinitatis* of Hildebert of Tours, an edition of which had recently been published in J Ussher, *De Romanae ecclesiae symbolo Apostolico vetere; aliisque fidei formulis* . . . (London, 1647). The Hebrew text, 'Massad hammikdash i.e. fundamenta Christiane religionis Hebraice descripta', has not been positively identified, but I am grateful to Professor M Feingold for help with the problem.

95 Innes, *Fasti*, 347. The books prescribed in 1676 were, for the second year, *The Whole Duty of Man* (1658); for the third, Grotius, *De veritate religionis Christianae* (1627); for the fourth, 'aither Paule's dialogues, Derlingcourt, or Protestant Triumphe'. The last may refer to M Poole, *A Dialogue between a Popish Priest and an English Protestant* (London, 1667) and C Drelincourt, *The Protestant's Triumph* . . . (English translation, London, 1664).

96 Innes, *Fasti*, 367.

97 AUL, MS K 130; Munro, *Old Aberdeen*, 2, 55, 71.

98 AUL, MS M 91/2; M 57, 1662; M 58, 1696–97.

99 A L Miller, 'The connection of Dr. James Anderson of the "*Constitutions*" with Aberdeen and Aberdeen University', *Ars Quatuor Coronatorum*, 36 (1923), 94–7. I am grateful to Professor D Stevenson for this reference.

100 'qui dexteritate publice precandi sine aliquo librorum subsidio non pollent': Innes, *Fasti*, 233.

101 Ibid., 367.

102 'Nimia quippe animi intensione, atque cogitatione . . . cerebrum supra modum desiccari, vel crudorum humorum sarcina, calorem nativum suffocari . . . Exercitationes maxime congruunt, quae cunctas corporis partes ex aequo moveant: Liddel, *Artis*, 442–3.

103 Innes, *Fasti*, 227–8, 244–5.

104 Aberdeen City Archives, Burgh Registers, 54, p. 14.

105 'pila palmari aut reticulari': Innes, *Fasti*, 245.

106 Orem, *Description*, 248. There is no reference to the construction of a billiard house as such in the building accounts of the New Work.

107 AUL, MS K 255/43, 44; K 278/2/10; K 278/7/44, Miscellaneous accounts and vouchers.

108 Munro, *Old Aberdeen*, 1, 113; 2, 58.

109 AUL, MS K 54/13, 1674–75; K 255/43; 255/44; 278/2/2; Orem, *Description*, 161. The location of the green is not known.

110 'Globis ferreis projiciendis': AUL, MS K 130.

111 Ibid., MS K 54/10, 1672–73; Innes, *Fasti*, 605. The location of the butts is not known.

112 Aberdeen City Archives, Burgh Registers, 53, p. 548; AUL, MS M 57, 1663; 1665; 58, 1687–88. See also J M Bulloch, *A History of the University of Aberdeen, 1495–1895* (London, 1895), 126.

113 Innes, *Rose*, 370.

114 'nemo admittitor nemo retinetor, in quo non sit verecundiae et diligentiae indicium, multo minus qui profligatae naturae vel indolis': Innes, *Fasti*, 226. Unless otherwise stated, the next three paragraphs are based on the codes of laws at King's. For related acts and injunctions: ibid., 328, 342, 347; AUL, MS K 37, f. 38r; K 41, f. 23v; M 91/9, 12, 14. Comparable information is not available for Marischal.

115 'qui studiis non Venere marcescunt, quibus oppidum carcer est, Musaeum et schola paradisus': Douglas, *Vindiciae*, 13, 33–5. For 'heavy smokers': 'herbae nicotianae haustus immodicus'.
116 coloris nigri vel fusci, vel alicujus gravioris aut severioris': Innes, *Fasti*, 254. The 'red or scarlet' gown had 'hanging sleeves': Middleton, *Appendix*, 42.
117 Vance, 'Mortifications', 291.
118 Innes, *Fasti*, 372.
119 Innes, *Fasti*, 366; AUL, MS M 58, 1693–94. According to Knight, 'Collections', p. 151, the rooms described as 'bilboes' also had a penal function, but there is some evidence that they provided ordinary accommodation: ibid., M 57, 1662, 1666, 1670, 1676; M 58, 1692–93.
120 AUL, MS K39, f. 5r.
121 Ibid., MS K 12, Oaths of allegiance etc., 5; K 37, f. 18v; Innes, *Fasti*, 241.
122 AUL, MS M 57, 1662, 1666; 'ratle', chain; 'slott', bolt; 'stensions', bars; 'brodes', shutters; 'hinggers', hangers; 'caisses', frames; 'transe', passage.
123 Ibid., MS K 12, 1–3; K 38, f. 16v; M 57, 1670; M 387/10/1/2.
124 'Immodesty' may possibly refer to sexual activity among the students; if so, it is the only one noted in the period covered by this book.
125 Innes, *Fasti*, 228, 234, 246, 422, 426; 'dissidii factionis rebellionis aut conjurationis': ibid., 242;'conjurationes, combinationes, aut foedera': AUL, MS K 12, 1671–72.
126 Smith, *Old Aberdeen*, 61–5; St Machar's Cathedral, MS CH2/1020/2, pp. 80, 81, 201.
127 *RPCS, 1665–1669*, 50–1. The students may have been tried by external visitors because the masters had initially been accused of connivance in the affair.
128 AUL, MS K 55/7, Accounts, 1685–86; K 255/ 43; *RPCS, 1684–1685*, 174; Innes, *Fasti*, 358–9.
129 AUL, MS M 58, 1685–86; Knight, 'Collections', pp. 153, 299.
130 It seems no coincidence that both assaults took place soon after the accession of James II; that the Privy Council took the first so seriously; that Marischal invoked the council's authority when sentencing its students; and that the master assaulted at Marischal, Thomas Burnet, held strongly conservative religious and political views: Anderson, *FAM*, 2, 39.
131 AUL, MS K 39, ff. 29v, 32r. There is no record of the incident in the burgh archives.
132 NLS, Adv. MS 35.5.11, f. 73; McLaren, 'Affrichtment', 3–8.
133 AUL, MS M 57, 1667; J Stuart, ed., *Extracts from the Council Register of the Burgh of Aberdeen, 1643–1747*, Scottish Burgh Records Society (Edinburgh, 1872), 247.
134 McLaren, 'Affrichtment', 9–11.
135 AUL, MS M 387/10/1/11.
136 Ibid., MS K 56, 1701–02; M 58, 1700–01.
137 Ibid., SBL 1689 NP2, R Reid, *The account of the Popes Procession at Aberdene . . . The 11th of January, 1689, which was delivered to the new Elected Magistrats and Council thereof . . . with The Students Letter to the saids Magistrats theranent* (Aberdeen, 1689). Reid was a magistrand; his co-author was probably one of several Alexander Irvines then in the college. The students attesting comprised 27 magistrands, 20 tertians, 26 semis and 26 bajans. There is no record in the council archives of an election at this time and no other corroborative evidence of the event.
138 NAS, PC/24, ff., 217–22. A Marischal student, prominent in this affair, was one of a crowd that disrupted services in St Machar's in 1694: NLS, Yester Papers, MS 7017, f. 98, copy libel, [1694]. I am grateful to Dr T Clarke for this reference. The

reference to the song 'Carle an the king come' antedates those gathered in: R Burns, *The Poems and Songs of Robert Burns*, ed. J Kinsley, 3 vols (Oxford, 1968), 3, 1334. I am grateful to Dr C Milton for his guidance on this.

139 A Bower, *History of the University of Edinburgh*, 3 vols (Edinburgh, 1817–30), 1, 346. It was under this act that Thomas Reid was fined in 1705.

140 NAS, Montrose Papers, GD 220, 6/1782/4, 'Memoriall concerning the Conduct of the Masters in The Kings Colledge of Aberdeen since the Rebellion began', undated; J Allardyce, ed., *Historical papers relating to the Jacobite period, 1699–1750*, NSC, 2 vols (Aberdeen, 1896), 2, xliii–xlvi, 585–96. Unless otherwise stated, information about Jacobitism at the colleges is taken from these two sources.

141 Where positive identifications can be made, two bursars participated in 1659; two in 1692–93; two, including Thomas Reid, in 1705; 18, however, attested the non-violent, politically-correct spectacle of 1689.

142 For another version of Aeneas' activities: D Sage, *Memorabilia Domestica; or, Parish Life in the North of Scotland* (Wick, 1889), 2–5 (hereafter Sage, *Memorabilia*). Unless otherwise stated, further information about him as a student is taken from this source.

143 The civilist's complaint of the incident was minuted but then deleted: AUL, MS K 41, ff. 6v, 7r.

144 Where positive identifications can be made, the distribution of magistrands (m), tertians (t), semis (s) and bajans (b) is as follows: 1659, Marischal, 9 m, 6 t, 1 s, 6 b (the presence of so many bajans may be explained by family ties); 1665, King's, 2 m, 1 t; 1668, King's, 2 m, 10 t, 3 s; Marischal, 2 m, 2 t, 1 s; 1685, Marischal, 2 m, 1 t; 1677, King's, 4 t, 1 s; 1692–3, King's, 1 m, 12 t, 6 s; Marischal, 6 m, 2 t, 4 s, 1 b; 1705, King's, 2 t, 1 s; 1715–16, King's, 2 m, 5 t.

145 St Machar's Cathedral, MS CH2/1020/7, p. 172; NLS, MS 1277, f. 117, 10 January 1690.

146 'male feriatorum ardelionum, huc et illuc circumcursantium': Douglas, *Vindiciae*, 34; NLS, Adv. MS 35.5.11, f. 73; NAS, PC/24, f. 220v.

147 AUL, MS M 91/12; NLS, MS 1277, f. 144, 31 March 1693.

148 AUL, MS M 57, 1670, 1672.

149 Ibid., MS K 41, f. 5r; Anderson, *FAM*, 2, 296.

150 AUL, MS 2538, J Fraser, 'Triennial Travels', 1670, part 1, ff. 5v, 6r; part 3, f. 165v, 166r. Unless otherwise stated, information about James as a student is taken from this source.

151 T Urquhart, *The works of Sir Thomas Urquhart of Cromarty, knight*, Maitland Club (Edinburgh, 1834), 263. Both colleges are said to have evacuated their premises during the plague but there is no hard evidence of this: Anderson, *FAM*, 2, 213.

152 Edinburgh topped 100 entrants for the first time in 1662; Glasgow entrants doubled to between 50 and 60: Horn, *Edinburgh*, 30.

153 AUL, MS M 91/12, 14; Innes, *Fasti*, 327, 332–3, 339–40.

154 AUL, MS K 39, f. 16v; Dunbar, *Moray*, 2.

155 AUL, MS K 26, Bursars' Bonds, 1668–1714.

156 Supporting evidence for this incident comes from an untitled and undated list of 12 names, including Ferguson's, written beside the list of matriculants in the class of 1650 at King's: AUL, MS K 9, f. 68v. Comparative analysis of the names suggests that a walk-out did take place at King's in 1654 on the scale described by Fraser, but that some participants thought better of it and returned to King's, either then or the following year, to complete their education there.

157 AUL, MS K255/33, 'Mr Alexander Middletone compte from January 63 to February 66', p. 14.
158 Innes, *Fasti*, 332, 346.
159 Based on an analysis of numbers at the high, second and bursars' tables: ibid., 585–99. An analysis of amounts of bread served at meals in November 1651 shows that there were 9–10 'sitters' and 21–2 bursars in the last week of November 1651. An analysis of bread bought and consumed in the last week of March 1652 indicates that numbers remained low but stable during the height of the academic session 1651–52: AUL, MS K 2, ff. 483r–487v, 498r–502v.
160 AUL, MS K 225/1, 'Catalogus studiosorum pernoctantium in Academia', 'Catalogus pernoctantium'. The latter contains names of students living and sleeping out; some of the names are marked with a cross and may have been marked off when they came in the next day.
161 Anderson, *FAM*, 2, 236, 262–4, 268–70, 286–90.
162 NLS, MS 1277, f. 184, 14 January 1704. Ages at entry of other named students: Andrew Cant, James Ogilvie, around 12; Robert Duff, 13; James Gatt, Thomas Ragg, William Duff, 14; John Spalding, between 15 and 16; James Fraser, Ludovic Reid, 17.
163 Vance, 'Mortifications', 282. Comparable information is not available for the new bursaries founded at King's.
164 Students from Moray accounted for 12.9% of the class of 1646; 25.5% in 1658; 29.9% in 1663; 5.1% in 1677. Students from Ross accounted for 25.8%, 13.7%, 9.1% and 15.2%.
165 C Withers, 'Highland migration to Aberdeen, *c.* 1649–1891', *NS*, 7 (1987), 26.
166 Based on the designations of students from landed families and the parishes of bursars, where recorded.
167 For example: Innes, *Fasti*, 227, 248, 430–1, 436–7; AUL, MS K 37, ff. 10r, 18r, 26r; K 39, f. 5v; M 57, 1651–52.
168 AUL, MS K, 26, K 54/8, 1668–69; Anderson, *Roll*, ix.
169 Innes, *Fasti*, 230, 238.
170 AUL, MS K 256/42/1, 'Compts of Master John Row', 1654–57; K 257/21/3, Memorial . . . Anent the Bibliotheck money', [1716]; MS K 257/21/1/1.
171 AUL, MS M 58, 1687–88. These accounts have been misprinted in Anderson, *FAM*, 2, 258.
172 For example: Anderson, *FAM*, 2, 249, 255.
173 Innes, *Fasti*, 226, 230.
174 Anderson, *FAM*, 2, 282–91. As 'secundars' (sons of gentlemen) at St Andrews, Kenneth Mackenzie and Thomas Mackenzie (both 1712) each paid three guineas Sterling each to their regent and their teachers of Greek and mathematics. They each paid £42 Scots at graduation, including sums to the rector, the examiner, the beadle; to the library; and for a 'treat': W C Dickinson, *Two Students at St Andrews, 1711–16*, St Andrews University Publications (Edinburgh, 1952), xxvii (hereafter Dickinson, *Students*).
175 AUL, MS K 36, f. 42r.
176 For example: ibid., MS 2379/1/10; K 257/1/3/3/1; K 278/3/36, K 278/9/69, K 278/2/44.
177 Ibid., MS K 257/18/1, p. 96; Orem, *Description*, 306. Neither of these sources refers specifically to muses. A note on the allocation of rooms in the New Work refers

to 14: six studies 'n[orth]', six 's[outh]', two 't[ranse]'. It also refers to 13 chambers: six occupied by students, one by a graduate, two 'in the low transe', 'the newk chamber' and three others. The document is undated but may be as early as 1659: AUL, MS K 278/12/1, 'First dyvision of the studies of the new work'.

178 Ibid., MS K 255/43; K 257/1/3/3/1.

179 Ibid., MS K 255/44.

180 Anderson, *FAM*, 2, 214, 236.

181 AUL, MS K 257/1/3/3/1.

182 Innes, *Fasti*, 590; AUL, MS K 2, ff. 486v, 501r.

183 Peter Stivin (Steven): Munro, *Old Aberdeen*, 1, 104.

184 NLS, MS 1277, f. 187, 18 April 1704.

185 AUL, MS M 57, 1666.

186 Innes, *Rose*, 370. At St Andrews, in 1712, Kenneth Mackenzie's gown had cost £7 17s Scots in materials and: £1 12s to make up: Dickinson, *Students*, xxxviii.

187 *Evidence* (1826), 203; AUL, MS 2379/1/10, 'A short Summe of the state of the old Colledge of . . . Aberdeen Cropt 1651', [1652]. The document refers to 24 bursars and, the steward's accounts of 1650, to upwards of 19. Nevertheless, the 'official' figure of 15 arts bursars recurs throughout the period: e.g., Middleton, *Appendix*, 43.

188 AUL, MS K 27, Bursars' vouchers, 1669–1724, ff. 16–38. Graduation, on 24 August 1680, was exceptionally late.

189 Vance, 'Mortifications', 189, 190, 305.

190 Ibid., MS K 36, f. 42v; Innes, *Fasti*, 230. For payments, 1653–57, 1659: AUL, MS K 256/42/1, 2; Innes, *Fasti*, 601. For payments, 1664: ibid., K 255/33, 'Spone silver'. For the purchase of silver spoons: ibid., K 256/42/1; K 278/7/28; Innes, *Fasti*, 601.

191 Innes, *Fasti*, 321, 329, 364; Anderson, *FAM*, 1, 318; Vance, 'Mortifications', 302.

192 AUL, MS K257/1/3/3/1.

193 Ibid., MS M 57, 1684–87; M 58, 1687–88.

194 Ibid., MS K 256/42/1; K 278/2/12, 21; Innes, *Fasti*, 590, 605–6.

195 Ibid., *Rose*, 359–60.

196 AUL, MS K 255/43.

Chapter 3, pp. 66–98

1 P L Gordon, *Personal memoirs* . . . 2 vols (London, 1830), 1, 1–30. Unless otherwise stated, further information about Pryse and his relatives as students is taken from this source.

2 A Dingwall Fordyce, *Family Record of the Name of Dingwall Fordyce in Aberdeenshire*, 2 vols (Toronto, 1885–88), 2, 15. Unless otherwise stated, further information about James as a student is taken from this source.

3 AUL, MS M 366, Bursary competition lists, 1787.

4 The earliest noted use of the term is 1759: AUL, MS K 255/44, letter, Thomas Reid to an unnamed correspondent, 25 December 1759.

5 D M Walker, 'The rebuilding of King's and Marischal Colleges, 1723–1889', *AUR*, 55 (1993), 123–45.

6 For the institutional and academic history of the colleges in the eighteenth century: Emerson, *Professors*; Wood, *Enlightenment*. There is no equivalent account for the early nineteenth century.

7 *Abstract of Some Statutes and Orders of King's College in Old Aberdeen. M.DCC.LIII. With Additions M.DCC.LIV* [Aberdeen], [1754], 13 (hereafter *Abstract*); AUL, MS K 44, p. 89; M 41, f. 42r.
8 AUL, MS M 222, p. 8.
9 Ibid., MS K 44, p. 89.
10 Ibid., p Lamda, Abd Univ, R le, [J Forbes], *A letter to the Students of Marischal College on the Subject of the Approaching Election* (Aberdeen, 1824), 6 (hereafter *Letter*).
11 For a sketch of the reform movement in the early nineteenth century: D J Withrington, 'The Idea of a National University in Scotland, *c* 1820–*c* 1870' in Carter and Withrington, *Scottish Universities*, 41–4.
12 *Letter*, 12; P J Anderson, ed., *Rectorial Addresses delivered in the Universities of Aberdeen, 1835–1900*, AUS 6, (Aberdeen, 1902), 347–50 (hereafter Anderson, *Rectorial Addresses*).
13 AUL, L Aa P1.2 Abe, *A full and correct report of the proceedings of the rectorial court held in Marischal College and University Aberdeen 14th November 1825* . . . (Aberdeen, 1825), 12 (hereafter *Proceedings*). For other accounts of the court: AUL, MS M 104, Report and Appendices, and 'Narrative of Proceedings . . .'.
14 Dunbar, *Moray*, 7.
15 *Evidence* (1826), 213, 284; Douglas, *General Description*, 198.
16 *Evidence* (1826), 123–6. Unless otherwise stated, further information about Abercromby as a student is taken from this source.
17 Ibid., 283–4; *OSA*, 139; AUL, MS M 104, Appendix 8.
18 AUL, MS K 43, pp. 371–2.
19 Ibid., MS K 46, ff. 4r–5r; *Abstract*, 11; *Evidence* (1826), 35; W Thom, *The history of Aberdeen . . . including . . . an account of . . . the two Universities* . . . 2 vols (Aberdeen, 1811) 2, 42.
20 AUL, MS M 404/2/1. Unless otherwise stated, further information about William as a student and professor is taken from this source and from MS 404/1.
21 AUL, Papers of Duff Family, Old Meldrum, Aberdeenshire, MS 2778/12/2/11/19, letter, James Urquhart to his father, 15 November 1774. Unless otherwise stated, further information about James as a student is taken from this source.
22 AUL, MS K 44, p. 93.
23 Orkney Archives, MS D3/265, letters of Alexander G Watt to his father, 1788–90. Unless otherwise stated, further information about Alexander as a student is taken from this source.
24 Anderson, *Officers*, 49.
25 *Evidence* (1826), 218, 293.
26 Ibid., 12, 75; Anderson, *FAM*, 2, 63.
27 AUL, MS M 104, 'Narrative of Proceedings'. For the relegation of Latin from colloquial use: Anderson, *FAM*, 2, 345.
28 Wood, *Enlightenment*, 124.
29 For an example of the first: AUL, MS M 158, W Knight, Moral Philosophy [1801–02]; of the second, MS K 166, 'A Manuscript of Moral Philosophy . . . written by Alexander Thomson . . . 1773–74'.
30 Wood, *Enlightenment*, 211, n. 58; *Evidence* (1826), 106.
31 *Abstract*, 20.
32 John Senex was a cartographer and engraver, who died in 1740.
33 AUL, MS K 41, f. 71r.

34 *OSA*, 90, 115, 121.

35 For William Malcolm: J M Bulloch, 'The King's College Class of 1808–12', *AUR*, 7 (1919–20) 233–5. For Alexander Thomson: G Smeaton, *Memoir of Alexander Thomson of Banchory* (Edinburgh, 1869), 6–12. Unless otherwise stated, further information about William and Alexander as students is taken from these sources.

36 G Colman, *Random Records . . .* 2 vols (London, 1830) 92 (hereafter Colman, *Records*).

37 J Mackintosh, *Memoirs of the Life of . . . Sir James Mackintosh* (London, 1835), 9–20. Unless otherwise stated, further information about James as a student is taken from this source.

38 AUL, MS 30/16, J Beattie, Sessional journals, 1761–93.

39 NLS, Mackenzies of Delvine Collection, MS 1314, pp. 29–30. Unless otherwise stated, further information about Charles as a student is taken from this source.

40 NAS, Leith Hall Muniments, GD225/13/14, 16, letters between Harriet Leith and Andrew Hay of Rannes, 1772–73; H Leith-Hay and M Lochhead, *Trustie to the end: the story of the Leith Hall family* (Edinburgh, 1957), 58–9. Unless otherwise stated, further information about John as a student is taken from these sources.

41 NLS, Yester Papers, MS 14677, ff. 12–15. Unless otherwise stated, further information about George as a student is taken from this source.

42 AUL, Collection of papers of Duff Family, compiled by A and H Tayler, MS 2226/173, letter, Thomas Gordon to [William] Rose of Montcoffer, 23 December 1791; 2226/289/1, 'Account of money . . . expended by John Rose . . . 1791 and 1792.' Unless otherwise stated, further information about John as a student is taken from these sources.

43 NAS, GD225/1043/8, accounts of James Leith with J A Angus, James Clerk, Mary Dyce, 1775–77. Unless otherwise stated, further information about James as a student is taken from this source.

44 R Helsham, *A course of Lectures on Natural Philosophy* and W Nicholson, *An Introduction to Natural Philosophy*; the editions are not stated. For other books bought by students: John Don [J M Bulloch], 'A Student's Expences at King's College in 1801', *AUR*, 2 (1914–15), 58–9 (hereafter Don, 'Expences'); Johnston, 'Beattie', 25–8.

45 For a brief account of the management of the college libraries in this period: C A McLaren, *Rare and Fair: a Visitor's History of Aberdeen University Library* (Aberdeen, 1995).

46 Colman, *Records*, 1, 61–116. Unless otherwise stated, further information about George as a student is taken from this source.

47 *Evidence* (1826), 74.

48 Unless otherwise stated, money is expressed in Sterling in this chapter.

49 AUL, MS M 104, Appendix 3.

50 *Abstract*, 11.

51 W MacGill, 'King's College, Aberdeen, Two Centuries Ago', *Scottish Historical Review*, 4 (1906–07), 108–10. Unless otherwise stated, further information about John as a student is taken from this source.

52 AUL, MS K 46, f. 36v.

53 *Abstract*, 19–20.

54 NAS, Ross of Pitcalnie Muniments, GD 199/265, letter, Thomas Blackwell to Alexander Ross, 22 February 1744.

55 *Evidence* (1826), 15.
56 For changes in its format at King's: J Ogilvie, ed., *Bursary Competition Versions* (Aberdeen, 1889), xii (hereafter Ogilvie, *Versions*).
57 'King's College in 1818', *AUR*, 5 (1917–18), 143–4. Unless otherwise stated, further information about George as a student is taken from this source. He subsequently became George Abercromby Young Leslie.
58 For Knight's translation, which 'would now-a-days hardly do credit to any bursar, much less to a first': Ogilvie, *Versions*, xviii.
59 J McGrigor, *The Autobiography and Services of Sir James McGrigor, Bart* . . . (London, 1861), 1–9. Unless otherwise stated, further information about James as a student is taken from this source.
60 W K Tweedie, *Life of John Macdonald* (Edinburgh, 1849), 37–42. Unless otherwise stated, further information about John as a student is taken from this source.
61 *Evidence* (1826), 205, 272. Libertines, in contrast, got off lightly: 'I had no hesitation,' Thomas Gordon, a master at King's, informed John Rose's father in 1791, 'after conversing with [John] and considering the letter you was pleased to write me, to advise his entering . . . for the Greek language and that he should at the same time attend . . . [the] Humanity class'.
62 AUL, MS K 41, f. 49v.
63 Ibid., MS K 48, ff. 118r–119r; *Evidence* (1826), 18, 73. John Rose referred to 'the blackstone lesson', in January 1792. The name came from the mediaeval end-of-session examination. For its origin: Cant, *St Andrews*, 20n.; Durkan and Kirk, *Glasgow*, 92–3.
64 *Evidence* (1826), 214–15, 287.
65 The reflecting quadrant, invented by John Hadley in 1730.
66 AUL, MS K 50, pp. 248–9; *Proceedings*, 46; *Evidence* (1826), 101, 287.
67 *Evidence* (1826), 37.
68 *Proceedings*, 46.
69 AUL, MS M 104, Report and 'Narrative of Proceedings'.
70 For example: *Evidence* (1826), 92.
71 Ibid., 289; Anderson, *FAM*, 2, 367.
72 Innes, *Fasti*, 213.
73 AUL, MS K 50, pp. 31–2; 43–4; 62–3; *Evidence* (1826), 18.
74 AUL, MS M 43, ff. 30r, 31r; *Evidence* (1826), 289.
75 *Evidence* (1826), 42, 92.
76 Sage, *Memorabilia,* chapters 10–12. Unless otherwise stated, further information about Donald as a student is taken from this source.
77 Anderson, *FAM*, 2, 339.
78 For example: AUL, MS K 41, ff. 32v, 72v.
79 Ibid., MS K 41, f. 71r.
80 Knight, 'Collections', 170; Douglas, *General Description*, 113.
81 Wood, *Enlightenment*, 94; *OSA*, 84.
82 AUL, MS M 41, f. 42r.
83 Anderson, *Officers*, 77.
84 These were first delivered in 1825: Anderson, *Studies*, 446–7; J M Bulloch, 'The Founder of the Murtle Lectures', *AUR*, 15 (1927–28), 40–3.
85 AUL, MS K 48, 67r; *Abstract*, 8; *OSA*, 90.
86 AUL, MS M 42. f. 88r.
87 Innes, *Fasti*, 209.

88 AUL, MS K 43, ff. 178, 206.
89 *OSA*, 90; *Evidence* (1826), 27.
90 'Fanaticis tremulorum aut superstitiosis papistarum conventibus assistere'.
91 *Evidence* (1826), 107, 289.
92 The college bowling green is mentioned as late as 1762, but there is no record of it in use: AUL, MS K 257/20/2/3.
93 Knight, 'Collections', 170.
94 Colman, *Records*, 92.
95 Douglas, *General Description*, 200.
96 AUL, SBL 1786 NP 4, [R Hamilton and J Stuart], *Reply to a Paper Intitled Memorial from . . . King's College . . .* [Aberdeen, 1786], 15–16.
97 For this and, more especially, its equivalent at Marischal: A H Young, 'The University's Disputing Society of 1795–96', *AUR*, 4 (1916–17), 45–8.
98 It seems to have been this society to which Alexander delivered a retrospective speech in 1819: University of Edinburgh, New College Library, Alexander Thomson of Banchory Papers, Tho 10. I am grateful to Michelle Gait for this reference.
99 AUL, MS K 255/44; Dunbar, *Moray*, 6.
100 For example: AUL, MS K 46, f. 7v.
101 Ibid., MS K 47, p. 117; M 387/10/2/1.
102 Ibid., MS M 41, f. 27r.
103 N Macpherson, *Notes on the Chapel, Crown, and other Ancient Buildings of King's College, Aberdeen* (Edinburgh, 1889), 9.
104 A Hobbs, 'Downie's Slaughter', *AUR*, 45 (1973–74), 183–91.
105 Maclean, *Life*, 303.
106 '*Kuphipolium*', as translated by Knight, 'Collections', p. 156; 'Ludis scenicis'.
107 AUL, MS M 42, ff. 33v–35r.
108 Ibid., MS M 43, pp. 70–2. The 'sealing of gowns' was prohibited at King's in 1720, but the practice is not described: ibid., MS K 41, f. 71r.
109 *Abstract*, 8; *OSA*, 91.
110 For conflicting interpretations of their purpose: AUL, MS M 104, 'Narrative of Proceedings'.
111 Knight, 'Collections', p. 158.
112 AUL, MS M 42, pp. 82–3.
113 Ibid., MS K 49, p. 279; M 42, f. 88r; *OSA*, 90, 121.
114 AUL, MS K 44, p. 56.
115 *Evidence* (1826), 89.
116 AUL, MS K 28; K 44, p. 56.
117 Ibid., MS M 16, 17, 'Burse Book, 1749–90', '1791–1836'.
118 At King's, in 1740, the deaths of three bursars were reported at a single meeting: ibid., MS K 43, p. 106.
119 Tertians from the King's class of 1752 entered Marischal as magistrands in the class of 1751.
120 In 1825 a student 'debarred' from King's was admitted to Marischal, after discussions confirmed that he had not been formally expelled and was therefore eligible to enter there: *Evidence* (1826), 107.
121 AUL, MS K 255/44.
122 Ibid., MS K 50, pp. 172, 242, 246; M 43, ff. 47r–48r; *Evidence* (1826), 109–10. For the context: J E Cookson, *The British armed nation*, 1793–1815 (Oxford, 1997).
123 *Evidence* (1826), 98.

124 Edinburgh soared from an overall population of over 750 in 1791 to over 2000 in 1825. Glasgow rose from 259 arts students in 1798 to 667 in 1825. St Andrews, recording 25 matriculants in 1777 and 85 in 1826 considered that it had made 'a great, though not a regularly progressive increase': *Report . . . by a Royal Commission of Inquiry into the State of the Universities of Scotland* (London, 1831), Appendix, 161, 263, 408, in AUL QL f. Aa P2 1826, 2.
125 AUL, MS K 42, ff. 19v, 66v.
126 Ibid., K 44, p. 347; K 255/44; *Abstract*, 5, 17.
127 AUL, MS K 257/20/7/14.
128 Ibid., MS K 47, p. 103.
129 *OSA*, 91; *Evidence*, 33.
130 A wright, a mason, a goldsmith, a staymaker and a brewery worker; after 1800 these occupations are distributed between the 'Intermediate' and 'Working class' categories. One of the farms was a spread of 166 acres, 'the most opulent in the parish': *OSA*, 14, 583.
131 A similar decline in students from the landed classes is found in Glasgow: W M Mathew, 'The Origins and Occupations of Glasgow Students 1740–1839', *Past and Present*, No. 33 (1966), 79 (hereafter Mathew, 'Origins').
132 AUL, MS K 46, f. 19r.
133 *OSA*, 121.
134 AUL, MS M 42, f. 76v; Knight, 'Collections', 803.
135 AUL, MS 30/16.
136 Ibid., MS M 42, f. 43v.
137 James picked up at the auctions 'the Death of Abel' (S Gessner, *Der Tod Abels*; 1758, English translation, 1761) and 'the Blackbird, a Collection of Songs' (*The Blackbird, containing . . . songs . . . Scots and English*, possibly the third edition, Edinburgh, 1771).
138 AUL, MS K 46, f. 3v.
139 Ibid., MS K 42, f. 66v.
140 K 44, p. 347; *Abstract*, 6.
141 Based on: MS K 257/20/3–11.
142 *OSA*, 91.
143 Dunbar, *Moray*, 7–8.
144 AUL, MS K 41, f. 62v; K 43, pp. 338, 361–2; *Abstract*, 10.
145 AUL, MS K 43, p. 361; K 257/19/2/28, 257/20/1/7; *OSA*, 90.
146 NAS, Grant of Bught Muniments, GD 23/ 6/512; AUL, MS K 51, p. 115.
147 *Abstract*, 17–18.
148 Wood, *Enlightenment*, 57; *Abstract*, 17; *OSA*, 21, 122. For a fuller account of this practice in the Aberdeen colleges and elsewhere: Johnston, 'Beattie', 13–14.
149 AUL, MS K 255/44.
150 *OSA*, 91.
151 Ibid., 122–3; NAS, Papers of the Sinclair Family of Freswick, GD 136/498/96, letter, Donald Grant to an unnamed correspondent, 5 November 1803.
152 Douglas, *General Description*, 198.
153 AUL, Papers of Duff Family, Braco, Banffshire, 1665–1869, MS 27271/38, letter, George Chalmers to Lord Braco, 12 October 1732.
154 *Abstract*, 3. Thus, bursars in the class of 1752, who had been awarded foundation bursaries on entering, received foundation bursaries plus Fullarton bursaries in 1753. This did not stop three of them migrating to Marischal in 1754: AUL, MS K 28, p. 36.

155 AUL, MS K 44, p. 57.
156 Douglas, *General Description*, 205.
157 Anderson, *FAM*, 1, 440–3.
158 A and H Tayler, *History of the Family of Urquhart* (Aberdeen, 1946), 181.
159 Walter Morison may have attended King's but has not been positively identified.
160 Based on examples in Knight, 'Collections', 797–804.
161 AUL, MS 30/16.
162 Ibid., MS K 43, pp. 364–5.
163 *Abstract*, 8.
164 AUL, MS K 42, f. 66v.
165 Ibid., MS K 44, p. 347; K 257/20/10/8.
166 Ibid., MS K 45, pp. 112–14, 138–42; *Abstract*, 10.
167 AUL, MS K 46, ff. 2v–4r.
168 For breakfast Pryse had bread and milk, 3s a month; for supper, bread, cheese, butter, smoked haddocks, small beer and other *luxuries*', around 4s; tea and sugar, 'once or twice a week', around 2s. He also patronised 'Sweety Nell, an old woman who sold *lollypops*'.
169 Don, 'Expences', 59. In comparison, a St Andrews bursar, Duncan Dewar (1818), spent on average £14 a session: rent for the rooms he shared at various times ranged from £2 to £2 5s; food in his first year, supplemented with supplies from home, cost £5 9s; P S Lang, ed., *Duncan Dewar, a Student of St Andrews 100 years Ago, his Accounts* (Glasgow, 1926), 108–12.
170 *OSA*, 90; Douglas, *General Description*, 113.
171 AUL, MS K 46, f. 3r.
172 See also: Don, 'Expences', 58.
173 Dunbar, *Moray*, 7.
174 NAS, GD 199/265.
175 Johnston, 'Beattie', 15 and following.
176 AUL, MS M 222, p. 12.
177 For example: Robert Morice (1787) followed his father, David (1751); he had as a classmate his brother, Alexander; he was followed by his other brothers, William (1791) and John (1795); and sent his sons, David (1830), James (1832), George (1835) and Arthur (1841): J A Henderson, ed., *History of the Society of Advocates in Aberdeen*, NSC (Aberdeen, 1912); W Johnston, *Genealogical Account of the Descendants of James Young . . . and Rachel Cruickshank 1697–1893* (Aberdeen, 1894).
178 A A MacLaren, 'Privilege, Patronage and the Professions: Aberdeen and its Universities, 1760–1860', in Carter and Withrington, *Scottish Universities*, 96–104.
179 W Hazlittt, *The Spirit of the Age* (London, 1904 edn), 147.
180 AUL, MS M 222, p. 1.

Chapter 4, pp. 99–132

1 G MacDonald, *George MacDonald and his wife* (London, 1924), 67–73. Unless otherwise stated, further information about George as a student is taken from this source. According to his son and biographer, many of MacDonald's own experiences as a student are assigned to 'Alec Forbes' and 'Robert Falconer', eponymous heroes of two of his college novels.
2 Bain, *Autobiography*, 29–32, 43–84. Unless otherwise stated, further information about Alexander as a student is taken from this source, which is helpfully arranged by session.

3 Walker, 'Rebuilding'; W Walker, *Reminiscences, Academic, Ecclesiastic and Scholastic* (Aberdeen, 1904), 12–20 (hereafter Walker, *Reminiscences*); W Geddes, 'Notes on King's College Quadrangle as it stood before 1860', *Scottish Notes & Queries*, 11 (1897–98), 113–15 (hereafter Geddes, *Notes*).
4 *Evidence* (1826), 14, 36.
5 *Report* MC (1826), 28.
6 'Song of the Student', *Aberdeen University Magazine* (1854), 91.
7 D J Withrington, 'The "mysterious" road to union: the making of the new University of Aberdeen, 1858–60', *AUR*, 55 (1993), 146–61.
8 *Evidence* (1826), 76, 81, 99, 108.
9 D Masson, 'Dead Men I Have Known', *Macmillan's Magazine*, 9 (1863–64), 325–43 (hereafter Masson, 'Dead Men').
10 For this and following paragraph: Anderson, *Rectorial Addresses*, 351–62. For the political and religious background: I G C Hutchison, *A Political History of Scotland, 1832–1924* (Edinburgh, 1986), chapters 1–3.
11 AUL, MS M 43, ff. 81v, 137r.
12 Ibid., MS K 51, pp. 46–7; Anderson, *Officers*, 21–2.
13 AUL, MS K 50, p. 448.
14 *Evidence* (1826), 36, 108; *Report* KC (1826), 35.
15 AUL, MS K 52, p. 271.
16 Ibid., K 52, pp. 148, 299, 365.
17 *Evidence* (1826), 214, 286–7. Changes in hours are recorded in the *Aberdeen Journal*; see also Maclean, *Life*, 353.
18 *Evidence* (1826), 214, 285–6.
19 NAS, GD 136/524/442–7, 558/2–9, letters, John Tulloch to William Sinclair, Thurso, 1827–30. Unless otherwise stated, further information about John as a student is taken from this source.
20 *Report* KC (1826), 35.
21 *Evidence* (1826), 74.
22 R Simson, *Elements of Euclid* (first edn, Glasgow, 1756).
23 *Evidence* (1826), 35.
24 Ibid., 87.
25 Masson, 'Dead Men'. Unless otherwise stated, further information about David as a student is taken from this source.
26 I M Harrower, *John Forbes White* (Edinburgh, 1918), 24–8. Unless otherwise stated, further information about John as a student is taken from this source.
27 For example: *Evidence* (1826), 43.
28 Maclean, 'University life', 276. Unless otherwise stated, further information about Neil as a student is taken from this source.
29 Maclean, *Life*, 2.
30 Walker, *Reminiscences*, 40–9, 62–72, 76–86, 226–30; *Additional Reminiscences* (Aberdeen, 1906), 3–10, 12–18. Unless otherwise stated, further information about William as a student is taken from this source.
31 Maclean, *Life*, 106.
32 W G Blaikie, *William Garden Blaikie: an autobiography . . .*, ed. N L Walker (London, 1901), 41–52 (hereafter Blaikie, *Autobiography*). Unless otherwise stated, further information about William as a student is taken from this source.
33 *Evidence* (1826), 26, 40, 92–3.

34 W Mair, *My Life* (London, 1911), 27–41. Unless otherwise stated, further information about William as a student is taken from this source.
35 *Evidence* (1826), 95.
36 *Report* KC (1826), 35; *Report* MC (1826), 33.
37 *Evidence* (1826), 85; P Forbes, *Syllabus of lectures on chemistry and natural history . . .* (Aberdeen, 1825).
38 *Evidence* (1826), 229; *Report* KC (1826), 29.
39 AUL, MS K 129/1–3. For 'Stewart's Outline', 'Reid's Inquiry': D Stewart, *Outlines of moral philosophy for the use of students in the University of Edinburgh* (first edn, Edinburgh, 1793); T Reid, *An inquiry into the human mind on the principles of common sense* (first edn, London, 1764).
40 *Evidence* (1826), 101, 304–5.
41 Ibid., 36–7; AUL, MS K 52, p. 256.
42 *Evidence* (1826), 28.
43 [J H Burton], 'The two great northern Universities', *Edinburgh Magazine* (1833), 182–91. Unless otherwise stated, further information about John as a student is taken from this source.
44 Maclean, *Life*, 49.
45 Ogilvie, *Versions*, xii.
46 Maclean, *Life*, 24; D Anderson, *Scottish folk-lore: Reminiscences of Aberdeenshire from pinafore to gown* (New York, 1895), 237–45. Unless otherwise stated, further information about Duncan as a student is taken from this source.
47 J Kennedy, *Old Highland Days: the reminiscences of Dr. John Kennedy* (London, [1901]), 61–72 (hereafter Kennedy, *Days*). Unless otherwise stated, further information about John as a student is taken from this source.
48 *Evidence* (1826), 16, 32, 33, 37, 287.
49 AUL, MS K 51, pp. 20–1. It is not clear how far these rules were applied.
50 Ibid., K 52, p. 317; *Report* (1857), 122.
51 *Report* KC (1826), 36.
52 *Report* (1836), 106–7.
53 *Evidence* (1826), 288.
54 *Report* (1836), 200.
55 Ibid., 107; W Johnston, *A Calendar of the University of Aberdeen for the sessions 1860/1 to 1863/4* (Aberdeen, 1900), 113–14.
56 *Report* KC (1826), 36; AUL, MS K 51, pp. 20–1.
57 Innes, *Fasti*, 221.
58 Anderson, *Rectorial Addresses*, 355.
59 *Report* KC (1826), 26, 36.
60 *Evidence* (1826), 37, 106.
61 Maclean, *Life*, 332–3.
62 Ibid., 334–7.
63 AUL, Lamda Gra j m, J A Grant, *Memoranda: J A Grant* (no place or date of publication), 3–4 (hereafter Grant, *Memoranda*).
64 *Autobiography*, 88.
65 *Report* KC (1826), 25; *Report* MC (1826), 21.
66 *Report* (1836), xxv.
67 D Dewar, *The Evidences of Divine Revelation* (Edinburgh, 1838).
68 Comparable information on this and subsequent topics is not available from Marischal.

69 AUL, MS K 51, p. 382; K 52, p. 256.
70 *Evidence* (1826), 33.
71 Kennedy, *Days*, 69–72; J Kennedy, *My Early Days* (London, 1886), 94. Unless otherwise stated, further information about James Kennedy as a student is taken from these sources.
72 MacDonald, *Falconer*, 231, 253.
73 Maclean, *Life*, 63; Anderson, *Community*, 41–2.
74 'A glance at the past history and present state and prospects of our universities', *Aberdeen Universities Magazine*, 1 (1849–50), 7.
75 Maclean, *Life*, 303–4.
76 Geddes, *Notes*, 113; AUL, MS K 52, p. 83.
77 D Fraser, *Autobiography of the late Donald Fraser, D.D.* (London, 1892), 5–7. Unless otherwise stated, further information about Donald as a student is taken from this source.
78 Maclean, *Life*, 66–7, 74, 210–22.
79 T Davidson, *Memorials of Thomas Davidson, the wandering scholar*, ed. W Knight (London, 1907), 11–13. Unless otherwise stated, further information about Thomas as a student is taken from this source.
80 Maclean, *Life*, 254–60.
81 *Forbes*, 2, 3–6.
82 AUL, MS K 52, pp. 35–6.
83 Ibid., MS K 146, Minutes, 1848–59. Unless otherwise stated, information in this and the following paragraph is from this source.
84 Ibid., MS U 325, Minutes, 1848–49.
85 Ibid., MS U 297, Minutes, 1853–59. I am grateful to Professor C OBoyle for assistance on this matter.
86 Ibid., MS M 43, ff. 124–5, 146.
87 Ibid., MS U 286, Hellenic Society, history and constitution.
88 For full bibliographical details of these periodicals: P J Anderson, 'The Forerunners of "Alma Mater"', *Alma Mater*, 21, 121–2.
89 R H Smith, *An Aberdeenshire village propaganda forty years ago* (Edinburgh, 1889), 56–62.
90 AUL, MS K 51, pp. 6–8; M 43, f. 109; M 44, pp. 63–4.
91 Ibid., MS M 43, ff. 124–5.
92 *Aberdeen University Magazine* (1853–54), 31–2; Maclean, *Life*, 50–2.
93 Maclean, *Life*, 55, 65, 76–7, 183.
94 AUL, MS K 52, pp. 229–42. For another side of Morrison: Maclean, *Life*, 363.
95 AUL, MS K 52, pp. 11–13, 124; Maclean, *Life*, 313.
96 AUL, MS K 51, p. 432.
97 Ibid., MS K 51, pp. 68–9; K 52, p. 38; Geddes, *Notes*, 113–14.
98 AUL, MS K 24; K 52, p. 256.
99 Maclean, *Life*, 156–9.
100 Ibid., 65, 114, 183, 199–208, 312–15.
101 MacDonald, *Forbes*, 2, 1.
102 AUL, MS K 51, pp. 417–18.
103 Ibid., MS K 50, p. 363; K 52, p. 174; G S Davidson, *Jottings* (no place of publication, 1902), 70–1 (hereafter Davidson, *Jottings*).
104 Maclean, *Life*, 107.
105 AUL, MS M 43, ff. 124–5; Grant, *Memoranda*, 4.

106 *Evidence* (1826), 16; Walker, *Reminiscences*, 33; Maclean, *Life*, 290.
107 Maclean, *Life*, 52–3, 91–2, 108, 245–6.
108 Ibid., 90; Blaikie, *Autobiography*, 42.
109 *Evidence* (1826), 44.
110 MacDonald, *Falconer*, 188, 196.
111 *Report* (1857), 14.
112 *Report* (1836), 25, 139; *Report* (1857), 119, 136.
113 *Evidence* (1826), 76.
114 Ibid., 109; AUL, MS K 50, p. 448; M 43, ff. 136–8.
115 Davidson, *Jottings*, 70.
116 *Report* KC (1826), 24.
117 *Report* MC (1826), 19. This does not, however, correspond with the evidence on which it is said to be based: *Evidence* (1826), 75.
118 *Evidence* (1826), 108.
119 *Report* (1857), 120, 143; Maclean, *Life*, 264–77.
120 *Report* (1836), 210; *Report* (1857), 141–2.
121 MacDonald, *Falconer*, 96–7, 188; *Forbes*, 1, 300.
122 *Evidence* (1826), 185–6, 249–50; *Report* (1857), 119, 137.
123 'Hutton's Course': C Hutton, *A course of mathematics* (first edn, London, 1798–1801).
124 *Evidence* (1826), 33.
125 AUL, MS K 51, p. 14; M 43, f. 152.
126 *Evidence* (1826), 202–5, 270–1; Innes, *Fasti*, 219–21; Anderson, *FAM*, 1, 492–536.
127 A H Duff, *Town and Country: Sketches* (London, 1866), 228–51. Unless otherwise stated, further information about Andrew as a student is taken from this source.
128 *Report* KC (1826), 12, 15–16; *Report* MC (1826), 7.
129 *Evidence* (1826), 82; *Report* (1836), vi.
130 AUL, MS K 24.
131 Maclean, *Life*, 243.
132 Ibid., 273.
133 *Evidence* (1826), 14.
134 For example: 'Ericson' in *Falconer*, 'Macleod' in *Life*.
135 Anderson, *FAM*, 1, 461.
136 Maclean, *Life*, 17.
137 Johnston, *Bajans*, viii.
138 Maclean, *Life*, 107, 153.
139 Anderson, *Officers*, 65.
140 MacDonald, *Forbes*, 1, 299.
141 *Evidence* (1826), 44.
142 *Report* (1857), 120.

Index

Note: the index focuses on individual students and the student community